Computer Literacy

A Hands-On Approach

First Edition Revised
Apple II Family Version

Other McGraw-Hill Computing Titles:

LOGO	Abelson	Apple Logo Logo for the Apple II TI Logo
	Tobias and Markuson	Adventures with Logo More Adventures with Logo
BASIC	Luehrmann and Peckham	Hands-On BASIC for the IBM PC jr.
	Mourlund	BASIC Programming for Computer Literacy
	Peckham	Hands-On BASIC for the IBM PC
	Peckham with Ellis and Lodi	Hands-On BASIC for the Atari 400/800/ 1200XL Hands-On BASIC for the Commodore 64 Programming BASIC with the TI Structured BASIC for the IBM PC
PASCAL	Belford and Liu	Pascal
	Luehrmann and Peckham	Apple Pascal: A Hands-On Approach
	Moshell	Computer Power

About the Authors

Arthur Luehrmann and Herbert Peckham are pioneers in the field of computer education. They have worked extensively with educators at all levels to develop methods for teaching about computers. They are the authors of many books and articles on programming, the computer curriculum, and computers. Each was trained as a physicist and has taught physics. Together with Martha Ramírez, they formed the partnership Computer Literacy to develop educational materials for a national computer curriculum.

Arthur Luehrmann did his undergraduate and graduate work at the University of Chicago. Dr. Luehrmann coined the phrase "computer literacy" in 1972, and he has worked to make the concept of computer literacy an integral part of American education. Formerly, he was associate director of the Lawrence Hall of Science at the University of California, Berkeley. He now devotes full time to writing and speaking about computer literacy.

Herbert Peckham graduated from the United States Military Academy and pursued further graduate studies. He has taught physics, computer science, and mathematics at Gavilan College. He is a widely published author of educational materials for use with computers.

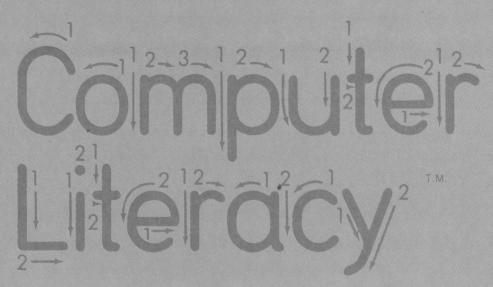

Computer Literacy

T.M.

A Hands-On Approach

First Edition Revised

Arthur Luehrmann

Herbert Peckham

Apple II Family Version

A

Computer
Literacy

BOOK

McGraw-Hill Book Company

New York   St. Louis   San Francisco   Auckland   Bogotá   Guatemala   Hamburg
Johannesburg   Lisbon   London   Madrid   Mexico   Montreal   New Delhi   Panama
Paris   San Juan   São Paulo   Singapore   Sydney   Tokyo   Toronto

Editor: Nola J. Hague
Editorial Assistants: Rudy Rodriguez, John Shane, Ray Simon, Kirby Urner
Design and Production Management: Suzanne LanFranchi
Art Direction: James Darby
Production: Judith Tisdale
Photo Editor: Safra Nimrod
Text and Cover Design: A Good Thing, Inc., Blaise Zito Associates

This book was set in 11 point Century Schoolbook by York Graphic Services, Inc.

ISBN 0-07-049242-5

2 3 4 5 6 7 8 9 10 VNHVNH 94 93 92 91 90 89 88 87 86

Acknowledgements

An advisory board of expert computer teachers carefully reviewed all initial drafts. Some 600 students at 16 test sites used the field-test edition of the work for a full semester. Extensive revisions were made based on classroom test results.

BOARD OF ADVISORS
The teachers listed below are computer teachers with many years of classroom experience.

Bobby Goodson, Co-founder of Computer Using Educators, Teacher of computing, Cupertino, California, President of International Council of Computers in Education

Helen Joseph, Resource Teacher in math, science, and computers, Novato Unified School District, California

Flora Russ, Teacher and Computer Science Coordinator, Berkeley Unified School District, California

COMPUTER-AWARENESS CONSULTANT
Ronald E. Anderson, Associate Professor of Sociology, University of Minnesota, and a national expert on the personal, societal, and ethical issues of computer literacy

FIELD-TEST-SITE TEACHERS AND STUDENTS

Texas
Hurst-Euless-Bedford Independent School District
  Carolyn Nixon, Wilshire Elementary School
  Anna Nohavitza, Trinity High School

California
Cupertino School District
  Bobby Goodson, Hyde Middle School
  Jim McCaig, Miller Junior High School
  Richard Pugh, Kennedy Junior High School
Gonzalez School District
  Jack Steadman, Gonzalez High School
Mt. Diablo School District
  Marilyn Cameron, Foothill Intermediate School
Piedmont School District
  Joan Liever, Piedmont Middle School
Richmond School District
  Marcia Hataye, Crespi Junior High School
  Linda O'Connor, Crespi Junior High School
  Maria Robledo, Crespi Junior High School

Minnesota
East Grand Forks School District
  Dwayne Hanson, East Grand Forks Senior High School

New Jersey
Highland Park School District
  Diane Marshall, Highland Park Middle School
  George Towne, Highland Park High School

Maryland
Baltimore County Public Schools
  Vincent J. DeBlase, Perry Hall Senior High School

Michigan
Detroit District
  Erryl J. Moody, Cooper Elementary School

EVALUATION TEAM

Throughout the field test, the five people listed below gathered and analyzed information. Dennis Phillips, Professor of Education and Philosophy, Stanford University School of Education, supervised their work.

Meg Korpi, Educational psychologist
John Agnew, Social studies teacher
Steve Leitz, Curriculum specialist
Stuart MacMillan, Computer software researcher
Kathleen Gilbert-Macmillan, Math/computer educator

TEACHER'S GUIDE CONSULTANTS

The Teacher's Guide incorporated explanations of teacher needs and pedagogy based on classroom experience.

John Agnew, Curriculum Development Specialist, Stanford California
Marilyn Cameron, Teacher, Mt. Diablo Unified School District, Walnut Creek, California
Steve Leitz, Teacher and Curriculum Specialist, Stanford, California

EDUCATIONAL ADMINISTRATORS

We benefitted from the writings of and conversations with these educators:

Elliot Soloway, Yale University

Richard Mayer, University of California, Santa Barbara

Pete Rowe, Computer-Advanced Ideas, Berkeley

Ronnie Banner, Director of Special Projects and Research & Development, Hurst-Euless-Bedford Independent School District, Texas

Mitchell E. Batoff, Institute for Professional Development, Princeton, New Jersey

Dave Berg, Computer Coordinator, Independent School District, East Grand Forks, Minnesota

Elizabeth D. Bjork, Math-Computer Specialist, Lincoln Public Schools, Lincoln, Massachusetts

Robert Engberg, Computer Teacher, Muirlands Junior High School, La Jolla, California

William J. Engelmeyer, Supervisor of Mathematics, Baltimore County Public Schools, Baltimore, Maryland

Ron Erickson, Director of Computer Technology, Highland Park School District, Highland Park, New Jersey

Myrna E. Garfunkel, Computer Teacher and Editor of Computer Learners, Users, & Educators (CLUES) Newsletter, New Jersey

George Haddad, Coordinator, Computer-Based Education, Hartford Public Schools, Hartford, Connecticut

John J. Hopton, K–12 Mathematics Supervisor, Franklin Township School, Somerset, New Jersey

Mary Hoqquist McDermut, Computer Student, Chicago, Illinois

Nancy Roberts, Associate Professor and Director of Computers in Education, Lesley College, Cambridge, Massachusetts

James H. Smith, Principal, Cooper Elementary School, Detroit, Michigan

Stanley A. Smith, Mathematics Coordinator, Baltimore County Public Schools, Baltimore, Maryland

Louise Thompson, Brookline Public Schools, Brookline, Massachusetts

Richard Thurman, Teacher of Mathematics and Computer Literacy, Hoover Middle School, San Jose Unified School District, San Jose, California

Joyce A. Tobias, Curriculum Coordinator for Computer Education, Brookline Public Schools, Brookline, Massachusetts

William Zachmeier, Acting Superintendent, Cupertino School District, Cupertino, California.

This entire project has been long and complex. It has required good planning, coordination among teams, communication, and careful monitoring. For these management skills, we owe much to Martha Ramirez, President, Computer Literacy. When free of these tasks, she has also contributed many helpful suggestions regarding content and form.

Contents

Introduction

What Is "Computer Literacy"?

We all believe that literacy is the most important goal of education: Every citizen should be able to read and write. Democratic government, career opportunities, and personal welfare all depend on these skills. But what about "computer literacy"? Is there anything so important about computers that every citizen should learn it?

The Age of Information Many social critics have characterized our time as a transition from the Industrial Age to the Age of Information. At the beginning of this century, most people in developed nations worked at blue-collar jobs in factories. By the end of this century, four-fifths of us will be information workers, not manual laborers. Put simply, our jobs will be to receive information from others, process information in various ways, and pass information along to others.

The information machine The computer is designed to do only three things: receive, process, and give back information—the very things that all information workers do. Therefore, computer literacy is likely to have a significant impact on daily life in much the same way that ordinary literacy has had in the past.

Thinking skills Computer literacy means being able to tell a computer to do what you want it to do. To tell a computer to do anything, you must first understand exactly what you want done. If the computer does not do what you want, you must think again about the instructions you gave. You may need to carry out experiments and revise your ideas. These are exactly the same kinds of things you do when writing a report or solving a problem.

About Programming

To tell the computer to do what you want it to do, you must use a programming language. Writing instructions for the computer is programming. Therefore, programming skills form the backbone of computer literacy.

Many languages There are many languages for telling the computer to do what you want. Some languages can be used only for a single application, such as using a data base, writing letters, or drawing graphs. Other languages have a more general purpose and can be used for many different applications.

Writing programs   Many people prefer not to write their own programs because it is usually easier to buy a ready-made program and learn the special-purpose language for a particular application. Writing simple programs of your own helps you to understand how a computer works, what its capabilities are, and what its limitations are. There is no better way to gain a general appreciation of computers than by learning to write programs for them.

About Computer Languages

There are about a dozen commonly used, general-purpose languages. For example, you may have heard of Pascal, Logo, FORTRAN, or COBOL. This book uses a hands-on approach to teaching BASIC.

No right language   Every computer language has loyal followers who say it is better than the others. Such partisan debate obscures an important truth: Most computer languages are far more alike than they are different from one another. The main ideas of programming can be learned in any of the common languages. People who work with computers often know two or three programming languages.

BASIC   This book teaches BASIC, despite certain flaws in the language, because some version of BASIC is available on almost every microcomputer. If you know how to express your ideas well in BASIC, you will usually be able to tell any computer to do what you want it to do.

Structured programming   In this book, you will learn problem-solving skills using methods called top-down design and structured programming. Structured programming involves analyzing a problem and dividing it into sections. Then the sections are programmed and integrated. Structured programming makes your programs more readable and easier to debug.

About Applications

An accompanying book, *Introduction to Computer Applications,* introduces productivity tools. Database management, word processing, and spreadsheets are the three applications most frequently used in business careers. You will come to appreciate how information is organized, shared, and treated as something of value.

To use the Applications book, you will need a copy of AppleWorks and our Computer Applications DATA Disk.

Introduction to the Development of Computers

Today, there are many sizes and types of computers all over the world. Their power, speed, application, and sophistication change constantly. Taxi drivers have computerized meters which print receipts. Subway systems, such as the one in Washington, D.C., are completely managed by computers. Hotels have replaced room keys with hole-punched cards in order to increase security. Many, many household appliances contain computers of various sizes in order to increase the efficiency and flexibility of their operations. People buying tickets for concerts, doing laundry, taking photographs, buying gasoline for cars, standing at the checkout lines in supermarkets are all using computers constantly in their daily lives.

The word "computer" comes from Latin words meaning "together" and "to reckon." So even though the coinage of the word is a response to the recent development of electronic calculating machines, the *idea* of computing is very old.

Computers have their roots in very ancient times as people developed the use of symbols to represent sounds and numerical quantities. Gradually, they also began to develop counting and calculating devices that not only made their trading activities easier, but allowed them to expand the number and complexity of the activities. People began by using hand-operated devices, which then became mechanical as people investigated ways to get the tools to do more things. The harnessing of electricity increased radically the operational speed of these mechanical inventions. Similarly, the development of semi-conductor microchips has pushed the execution speed of modern computers to limits incomprehensible to most people.

The first computers were extremely large and used vacuum tubes for their operations. Even though they were impressive in their abilities, their memories were no larger than you can find now in a small calculator. The vacuum tubes heated up, burned out, and required tremendous amounts of electricity. The computer itself required an entire room to house, programming was tedious and difficult, and compared to today, slow.

The next stage in the development of computers (sometimes called the second generation) involved the introduction of transistors to replace vacuum tubes. Most people knew the transistor from their transistor radios. Now computers were both faster and much smaller. However, most computers still had no more memory than a tiny home computer.

The next stage involved the development of integrated circuits, etched on tiny silicon chips which made possible much larger memories in much less space. Each chip contained the equivalent of hundreds of transistors. People began to develop minicomputers and supercomputers, and to research further compression of the space required for different operations.

Large Scale Integration (LSI) and Very Large Scale Integration (VLSI) made the microprocessor a reality by packing tens, then hundreds of thousands, of circuit elements on the tiny chips. Now, computers about the size of a typewriter could perform many operations. The appearance of microcomputers made possible the introduction of the computer into the classroom and the home.

As you look at the History of the Development of Computing, remember that these milestone events are only highlights in a fascinating story of discovery. You may wish to do more research about many of these people and events.

Things that the Balinese made and stories they told suggest that human beings living about 30,000 years ago knew how to navigate. As navigators, they had to compute.

The earliest forms of writing date from about this time. Clay tablets from Mesopotamia are the first known materials on which people wrote.

From the Sumerian ideograms (symbols for ideas) and phonograms (symbols for phonetic values) come the Mesopotamian script, called cuneiform. The earliest script is thought to have had as many as 2,000 different symbols.

Caravans travel between India and Mesopotamia. Merchants traveling by land and sea exchange ideas about how to compute values.

prehistory   6000 BC   5000 BC   3200 BC

1700 BC

By the time of the Hammurabi dynasty in ancient Babylon, numerical, algebraic, and geometrical methods of computation are well-developed. The Babylonians use place-value notation, spherical geometry, and a base-60 numbering system.

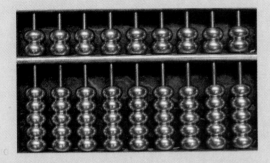

The abacus, probably developed by the Babylonians, is used a lot in the Far East. The abacus is both a computational tool and a device for storing information.

In India, papers on astronomy called *The Siddhantas* discuss astral geometry using Hindu numerals.

600 BC   400 BC

c. 1800–1400 BC

An ancient culture creates Stonehenge in England. Stones weighing up to 50 tons are placed in a circular pattern. The arrangement of the stones enables people to compute astronomical calendar events.

The invention of paper by the Chinese, indispensable to the development of printing, is destined to become the prime storage media for information, only recently challenged by photographic and electronic storage media. Paper moves through Asia to the Mediterranean (from Egypt to Morocco and Spain). Paper is found in Italy in 1270, in Nuremburg in 1390, in England in 1494, and in Philadelphia in 1690.

The first printed books exist by this time. The Chinese printed them from wooden blocks on which text and illustrations were engraved. A book, dated A.D. May 11, 868, with a woodcut frontispiece survives to the present.

Leonardo Fibonacci publishes *Liber Abaci,* in which he suggests the use of Hindu (Arabic) numerals and includes some material on algebra. The superior numbering system of the Hindu-Arabs is slow to catch on. Florentine merchants pass a law against the "new fangled [Hindu] figures."

The first European block books appear at about this time.

105 AD   868   1202   1350

100 BC   900

The Antikythera, a sophisticated device for predicting the motion of stars and planets, is used by the Greeks.

Abu Rayhan Muhammad ibn Ahmad al Biruni gives a clear presentation of Hindu numerals and their uses.

Gutenberg, a German printer, uses the techniques of textile printing and metalwork for printing on paper. He invents printing with movable type. It seems that the earliest piece of printing that exists (about 1444–1447) is a fragment of the *World Judgement* (Gutenberg Museum, Mainz).

1454

c. 1600

John Napier [1550–1617] invents logarithms, which are a series of numbers that allow people to do division and multiplication using subtraction and addition. He also invents Napier's Bones, which are popular calculating kits.

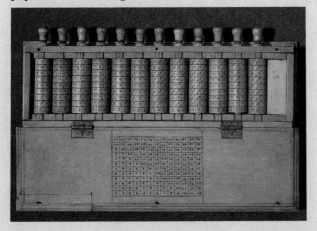

1623

Wilhelm Schickard invents a Calculating Clock.

Henry Briggs [1561–1630] develops extensive log tables.

William Oughtred [1574–1660] and Richard Delamain invent the slide rule based on log tables. With it, people can perform calculations more quickly.

To help his father perform
business accounting computa-
tions, Blaise Pascal invents
the first calculator. It multiplies and divides using repeated addition and subtraction.

1642

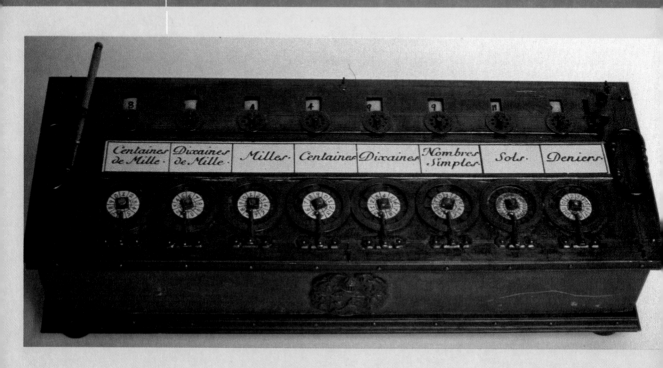

Gottfried Wilhem von Leibnitz invents the Stepped Reckoner (completed in 1694), a mechanical calculator that uses a new kind of gear called the Leibnitz wheel. Using repeated addition, the Stepped Reckoner multiplies, divides, and finds square roots.

Liebnitz helps bring the binary system to the West. The binary system, which uses only two numerals—0 and 1—to express all numbers, is crucial to the operation of all modern computers.

1671

1801

The Jacquard Loom uses cards with punched holes to store the details of a textile pattern. The movement of small wooden pins through the holes controls the operation of the loom. Similar cards are later used by Babbage (1835) and Hollerith (1880) to store other kinds of information.

Charles Babbage begins work on the Difference Engine, which can do calculations more accurately than by hand. His designs are too complicated for the machine makers of the day, and a successful working model is never completed.

1823

1835

Babbage proposes the Analytical Engine, a machine that can solve any mathematical problem. It uses two sets of punched cards (Jacquard cards) in a way similar to that used by many 20th-century computers: one had punched coded data, the other the sequence of operations.

The Analytical Engine has a storage unit and an arithmetic unit. It can print, compare quantities, and carry intermediate results to the next step of a programmed sequence.

George Boole develops Boolean algebra, which enables mathematics to be applied to nonmath ideas, such as logic. Boolean algebra is fundamental to many modern devices such as telephone communications and is very important to computer design.

Dorr E. Felt invents a machine that is a combination of a keyboard, calculator, and printer. It is called a Comptometer. It is a major advance in calculating machines. No longer do operators have to record results by hand.

Advances in engineering and machinery make improvements in mechanical calculators possible. Wide interest among inventors and the public brings calculators into the office.

Ada Augusta Byron, daughter of the poet Lord Percy Byron, writes the documentation for the Babbage Difference Engine. Her symbolic treatment of computation earns her the title of the First Computer Programmer.

1835

1854

1872

1885

1886

Herman Hollerith works on the 1880 census. He suggests using cards with holes punched in them that represent arithmetic sums.

It works, and the 1890 census is completed in one-third the time. Later, Hollerith establishes the Computing Tabulating Recording Company, which became IBM in 1924.

Alan Turing publishes "On Computable Numbers" in 1937. In it, he introduces the Turing machine, an imaginary machine that could solve almost any logical problem using very simple procedures. Because it could theoretically be taught to imitate or control almost any other machine, Turing's hypothetical model was really a computer.

John Atanasoff invents the first electronic digital computer. It is the first computer to use vacuum tubes.

1937

1939

1892

1937

1938

William Burroughs patents a calculator/printer that is extremely popular. The Burroughs Adding Machine Company grows to be a giant in the industry. Over the next decades, calculators become commonplace in finance, commerce, and the university.

Vannevar Bush, inventor of a differential analyzer at MIT, proposes his MEMEX idea. He looks forward to a peaceful time when scholars will work together to create a super data base that stores all human knowledge. A MEMEX version of this timeline would let you get more pictures and information just by touching the computer monitor at any entry.

Claude Shannon explains how electrical circuits can be controlled by Boolean logic. This is a very important development because it means that information in any form, not just numbers, can be manipulated by a machine.

Konrad Zuse creates the Z3, which uses electrical relays and reads programs from punched tape. The machine uses binary mathematics to compute data.

John Mauchley, J. Presper Eckert, and John von Neumann build ENIAC, a huge programmable calculator weighing over 30 tons. ENIAC proves that electronic computers have a bright future.

Max Newman, F.C. Williams, and others build the Manchester Mark I, the first computer to read stored programs from an internal electronic memory.

J. Presper Eckert, Jr., and John Mauchly create UNIVAC, the first commercially successful general-purpose electronic computer. UNIVAC began to convince people that the computer business can make money.

John Backus, Irving Ziller, and others create FORTRAN, the first high-level programming language. For the first time in history, people who are not engineers can give instructions to a computer.

1941   1946

1948   1951

1957

1947

John Bardeen, William Shockley, and Walter H. Brattain create the first transistor. Transistors, which dramatically reduce the size of computers and increase their speed and reliability, quickly begin to replace the vacuum tube.

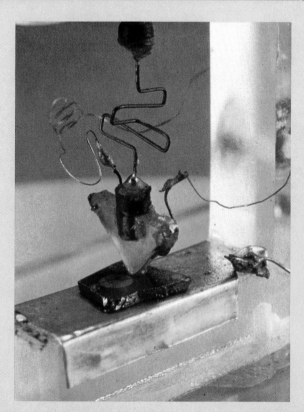

A European design team invents a new computer language called ALGOL, the ALGorithm Oriented Language. ALGOL, which is suitable for business, replaces FORTRAN in most European countries.

Grace M. Hopper heads a team that develops the COBOL language. COBOL, which is designed to be easy to read, is used for many business applications.

John Kemeny and Thomas Kurtz create BASIC, which is often used to introduce programming to students. BASIC, one of the easiest computer languages to learn, is used for many applications in entertainment, education, and business.

1958   1960   1963

1958–1959

John Kilby and Robert Noyce invent the silicon chip. These very small chips permit Very Large Scale Integration (VLSI). Computers that would have filled a school room can now be the size of a tiny chip. Computer designs that were originally too complicated for people to build can now be manufactured.

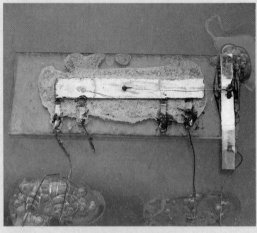
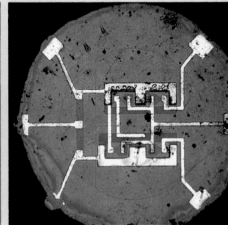

Nicklaus Wirth invents Pascal. Named for Blaise Pascal, this language is the model for several important languages to follow. It is an ideal language for structured programming. Structured programming lets you break a big problem into smaller problems, solve the smaller ones, and then put them all back together to arrive at the final solution.

Gary Kildall creates PL/I for the Intel 4004. Kildall uses PL/I on a mainframe computer to simulate the operations of a microcomputer. Such simulations help designers make new computers. The computer is now a tool-making tool.

IBM markets the floppy disk.

Kenneth Iverson creates A Programming Language (APL). APL starts out as a chalkboard notation to represent complicated algorithms in a very compact code. APL uses a unique set of symbols for its powerful functions.

1972

1969

1972

Ted Hoff, Stan Mazer, Robert Noyce, and Federico Faggin design the first microprocessor, the Intel 4004. A microprocessor is at the heart of every modern computer. Although a whole computer system may include things such as a monitor and a keyboard, it is really the tiny microprocessor that does all the work of computing. In a very real sense, the microprocessor—smaller than a fingernail—is the actual computer.

Intel invents the 8080, a relatively inexpensive 8-bit microprocessor. Inexpensive mass-produced microprocessors are what make the personal computer industry possible.

Edward Roberts invents the first personal computer. It is named the Altair, after a planet in a "Star Trek" episode. Computer whiz kids Bill Gates and Paul Allen develop a version of BASIC for the Altair.

Gary Kildall and Dorothy McEwen successfully market CP/M (control program/monitor), an operating system for the 8-bit microcomputer.

Apple Computer Company is founded by Steve Jobs, Stephan Wozniak, and A.C. Markkula.

The Apple II, the Commodore Pet, and the first TRS-80 appear on the market in the late seventies.

1975   1976

1976

Magnetic bubble storage and laser disk technology develops.

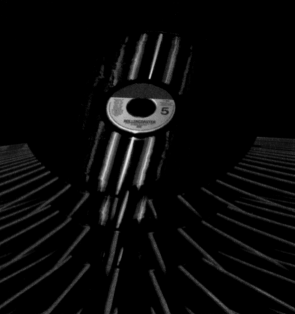

Electronic mail becomes increasingly popular. Banking continues to expand its use of Electronic Funds Transfer technology (EFT) and Automatic Teller Machines (ATMs).

Personal computers use powerful word processors, organizers, database managers, and spreadsheets.

The U.S. National Bureau of Standards develops encode/decode procedures for protecting the confidentiality of information.

1980s →

Ada develops. Named for Ada Byron, this programming language is designed for the real-time control of weapons systems.

World Game researchers develop software for a computer-controlled geoscope. A geoscope is an illuminated sphere that displays global patterns and trends in a highly visual and comprehensible form.

IBM PC and PCjr are introduced.

R. Buckminster Fuller publishes *Critical Path*. Critical path computer programs are used to manage large-scale projects such as NASA's space projects and Disney's EPCOT.

The Apple Macintosh makes its market debut. A new concept, this personal computer uses a mouse to point to graphic symbols to control operations. (Photo courtesy of Apple Computer, Inc.)

Artificial Intelligence researchers pioneer the first Expert Systems. Expert Systems make routine decisions based on large amounts of complex information, freeing the human expert to address more complicated decisions requiring more intuitive responses.

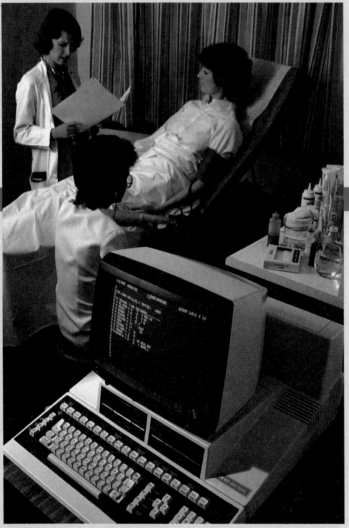

1980s

Inventors develop "talking" computers that can also interpret human speech.

Researchers look for ways to construct circuits that will self-replicate and self-repair. So-called biocomputers may help us understand the structure and function of the human brain.

omputer graphics technology
ontinues to evolve. Popular
lms use the ability of Cray su-
ercomputers to animate real-
tic science fiction scenes.

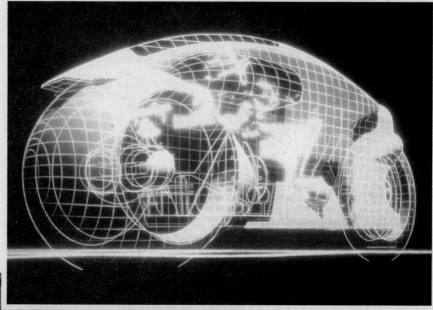

2000

The New York Insti-
tute of Technology,
Lucasfilms, Bell Labs,
and Walt Disney Pro-
ductions are principal
training grounds for
new generations of
computer graphics art-
ists. Programmers dis-
cover how to create
images of landscapes,
clouds, and rough sur-
faces.

Part

Taking Control

Computers are everywhere. There is one in every digital watch and every pocket calculator. New cars, television sets, microwave ovens, and typewriters often have computers. Without computers, there would be no video games and no electronic toys. At the office, computers help people type, file information, and send messages back and forth. In the factory, computers guide robot arms that build cars.

Slaves or masters? Computers are making revolutionary changes in the way we live, play, and work. Are these good changes? Some people worry that we may become slaves to this new machine, totally dependent on it and no longer in control of our own lives. Others see a brighter future in which people are masters and machines are helpers. Which future will actually happen?

Computer literacy The answer to that question depends on what you decide to do about the computer. You can decide that computers are too difficult and leave the whole subject in the hands of the "experts." Or you can decide to learn about computers and take control of them yourself. In other words, you can become **computer literate**.

Literacy and freedom It took you many years to master the skills of reading and writing, but these skills gave you *freedom*. You do not have to depend on others to read street signs for you, or to tell you the latest news, or to write your letters to friends or representatives in Congress. You do not have to trust experts: You are *literate*. In the same way, your "math literacy" gave you freedom: You do not have to trust a math expert to tell you whether three oranges for 80 cents is a better buy than one orange for 25 cents. You are in control.

Controlling the computer Computer literacy is like these other skills: It takes time and practice to learn, but it puts you in control of the computer and frees you from having to depend on and trust a computer expert. When you become computer literate, you will know two important things: (1) what things a computer *can* do and (2) how to tell a computer to do the things *you* want it to do.

The Computer in Your Life

IN THIS SESSION YOU WILL:
• Learn some ways people use computers.
• Learn how computers are important in everyday life.
• Learn the difference between dedicated computers and general-purpose computers.
• Learn that controlling computers can be useful and fun.

Computers and People

January of 1980 is an important month in the history of computers and people. During that month, more computers were built than children were born.

A computer for everyone? For the first time, it began to seem possible that any person who wanted a computer could own one. In fact, only three years later there were as many computers in the world as people. Where are all those computers?

Computers in calculators Have you used a pocket calculator? There is a computer inside a pocket calculator. It notices each key that you press, knows all the rules of arithmetic, and writes answers on the display. The calculator can do arithmetic because a computer tells it how.

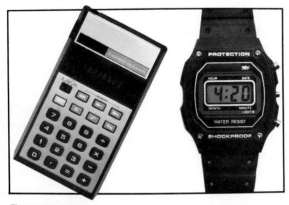

There are computers in this calculator and in this digital watch.

Computers in watches There is also a computer inside each digital watch—see the digital display on the watch in the photo. The watch contains a tiny quartz crystal that vibrates many times every second. The computer counts each beat of the crystal, adds up all the beats, and writes the time on the display. The watch shows the time because a computer tells it how.

Computers in typewriters Some typewriters let you type whole letters or compositions into a part called the "memory." Later you can call up what you have written, correct spelling errors, and rewrite as much as you want. After that, you can have the typewriter type a perfect copy automatically. This typewriter remembers because a computer inside tells it how.

Computers in stereo and TV sets To pick a station on older stereo and TV sets, you turn a knob that moves some metal parts inside the set. To pick a station on newer units, you just touch a small button. A computer notices which button you touch, makes electrical changes inside the unit, and writes the new channel number or station frequency on a small digital display. The computer may also remember your favorite stations and how loud you like the sound.

Computers in games and toys Have you used a video game or an electronic toy? An electronic chess game? Usually, a computer tells these games what to do and how to do it.

Same parts in all It might surprise you that there are computers inside all these household appliances. Most people probably think that a pocket calculator and an electronic game must look very different inside. In fact, the parts of one are much like the parts of the other. The main difference is that one computer "knows" the rules of arithmetic and the other computer "knows" the rules of chess.

Who Tells the Computer?

The fact that a computer can store knowledge is very important. This ability makes computers different from every other machine ever invented.

The stored program Before a computer can play chess, it must be told the rules and tactics of the game. This information is contained in a **computer program**, or simply, a **program**. *A program is a list of instructions that the computer carries out one at a time.* With a different program, the same computer that carried out the steps of a chess game can carry out the steps of a multiplication problem.

This chess game has a dedicated computer.

Writing programs The knowledge inside any computer was put there by a person. Before a computer can play chess, a good chess player has to write the rules and tactics into a program and then put the program into the computer. After that, the computer can play chess, but only as well as the person who wrote the program. *Whenever you see a computer in use, remember that it is doing only what some person told it to do.*

Dedicated computers You cannot easily change the program in a chess game, a typewriter, a TV set, a watch, or a calculator. Each program is a permanent part of the appliance. We say that each of these computers is **dedicated** to carrying out the steps of one program. It could have a different program, but there is no easy way for you to change programs.

General-purpose computers   The programs in the computers you will use are easily changed. These computers are called **general-purpose computers** because, by changing programs, you can easily change the purpose of the computer. If you put a chess-playing program into the computer, in a few seconds it will play chess. If you put a type-writing program in, it will help you type letters. If you put a calculator program in, it will help you do arithmetic problems.

Taking Control

If you want to do more than use other people's programs, you must learn how to tell the computer to do what you want it to do. In other words, you must learn to write programs of your own.

Computer language   You will learn a simple language especially made up for writing programs. As you learn the words of this language, you will be able to do more with your computer. You will learn to give the computer commands, and you will learn which commands are easy and which are difficult to give. You will learn how to do many new things with the computer, but you will also see its limitations.

Loading and running programs   The first computer words you learn will let you load other people's programs into the computer and find out what those programs tell the computer to do. (If you have played games on a computer, you probably know how to do this already.)

These students are using a graphics program.

Reading programs   Another word will allow you to read the instructions in a program. The best way to start learning about writing programs is by reading what other people have written and getting new ideas.

Drawing pictures   Before long, you will find out how to write programs of your own. In just a few days, you will be able to tell the computer to print on the TV screen pictures made up of letters. In a few weeks, you will learn how to tell the computer to draw pictures in color or shades of gray.

Doing math, playing games, and more   As you learn more about writing programs, you will be able to tell the computer to do more things for you. You can tell it to help you do math calculations. Or you can give it the rules of a game you invent and make the computer play it with you.

QUESTIONS

1. How are calculators, digital watches, and electronic games alike? How are they different?

2. Have you seen other machines that might contain computers? (Hint: look for pushbuttons, keyboards, and digital displays.)

3. Do you or your family ever get mail that seems written by a computer? What makes you think so?

4. What makes the computer in a chess game behave differently from the same computer in a pocket calculator?

5. Think again about letters that seem written by a computer. What or who told the computer how to write those letters?

6. What is the difference between a dedicated computer and a general-purpose computer?

7. Before you can give instructions to a computer, what will you need to learn?

8. What are some of the things you will be able to tell your computer to do?

Getting Started

- Use the LOAD command to move a program from a diskette into the computer.
- Use the RUN command to tell the computer to carry out the instructions in a program.
- Use the NEW command to erase a program from the computer.
- Use the CATALOG command to see what programs are on a diskette.

Starting the Apple II

You may have separate instructions for starting your Apple II computer system. If so, follow those instructions. If not, follow the instructions below.

How to Start Your Computer

Before doing anything, take a close look at the computer system. It has three important parts. The main unit has a **keyboard** like the one on a typewriter. On top of the main unit is a **TV screen** (also called a **monitor**). Your system also has a **disk drive** which is either in the main unit or in a separate cabinet. The drive is behind a long horizontal slot covered by a latch. In a moment, you will be putting your Computer Literacy diskette into this slot. (If your computer has two drives, you will always use the one labeled "Drive 1.")

Step 1.   Be sure the TV set or monitor is turned on. If there is a volume control, turn it down.

Step 2.   Be sure the (CAPS LOCK) key is in the down position. You will be using capital letters only. (If there is no (CAPS LOCK) key, skip this step.)

Step 3.   Insert the diskette labeled COMPUTER LITERACY into the disk drive. Open the latch in front of the disk drive slot. Hold

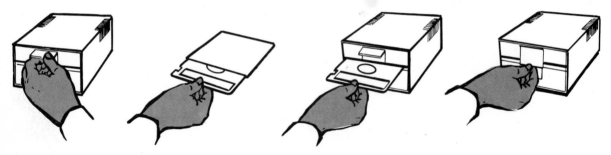

the diskette with your thumb on the label and the label up. Gently slide the diskette all the way into the slot. Close the latch tightly.

Step 4. If the computer's POWER light is off, just turn the power switch on. To do this, reach with your left hand around the back of the computer. You will feel a small on/off toggle switch. Turn it on. The POWER light should come on. Go to step 5.

If the POWER light is already on, enter the PR#6 command, as shown below. Don't worry about the meaning; think of PR#6 as a magic phrase, like "open sesame." Here is how to type it. (If you make a mistake, just press the (RETURN) key and then start over.)

Press and release the (P) key.
Press and release the (R) key.
Hold down the (SHIFT) key and, at the same time, press the (3) key.
Then release both keys.
Press and release the (6) key.
Press and release the (RETURN) key.

Step 5. Watch for this: The red disk drive light should come on. You may hear clicks and whirrs coming out of the disk drive. The red light should turn off, and your screen should look like this:

SUCCESS!!!
WELCOME TO COMPUTER LITERACY
]■

You may have to adjust the screen to make it more readable. The symbol] is called the **Applesoft BASIC prompt character.** The little box after the prompt character is called the **cursor.** It should be flashing on and off. The prompt character and flashing cursor tell you that you have started the computer correctly. If your screen does not look like this, turn your computer off and start over with step 1.

1. How do you know whether the computer is on?
2. How do you know you have started the computer correctly?
3. When should you type PR#6?

Using This Book with the Computer

The even-numbered sessions in this book will guide you in learning to use a computer. You will not need additional help, but you will have to read carefully. The book should be open and next to the computer or in your lap where you can easily read it while typing on the keyboard. On many pages, there are words printed in color at the left border. These words have a long, colored line under them. The line leads to a sentence at the right. When you see a page like this, here is what you should do:

> **How to use this book**
>
> **1.** Always read the words at the left and the sentence at the right before you do anything.
> **2.** Type the letters shown in the left column.
> **3.** Press the (RETURN) key after each line.
> **4.** Then see what happens, and reread the sentence at the right.

Messages to the Computer

All right, let's get started. The prompt symbol (]) should be at the left of the screen. The flashing cursor means that the computer is waiting for you to type something. Type the following letters:

ZZZZ ....and press the (RETURN) key at the right side of the keyboard.

As you pressed the keys, you should have seen the same letters show up on the screen. The cursor tells you where the next letter will go. When you pressed the (RETURN) key, the computer beeped and printed the message ?SYNTAX ERROR. You did nothing wrong. The computer says ?SYNTAX ERROR when it does not understand a message you typed.

HOUSE ....and press the (RETURN) key. The computer does not understand HOUSE either.

HOME ....and press (RETURN). The computer understood what you typed. It cleared all words from the screen and moved the cursor to the upper left corner.

4. What does ?SYNTAX ERROR mean?

5. If you want to clear the TV screen, what word should you type?

6. When you are through typing a line, what key should you press?

Loading Programs from Diskettes

Let's see how we can make the computer do something more interesting. (If you get the ?SYNTAX ERROR message, just retype the line.)

LOAD HI THERE   ...and press the (RETURN) key. Be sure to include the spaces in your message.

HI THERE is the name of a **program** stored on your diskette. When you pressed the (RETURN) key, you should have seen the red light on the disk drive come on. While this was happening, the cursor disappeared. After a few moments, the cursor and the prompt symbol (]) should have reappeared on the screen.

RUN   ...and press the (RETURN) key.

Answer the question by typing your name and pressing the (RETURN) key.

RUN   ...and press the (RETURN) key. Try it again with a friend's name.

NEW   ...and press the (RETURN) key.

RUN   ...and press the (RETURN) key. Nothing happened because NEW erased HI THERE from the computer.

Do you think HI THERE is totally lost now? Let's see.

LOAD HI THERE   ...and press (RETURN).

RUN   Answer the question and press (RETURN).

The original version of program HI THERE is still on the diskette. The LOAD command only loads a *copy* of the program into the computer.

If everything worked, you found out how you can use three **commands**. The LOAD command told the computer to move HI THERE from the diskette into the computer. The RUN command told the computer to perform HI THERE. The NEW command told the computer to erase HI THERE. You used the (RETURN) key to send each message to the computer.

Let's try these commands again. If you make a typing error, just retype the line. **Remember to press the ⌜RETURN⌝ key at the end of each line.**

```
LOAD ROCKET
RUN
```
Now you should see a rocket drawn on the screen.

```
NEW
RUN
```
The `NEW` command erased program `ROCKET` from the computer.

```
LOAD BLAST OFF
RUN
```
This program shows the rocket taking off.

```
RUN
```
Launch it again.

```
NEW
RUN
```
Now the program is gone from the computer.

```
LOAD BLAST OFF
RUN
```
But you can bring it back from the diskette.

7. Suppose you have a program named `CIRCLES` on your diskette. How would you load this program into the computer and tell the computer to perform it?

8. If you just ran a program named `AIRPLANE`, how would you tell the computer to erase `AIRPLANE` from the computer?

9. What have you used the ⌜RETURN⌝ key for?

Finding What Programs Are on a Diskette

Your diskette contains many programs. Here is how you can discover what is there.

```
CATALOG
```
This is a new command.

The `CATALOG` command tells the computer to show you the names of the programs on the diskette. Can you find `HI THERE`, `ROCKET`, and `BLAST OFF` in the list? There is also a program named `BOXES`. Try loading it and running it.

```
LOAD BOXES
RUN
```
Your Apple computer can draw with colors (or shades of gray on a black-and-white TV).

```
NEW
RUN
```
`NEW` erased the program from the computer.

Errors While Loading

If you made no typing mistakes, you saw no error messages on the screen. There are other errors besides typing errors. Let's make one happen now.

Open the door on the disk drive and remove the diskette.

LOAD HI THERE

...and press the (RETURN) key. After some buzzes and clicks, you should see an error message on the screen.

I/O is an abbreviation for **input/output**. So, I/O ERROR means the computer had a problem with input or output. You know why. The computer was trying to load HI THERE, but you removed the diskette containing HI THERE. The error was that there was no diskette in the drive. The same error message will appear if the door on the disk drive is open or if the diskette is upside down. Put the diskette back in the disk drive and close the door.

CATALOG

Check the list of programs on the diskette.

LOAD AIRPLANE

But AIRPLANE is not on the diskette.

This time you should have seen this error message on the screen: FILE NOT FOUND. Programs are stored in **files** on the diskette. There is no file named AIRPLANE on the diskette, so the computer said it could not find the file.

10. If you try to load a program from the diskette, but accidentally leave the disk-drive door open, what message will the computer print?

11. In the message I/O ERROR, what does I/O stand for?

12. If you try to load a program that is not on the diskette, what error message will you get?

If you have extra lab time:

- There is an interesting program called TURTLE TROT on the diskette. Find out what it does.
- See what programs SYMMETRY and QUILT do.

  When you leave the computer, it is a good idea to turn off the TV. Leave the computer on, however. Be sure to take your diskette out of the drive.

Communicating with Your Computer

IN THIS SESSION YOU WILL:
- Review the system commands LOAD, RUN, NEW, and CATALOG.
- Learn what a computer language is.
- Learn how information flows between the computer and the person using it.
- Define all computer activities as one of three things: input, processing, or output.
- Learn how keyboard input leads to screen output.

Review

In Session 2, you learned how to turn your computer on, and you experimented with typing letters and words on the **keyboard**. You found that the computer did not recognize some words and gave you an **error message**. It recognized the words LOAD, RUN, NEW, and CATALOG, however, and carried out your instructions. These four words are examples of **commands**. A command usually tells the computer to do something with a **program**.

LOAD You saw that the LOAD command tells the computer to move a *copy* of a program from the **diskette** into the computer.

RUN The RUN command tells the computer to perform the program now in the computer. What the computer does after that depends on what program is in the computer. If there is no program in the computer, it will do nothing.

NEW The NEW command tells the computer to erase the program from the computer, but *not* from the diskette. In sessions to come, you will enter programs by typing them on the keyboard. You will need the NEW command to erase an old program before typing a new one.

CATALOG If you have many programs on a diskette, you may not remember exactly what is there. The CATALOG command tells the computer to show you the names of the programs on the diskette in the disk drive.

The Language of the Computer

To use a computer, you must be able to *communicate* with it. You must tell the computer what you want done and must understand the messages that come back from the computer. In short, you need to know a **language**.

BASIC The language your computer uses has a name. It is called BASIC, which stands for Beginners All-purpose Symbolic Instruction Code. BASIC was invented in 1963 by John Kemeny and Thomas Kurtz to teach students how to use a computer. Today more people know BASIC than any other computer language. BASIC is used in homes, businesses, science labs, and schools.

Applesoft The version of BASIC you will use is called Applesoft BASIC. There are other versions of BASIC, but their main parts are very much alike. We will call these common parts Standard BASIC. When there is an important difference between Applesoft and Standard BASIC, we will point it out.

Very small vocabulary From your activities in Session 2, you are beginning to understand what kind of language your computer speaks. There aren't very many words in the computer's vocabulary. In fact, you will need to know only about two dozen words and a dozen symbols. After that, you will be able to say almost anything that can be said to your computer.

Other languages There are many other computer languages. They have names such as FORTRAN, COBOL, PL/I, Logo, Pascal, and Ada. People have written hundreds of thousands of programs in each language, and it seems unlikely that any one language will win out over the rest. Some people argue that their own favorite language is best, but most computer languages are really very much alike. They all have very tiny vocabularies, and it is usually easy to translate from one computer language into another. Most people who work with computers know three or four computer languages.

Learning new languages Although you will be using BASIC in this course, you will be learning things that apply to any other computer language you might learn later. Usually, all you will have to do is learn a few new words and punctuation rules. Your basic tools will be the same in any language.

Talking with the Computer

In Session 2, you found that working with a computer is a lot like having a conversation with another person. There is a time to talk and a time to listen. You "talk" to the computer by typing on its keyboard, and you "listen" by reading words on the screen. If you talk when you should be listening, the conversation gets confusing.

The cursor The computer has a way of signaling when it is ready to listen to you. It puts its **cursor** on the screen. On the Apple II computer, the cursor is a small square of light that flashes on and off. *If the cursor is not on the screen, the computer is not paying attention to the keyboard.*

The RETURN key You also have a way of signaling that you have finished talking to the computer. *After typing your message, you must* *press the* ⌐RETURN⌐ *key.* After that, the computer accepts your message, does what you asked, and puts the cursor back on the screen.

What Is a Computer?

Until now, we have been using the term *computer* without saying clearly what it means. From your experience in Session 2, you already know a lot about what a computer is, because you know some things it can do. You will learn more about how computers work later. At this time, you should not worry about how the computer does things. You don't need to know how it works to understand how it behaves. You understand and get along with your friends without knowing how their brains, hearts, and stomachs work. Likewise, most people who use computers every day don't know much about how the parts make the whole machine work.

Input, processing, and output A computer *is* what it *does:* Remember when you ran the program HI THERE and entered your name? The computer was performing **input**. After you pressed ⌐RETURN⌐, the computer combined your name with the phrase IS GREAT!!. The computer was **processing** the information you gave it. Finally, the computer printed CHARLIE (or whatever your name is) IS GREAT!! many times. The computer was performing **output**.

The three main activities of a computer

1. **Input:** The computer takes in information.
2. **Processing:** The computer does something with the information.
3. **Output:** The computer gives out information.

Listening, thinking, and talking In human terms, input is like listening, processing is like thinking, and output is like talking. Some people try to do all three at once, but computers usually do one at a time. For example, when you typed LOAD HI THERE, the computer began to input HI THERE from the diskette. While doing that, the computer turned off the cursor. It was not ready for input from the keyboard.

Other inputs and outputs In this course, you will usually use your keyboard for input and your screen for output. If you play computer games, you often use knobs and buttons for input, and you may get music or sound as output. The computer in a new car uses many different input devices: Thermometers, pressure gauges, light switches, and speedometers are a few. The car computer uses dials, lights, and beepers for output. Someday the car computer will get input from a radar beam, and it will use the brakes as output if the car is about to hit something.

Keyboard Input and Screen Output

When you first started using your computer, it probably seemed to you that the keyboard was "connected to" the screen. When you pressed the Ⓗ key, the letter H appeared on the screen right away. The computer behaved like a typewriter.

The keyboard is really just a set of switches. They are connected to the computer **processor**, not the screen. The screen, which is also connected to the processor, shows what you type *only* if the processor says so.

Keyboard input Each time you press a key, the computer performs input, processing, and output. The computer usually checks the keyboard about a thousand times a second to see if you have pressed a key. If so, the computer *inputs* information that tells which key you pressed. Next, the computer *processes* that information and decides what to do. When you press most keys, the computer *outputs* that letter or symbol on the TV screen. It puts the letter where the cursor is and then moves the cursor to the right. When you press certain keys, such as (RETURN), the computer performs a different kind of processing and output.

Modern offices often contain hundreds of computers with keyboards and monitors.

QUESTIONS

1. What do commands usually do?
2. What commands must you type to put the program named BOXES into the computer and perform it?

3. What is the purpose of a computer language?

4. About how many BASIC words will you need to learn to communicate with your computer?

5. What computer language is most used in the world?

6. What are two computer languages other than BASIC?

7. When the cursor is on the screen, what is the computer ready to do?

8. What is the (RETURN) key used for?

9. What three main activities does every computer perform?

10. If you experimented with the program TURTLE TROT, what part of what you saw was input, processing, and output?

11. Today, you can use an automatic teller to get money out of a bank. The automatic teller is connected to a computer. You must put a plastic bank card into a slot. Your account number is on the card. You must then press keys that let the teller know your secret password and how much money you want. The teller checks your password and checks whether there is enough money in your account. If everything is OK, the machine gives you the money. Think of what happens when you use an automatic teller. What information is input? What processing does the teller do? What is output?

12. A home thermostat turns your heat on and off as the temperature of the room goes down and up. Some new thermostats are actually computers. What information is input to such a thermostat? What processing does the thermostat do? What information is output?

13. Some supermarkets have computers that figure out your bill at the checkout counter. The clerk passes each product over a "reader." It reads the stripes on the package that tell exactly what the product is. Quickly, the computer shows the price on the cash register. Can you explain what information is input? What processing the computer performs? What the output is?

14. At the computer, you typed ZZZZ on the keyboard and then pressed the (RETURN) key. For each key you pressed, can you describe what was input? What processing the computer did? What was output?

15. Is it true that whenever you press a key on the keyboard, the computer prints a letter or symbol on the screen? Explain your answer.

Reading and Changing Programs

IN • THIS SESSION YOU WILL:
- Use the LIST command.
- Use the arrow keys to correct typing errors.
- Read program ROCKET.
- Make changes in a BASIC program.

Starting the Computer

Every hands-on session in this book begins the same way. You must start the computer with your diskette as you did in Session 2. Follow the steps below. If you need more details, see pages 6 and 7.

1. **Turn on the TV or monitor.**
2. **Be sure the** (CAPS LOCK) **key is down.**
3. **Insert your diskette into the drive.**
4. **If the computer is on, type** PR#6 **and press** (RETURN). **If it is off, just turn it on.**
5. **Wait for the** WELCOME TO COMPUTER LITERACY **message.**

A New BASIC Command

You already know several commands that tell the computer to do something with a program. Let's start with some of the commands you have used. Remember, if you make a typing error, just press the (RETURN) key and retype the lines.

LOAD ROCKET

This brings program ROCKET into the computer from your diskette.

RUN

This tells the computer to perform the program.

You have used the LOAD and RUN commands before. Here is a command you have not used.

LIST

This tells the computer to print the program lines on the screen.

You are now looking at the BASIC program named ROCKET. It tells your computer how to draw a picture of a rocket. Each line starts with a number. In program ROCKET the top line number is 100; the bottom

number is `290`. Notice that all but two of the lines use the word
`PRINT`. The `LIST` command tells the computer to list the lines of the
BASIC program now in the computer.

`HOME` _____	This tells the computer to clear the screen.
`LIST` _____	Program `ROCKET` is still in the computer.
`CATALOG` _____	Do you think this command erased `ROCKET` from the computer?
`LIST` _____	No, `ROCKET` is still in the computer.
`NEW` _____	Is `ROCKET` still there now?
`LIST` _____	Now it's gone.

`LIST` is a useful command. Any time you want to see the BASIC program in the computer, type `LIST`.

1. If you use `HOME` to clear the screen, does it also erase the program
   from the computer?
2. How can you see the lines of a program stored in the computer?

Correcting Typing Errors

If there is a typing error in a command you give to the computer, you
will usually get the `?SYNTAX ERROR` message. If you make mistakes
but notice them before pressing the (RETURN) key, you can correct the
errors. You will find out how to do that in this section. Start with this
error.

`LOAD SOCKET` _____ Whoops! There is no program named
`SOCKET` on your diskette.

We intentionally had you misspell `ROCKET`. As soon as you pressed
(RETURN), the computer tried to find a program named `SOCKET` on your
diskette. There was no `SOCKET`, so the computer beeped and said `FILE
NOT FOUND`. (Remember, programs are stored on the diskette in files.)
   Let's suppose you saw the typing mistake before you pressed the
(RETURN) key. You would probably want to fix the error before pressing
(RETURN), so the computer would not waste time looking for the wrong
program. Type `LOAD SOCKET` again, but don't press (RETURN) this
time! Here is how to use the **arrow keys** to change the `S` to an `R`. (The
two arrow keys are located below the (RETURN) key.)

1. Press the left-arrow key (←) until the flashing cursor is over
   the `S` in `SOCKET`.
2. Type (R) to correct the spelling mistake.

3. Then use the right-arrow key $\rightarrow$ to move the cursor out past the end of the line.
4. Then press the (RETURN) key.

You know you corrected the error because this time there was no FILE NOT FOUND message.

Step 3 is very important. Let's see what happens when you leave it out by accident. Type LOAD SOCKET again, but don't press (RETURN) yet. Now carry out steps 1, 2, and 4 in the instructions above. What happened?

When you pressed (RETURN), all the letters to the right of the R disappeared. Your command became LOAD R. There is no file named R on your diskette, so you got the FILE NOT FOUND error message. *Moral: You must always use the right-arrow key after fixing any errors in the middle of a line. Move the cursor to the right, past the end of the line.*

3. Suppose program BLAST OFF has been loaded into the computer. You type RUNAWAY, press the left-arrow key four times, and then press the (RETURN) key. What will happen?
4. If you type LOAD HITHERE, what must you do to put a space after HI?

Reading a Program

A good way to start learning to write a program is by reading programs other people have written. Let's start by reading program ROCKET.

LOAD ROCKET
LIST
          You should see a listing of ROCKET on your screen.

All but the first two lines contain the word PRINT and some characters between quotation marks. Look at these characters carefully. Let's see what PRINT tells the computer to do.

RUN
          Now you know what the program tells the computer to do.
LIST
          Now you see the program again.

You have probably figured out that PRINT tells the computer to print on the TV screen whatever characters are inside the quotation marks. Try out this idea.

HOME
PRINT "ROCKET"
          You have to hold down the (SHIFT) key and type the (2) key to get the quotation mark. Notice the words under the line you typed.
PRINT "BLAST OFF"
LIST
          List the program.

Now you know what PRINT tells the computer to do. You also know that HOME (in line 110) tells the computer to clear the screen. But what does line 100 mean? The word REM is short for "remark." The writer of this program used REM to put a title at the beginning of the program. When the computer performs the program, it simply ignores REM and the rest of line 100.

5. How can you tell the computer to put the sentence CHARLIE IS GREAT!! on the screen? (Try it and see if you are right.)

6. How can you put the phrase PART 1 into a program without having it appear on the screen when you run the program?

Making Changes in Programs

Throughout the rest of this book, you will constantly be making changes in programs. Let's change program ROCKET. (Load it if it is not already in your computer.)

LIST _____ You should see a listing of ROCKET on your screen.

This program listing should be on your screen:

```
100 REM --PROGRAM ROCKET
110 HOME
120 PRINT "          ^ "
130 PRINT "         # #"
140 PRINT "        #   #"
150 PRINT "        # M #"
160 PRINT "        # O #"
170 PRINT "        # O #"
180 PRINT "        # N #"
190 PRINT "        #   #"
200 PRINT "        # R #"
210 PRINT "        # A #"
220 PRINT "        # K #"
230 PRINT "        # E #"
240 PRINT "        # R #"
250 PRINT "       #     #"
260 PRINT "      #       #"
270 PRINT "     #  #####  #"
280 PRINT "# #          # #"
290 PRINT "#              #"
```

This is the program that draws a picture of a rocket. Notice that each line begins with a **line number**. You have already seen that PRINT tells the computer to print characters on the screen. Now for a few changes. *When you type the next lines, make certain you use the number keys for 1 and 0. Don't use the ⌶ key or the letter ⓞ key for these numbers.*

```
160   PRINT "   ## 0 ##"
```
There are three spaces after the first quotation mark and one space before and after the 0.

```
170   PRINT "  # # 0 # #"
```
There are two spaces after the first quotation mark.

What do you think the program looks like now? Let's list it and see:

```
LIST
```
The old lines 160 and 170 are gone. The new ones you just entered have taken their place.

```
RUN
```
You have added forward fins to the rocket.

If you want to change a line in a BASIC program, simply retype the complete line, using the same line number. The new line will take the place of the old one.

```
180
```
...and press the (RETURN) key.

```
LIST
```
Line 180 is missing.

```
RUN
```
The rocket is a little shorter now.

To remove a line from a program, type only the line number and press the (RETURN) key. The computer then removes the line from the program.

```
122   PRINT "      ###"
124   PRINT "      ###"
126   PRINT "      ###"
```
There are now five spaces after the first quotation mark.

```
LIST
```
Now there are three new lines in the program.

```
RUN
```
You have added a capsule to the top of the rocket.

To insert a new line, use a line number not already in the program. The computer will place the new line in numerical order among the other lines.

7. How do you remove a line from a BASIC program?

8. How do you change a line already in a BASIC program?

9. How do you insert a new line into a BASIC program?

If you have extra lab time:

- Remove line 110 from program ROCKET. Run it a few times. What does the computer do now?

- Do you think the changes you have made to ROCKET have also changed the version on your diskette? Load it and see.

- Load program HI THERE. Run it, and then list it. Find the line that contains PRINT. Change the line so that GREAT becomes SMART, but everything else stays the same. Run the new version.

- Change the 50 to a 5 in line 140 in program HI THERE. Run this version. Now change the 5 to 100 and run.

 Before leaving the computer, turn off the TV and take your diskette out of the drive.

Program Lines and Statements

IN THIS SESSION YOU WILL:
- Learn what a program listing is.
- Learn the difference between a command and a statement.
- Learn what the PRINT, REM, and HOME statements do.
- Learn the difference between immediate mode and program mode.
- Learn how line-number editing works.
- Learn what a user trap is.

Review

In Session 2, you learned to use the LOAD and RUN commands to put a program into the computer and run it. But you did not see the program itself. Then in Session 4, you discovered the LIST command. It tells the computer to show you the actual lines of the program.

Disk input As we have said, a computer is always doing one of three things. When you entered the LOAD command, your computer began to input a program that was stored on the diskette in the disk drive.

Processing When you entered the RUN command, the computer processed all the lines of the program. The computer processes a program by reading one line at a time and carrying out whatever instructions are written there.

Screen output Certain program lines contain the word PRINT. The PRINT statement tells the computer to output characters on the TV screen. The LIST command also tells the computer to process (read the program lines) and output (print them on the screen).

You used the computer to draw a rocket. Computers are used to control real rockets too.

The program listing In Session 4, you loaded program ROCKET into your computer. Then you typed the LIST command. The computer responded by printing these lines on the screen:

```
100    REM  --PROGRAM ROCKET
110    HOME
120    PRINT "         ^"
130    PRINT "        # #"
140    PRINT "       #   #"
150    PRINT "       # M #"
160    PRINT "       # O #"
170    PRINT "       # O #"
180    PRINT "       # N #"
190    PRINT "       #   #"
200    PRINT "       # R #"
210    PRINT "       # A #"
220    PRINT "       # K #"
230    PRINT "       # E #"
240    PRINT "       # R #"
250    PRINT "      #     #"
260    PRINT "     #       #"
270    PRINT "    # ##### #"
280    PRINT "# #       # #"
290    PRINT "#          #"
```

These lines are called a **listing** of the program. The listing of program ROCKET shows all the instructions the computer follows when drawing a picture of a rocket ship.

Program lines Every BASIC program is made up of a list of **lines**. Every line begins with a **line number**. The rest of the line is a **statement**. For example, program ROCKET contains this line:

```
130    PRINT "        # #"
```

This line is called "line 130." The statement on line 130 is

```
PRINT "        # #"
```

The PRINT statement You found in Session 4 that PRINT tells the computer to print on the TV screen all the characters between the two quotation marks. We say that "line 130 contains a PRINT statement," which means that the word after the line number is PRINT. All but two lines in program ROCKET contain PRINT statements. They tell the computer how to draw the rocket.

The REM statement Program ROCKET begins with a REM statement. The REM statement allows the writer to put a **remark** into a program listing without changing the way the program runs. The computer ignores all REM statements when performing a program. You will use the REM statement often to make your programs easier to read.

The HOME statement Line 110 of program ROCKET contains a HOME statement. It tells the computer to clear the TV screen before it begins to print the rocket in lines 120 through 290. It is usually a good idea to start programs with a HOME statement.

Commands The words LOAD, RUN, LIST, and NEW are examples of **commands**. A command usually tells the computer to do something with a program. The LOAD command says to put a program into the computer. RUN tells the computer to run the program. LIST says to show the program lines on the screen. NEW says to erase the program from the computer, but not from the diskette.

Statements The words PRINT, REM, and HOME are examples of **statements**. Statements do not tell the computer what to do with programs. Statements make up a program.

Program mode Before you can add a statement to a BASIC program, you must give the statement a line number. The computer does not perform the statement right away, but stores it along with any other statements you type. The computer performs the statement only when you enter the RUN command. This is called the **program mode** of using a statement.

Immediate mode But you found in Session 4 that you could also enter a statement without a line number. For example, you typed

```
PRINT "BLAST OFF"
```

and the computer printed BLAST OFF on the screen immediately. You also used the HOME statement without a line number and the computer cleared the screen immediately. Whenever you type a BASIC statement without a line number, the computer performs it right away. This is called the **immediate mode** of using a statement.

Spaces in programs When you type a program into the computer, put spaces after line numbers and between words. Applesoft BASIC does not usually require spaces, but Standard BASIC does. So you should get into the habit of putting in spaces now. Applesoft BASIC will sometimes add extra spaces to the listing, but you should not worry about them. All program lines in the rest of this book will show only the spaces you should type.

Line-Number Editing

In Session 4, you learned how to use the LIST command to see the lines of a program. You also learned how to make changes in a program. The process of changing a program is called **editing**. Most of your time at the computer will be spent editing. It is very easy to edit BASIC programs. Suppose you start by entering this program:

```
10 PRINT "HOW"
20 PRINT "PURPLE"
30 PRINT "THE ELEPHANT"
40 PRINT "IS"
```

Changing a statement To change a statement, all you have to do is retype the line and use the same line number. Example: If you enter the line

```
30 PRINT "COW"
```

your program will change to this:

```
10 PRINT "HOW"
20 PRINT "PURPLE"
30 PRINT "COW"
40 PRINT "IS"
```

Removing a statement Getting rid of a statement in a program is easy. All you have to do is type its line number and press the (RETURN) key. Example: If you now enter the line

```
40
```

your program will change further to this:

```
10 PRINT "HOW"
20 PRINT "PURPLE"
30 PRINT "COW"
```

Adding a statement To put a new line *between* the first and second lines of your program, you must pick a line number between 1 1 and 1 9. (You may not use decimal points.) The computer will then put the line into the program at the right place. Example: If you next enter the line

```
15 PRINT "NOW"
```

the program would change once more to this new form:

```
10 PRINT "HOW"
15 PRINT "NOW"
20 PRINT "PURPLE"
30 PRINT "COW"
```

User traps Line-number editing is a tool that helps you write and change programs. Like any tool, it can also cause damage by accident. You should watch out for **user traps**: common mistakes that are likely to cause accidents. For example, suppose you want to type this line

```
20 PRINT "BROWN"
```

but by mistake you type the letter ⓞ for the number ⓪. When you list the program, you find that line 2Ø is *unchanged,* and there is a *new* line 2! Your program looks like this:

```
2 O PRINT "BROWN"
10 PRINT "HOW"
15 PRINT "NOW"
20 PRINT "PURPLE"
30 PRINT "COW"
```

Why? Because the line number you typed was really 2. You next typed the letter O. Since O is not a number, the computer assumed you had finished the line number. *Line numbers give you a powerful way to change a program, but mistakes in line numbers can hurt a program.*

Blank lines One problem with line-number editing in BASIC is that you cannot enter a line with just a line number. Such lines are very important because they make your programs easy to read. The closest you can come in Applesoft BASIC (the version of BASIC on your computer) is a line number followed by a colon (:). As you explore the programs on your diskette, you will see many examples of such "blank" lines.

QUESTIONS

1. What command tells the computer to show you the lines of the program in the computer?

2. What are the two parts of any line in a BASIC program?

3. What are the three different types of BASIC statements in program ROCKET?

4. What is the difference between a *command* and a *statement*?

5. What is the difference between *immediate mode* and *program mode* of using a statement?

6. Suppose you intended to enter the line

   ```
   20 PRINT "BROWN"
   ```

   but typed the letter Ⓞ rather than the number ⓪.
   Your program ended up with this line:

   ```
   2 O   PRINT "BROWN"
   ```

   How would you fix your mistake?

7. What would you type to add the statement PRINT "OLD" between the two statements in the following program?

   ```
   20 PRINT "GOOD"
   30 PRINT "BOY"
   ```

8. In the program in question 7, what would you type to change the last statement to PRINT "GIRL"?

9. In the program in question 7, what would you type to get rid of the last statement?

10. In the program in question 7, what statement would you add to the beginning of the program to tell the computer to clear the screen?

Writing a Program and Saving It

IN THIS SESSION YOU WILL:
- Use PRINT statements to write a new BASIC program.
- Use line editing to change the program.
- Use the SAVE command to move the program to the diskette.
- Use the DELETE command to remove the program from the diskette.

Writing a Program

You have looked at a few programs on your diskette. Now it is time for you to write your own program. For this first program, you will be told exactly what to do. Later in this session, you will have a chance to write several programs without help.

Start the computer just as you did in Sessions 2 and 4. Turn on the TV. Check the (CAPS LOCK) key. Insert your diskette. If the computer is on, type PR#6 and press (RETURN). If not, just turn it on. Wait for the WELCOME TO COMPUTER LITERACY message.

`NEW` — This erases whatever is in the computer.

Always type NEW *before entering a new program from the keyboard.* Otherwise you will be adding lines to whatever program is already in the computer. Now type the following four lines. Remember to use the (SHIFT) key to get the quotation marks. Be sure to use the number keys for the line numbers.

```
100 PRINT "YOUNG"
110 PRINT "MARTIANS"
120 PRINT "EAT"
130 PRINT "SNAILS"
```
— Now you have a four-line program.

`HOME` — Clear the screen.

`LIST` — Look at the program.

`RUN` — If you get a ?SYNTAX ERROR message, retype the line with the error.

When running the program, the computer performed each statement in *numerical order*. Each statement told the computer to print a single word on the screen.

1. What is the purpose of line numbers in a BASIC program?
2. When a computer runs a BASIC program, which line does it perform first?

Editing the Program

Here is what the program should look like now:

```
100 PRINT "YOUNG"
110 PRINT "MARTIANS"
120 PRINT "EAT"
130 PRINT "SNAILS"
```

Suppose you wanted to change the order of the column of words on the screen. You want to see SNAILS, EAT, YOUNG, and MARTIANS. You have learned how to add and delete lines. That is all you will have to do, so try some editing now:

First, clear the screen and list the program. Then edit it to look like this:

```
80 PRINT "SNAILS"
90 PRINT "EAT"
100 PRINT "YOUNG"
110 PRINT "MARTIANS"
```

After you finish that editing job, change the line that says YOUNG to say GREEN.

3. How do you change a line in a BASIC program?
4. If you type only the line number of a line in a BASIC program and press the (RETURN) key, what will happen?
5. How do you put a new line into a BASIC program?

Saving the Program

Now, let's see how to move this program from the computer to your diskette. First, let's check the names of the programs on the diskette.

```
HOME
CATALOG
```
Look at the names. There is nothing named SNAILS.
```
LIST
```
Check out the program.
```
SAVE SNAILS
```
Be sure to remember the space between the words. Notice that the red light on the disk drive came on.
```
LIST
```
A copy of your program is still in the computer.
```
CATALOG
```
SNAILS should be in your diskette catalog now.

```
NEW
LIST
```
Now your program is gone from the computer.

But `SNAILS` is still on the diskette.

```
CATALOG
LOAD SNAILS
LIST
```
Now your program is back in the computer. You recalled it by loading `SNAILS`.

The `SAVE` command tells the computer to move a copy of a program from the computer to the diskette. `SAVE` should be followed by a space and the file name you want to give the program.

6. Suppose you have just used the `SAVE` command to move a copy of program `FOXES` from the computer to the diskette. Is program `FOXES` now erased from the computer?

7. How would you move a program with the name `MESSAGE` to the diskette?

Removing a Program from the Diskette

If you use the `SAVE` command often, sooner or later your diskette will not hold any more programs. In this section, you will learn how to remove programs from your diskette when you no longer need them. If `SNAILS` is not in your computer now, type `LOAD SNAILS`.

```
CATALOG
```
Check that `SNAILS` is still on your diskette.

```
DELETE SNAILS
```
Notice that the red light on the disk drive came on.

```
CATALOG
```
`SNAILS` should be missing from the diskette now.

```
HOME
LIST
```
But `SNAILS` is still in the computer.

```
NEW
LIST
```
Now `SNAILS` is gone from the computer, too.

The `DELETE` command tells the computer to remove a file from the diskette. `DELETE` has no effect on the program in the computer.

8. Which command do you use to remove a program from the computer?

9. Does the `DELETE` command automatically erase whatever program is now in the computer?

SAVE and LOAD User Traps

Before doing anything further, have a look at your keyboard. Soon you will be using two new keys. Look now for the RESET key, but do not press it yet. On most Apple computers it is near the upper right-hand corner of the keyboard. It may be recessed. Next look for the CONTROL key. It is at the left end of the keys, and the label may be spelled CTRL on your computer. In this section you will use the RESET key and perhaps also the CONTROL key.

You learned in Session 5 what a user trap is. There are a few user traps to watch out for with SAVE and LOAD. It is easy to forget to put a program name after SAVE and LOAD. Let's see what happens.

LOAD ——————————————————————— Notice that the cursor is gone.

 On some computers the cursor will still be present. If it is still visible on your screen, you will not experience the user trap that we are exploring here. Skip the rest of this section.

The red light on the drive did not come on. Nothing is happening. It looks like your computer is broken. Press a few keys on the keyboard. It looks bad. Here is the way out: Hold down the CONTROL key and at the same time press the RESET key. Release both keys. (In the future we'll call this double-action CONTROL | RESET. On some computers, by the way, the RESET key alone has the same effect as CONTROL | RESET.) The cursor returns, and all is well again. Now let's see what happens with SAVE.

SAVE ——————————————————————— Again, the cursor is gone.

This is the same problem. Press CONTROL | RESET again. The cursor should be back once more. No damage is done by falling into these user traps, but you do need to know how to get out.

 Do not press the CONTROL | RESET key while the red light on the disk drive is on. If you do, you may destroy information on the diskette.

You are probably wondering why the Apple computer "hangs up" when you forget the program name. The LOAD command without any program name tells the computer to try to load a program from a **cassette tape recorder**. If no tape recorder is attached, or if there is one but it is turned off, the Apple waits *forever* for the program. SAVE followed by no program name also refers to the cassette recorder.

 10. If the cursor disappears after you type LOAD or SAVE, what should you do to get it back?

If you have extra lab time:

- Write a program to print your first name on one line and your last name on the line below it.

- Write a program to print a message of your choice, with one word on each line.

- Find out whether you can save the same program on your diskette in two files with different names.

- Find out what happens when you try to save a program with the name ROCKET or BOXES.

Before leaving, use DELETE to remove any programs you do not want on your diskette. Then turn off the TV and remove your diskette.

Patterns with the PRINT Statement

- Review diskette commands.
- Learn to use LOCK and UNLOCK commands.
- Understand that computer information can be lost, stolen, and damaged.
- Plan a program using PRINT statements to make a design on the screen.

Review of Diskette Commands

You have now used all four of the commands that move copies of programs back and forth between the diskette and the computer and that erase copies of programs in either place. Now is a good time to review these four commands: LOAD, SAVE, DELETE, and NEW.

Information is erased *Every one of these commands is potentially dangerous because it erases something.* To stay out of trouble, you have to know what is going to be lost: NEW erases the program in the computer. DELETE PIG erases file PIG from the diskette. But LOAD PIG *also* erases something, and so does SAVE PIG.

Effect of commands The table below shows the danger spots for these commands. Suppose there is a program in the computer now. Let's call it HOG. There is a *different* program on the diskette in a file named PIG. This table shows what would happen to HOG and PIG if you typed any one of the commands below.

Command	Effect
NEW	Erases HOG from the computer. Does nothing to any diskette file.
DELETE PIG	Erases file PIG from the diskette. Does nothing to program HOG in the computer.
LOAD PIG	Erases HOG from the computer. Then puts a copy of file PIG into the computer.
SAVE PIG	Erases file PIG from the diskette. Then puts a copy of program HOG into file PIG.

The LOCK command The diskette copy of a program is usually important. You don't want to lose it by accident, but accidents can happen. Suppose that PIG is an important program on your diskette. But you forget its name, and then you decide to save a different program with the name PIG. As soon as you type SAVE PIG, your precious old program is erased. You can prevent this accident by **locking** the programs on your diskette. The command

    LOCK PIG

does the job for program PIG. After that, if you type DELETE PIG or SAVE PIG, the computer will beep and say

    FILE LOCKED

Before you can erase PIG, you must first type

    UNLOCK PIG

Locked files on your diskette   All the programs on your diskette were locked before you got it. You can easily tell which files are locked by typing the CATALOG command. If there is an asterisk (*) at the start of a line in the catalog listing, that file is locked.

Protecting Your Information

After you spend several hours writing and improving a program, you don't want to see it disappear from your diskette. If that happens by accident, no one is to blame. But another person who has access to your diskette might think it would be fun to wipe out a few of your programs—just as a joke. It is *not* a joke to damage or to take information that belongs to someone else.

Huge amounts of information are stored in computer centers.

Information is property   Every year our society depends more and more on systems of information. It takes time and costs money to collect information and write the computer programs that process that information. Citizens in an information society need to develop respect for information that does not belong to them. Just as law-abiding citizens do not steal cars or set someone's house on fire, they should not steal or damage information.

Protecting information   People who make or collect information need to learn that they should protect it, just as they would lock their bikes, cars, and houses. The LOCK command on your computer offers some protection, but not much: Anyone who has your diskette can unlock a program and destroy it. People who design computer systems have not worried as much as they should about this problem. And so it is up to you to think carefully about the privacy and safety of any information you allow to be put on a computer system. Who else will be able

to see and use your information? Can someone copy it without asking?
Can someone destroy it?

Screen Designs with PRINT

In Session 6, you wrote complete BASIC programs that contained only
PRINT statements. Each of the PRINT statements told the computer to
display words on the screen. The characters displayed by the PRINT
statement need not be words; they can be almost any characters. In this
session, you will learn to create your own design by using only PRINT
statements and the characters on the keyboard of your computer. Program ROCKET is an example of this type of design.

Plan the design A little advance planning will save you some confusion later on. First, you should use no more than 19 characters inside
the quotation marks in each statement. (If you type lines in a program
that are more than 32 characters long, they run over to the next screen
line and make it very hard to see what the pattern is.) Next, use no
more than 20 PRINT statements for the whole pattern. (If you use too
many lines, the pattern will not fit on the screen.)

Here is the kind of "form" you will use for a design program that
follows the rules above.

```
100 PRINT ". . . . . . . . . . . . . . . . . . ."
110 PRINT ". . . . . . . . . . . . . . . . . . ."
120 PRINT ". . . . . . . . . . . . . . . . . . ."
130 PRINT ". . . . . . . . . . . . . . . . . . ."
140 PRINT ". . . . . . . . . . . . . . . . . . ."
150 PRINT ". . . . . . . . . . . . . . . . . . ."
160 PRINT ". . . . . . . . . . . . . . . . . . ."
170 PRINT ". . . . . . . . . . . . . . . . . . ."
180 PRINT ". . . . . . . . . . . . . . . . . . ."
190 PRINT ". . . . . . . . . . . . . . . . . . ."
200 PRINT ". . . . . . . . . . . . . . . . . . ."
210 PRINT ". . . . . . . . . . . . . . . . . . ."
220 PRINT ". . . . . . . . . . . . . . . . . . ."
230 PRINT ". . . . . . . . . . . . . . . . . . ."
240 PRINT ". . . . . . . . . . . . . . . . . . ."
250 PRINT ". . . . . . . . . . . . . . . . . . ."
260 PRINT ". . . . . . . . . . . . . . . . . . ."
270 PRINT ". . . . . . . . . . . . . . . . . . ."
280 PRINT ". . . . . . . . . . . . . . . . . . ."
290 PRINT ". . . . . . . . . . . . . . . . . . ."
```

Each of the dots in the pattern can be any character you want in
your design. Be sure to remember the quotation marks.

Sample Design

On the next page is a sample design created with PRINT statements.
This design uses only the +, -, /, !, and space characters.

```
100 HOME
110 PRINT "          +----------+"
120 PRINT "         /!         /!"
130 PRINT "        / !        / !"
140 PRINT "       /  !       /  !"
150 PRINT "      /   !      /   !"
160 PRINT "     /    !     /    !"
170 PRINT "+---------+    /    !"
180 PRINT "!         !   /     !"
190 PRINT "!         !  /      !"
200 PRINT "!         ! /       !"
210 PRINT "!    +----!-----+"
220 PRINT "!   /     !    /"
230 PRINT "!  /      !   /"
240 PRINT "! /       !  /"
250 PRINT "!/        ! /"
260 PRINT "!/        !/"
270 PRINT "+---------+"
```

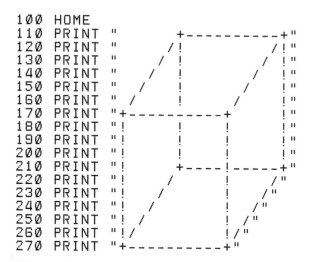

When the computer performs this program, you see an outline drawing of a box.

When you start a design of your own, probably the easiest way is to use graph paper (or make your own graph paper). Draw an outline that has 19 small squares across and 20 down. Each square will hold one character. All the characters in one row will be the "message" in one PRINT statement.

Create a Design

Now it is time to plan a design of your own. Remember that you can use any of the characters on the keyboard (except the quotation mark) to create your design. In the next session, you will enter your program into the computer and make improvements.

QUESTIONS

1. Which commands can erase the program in the computer?
2. Which commands can erase a file on the diskette?
3. What do the LOCK and UNLOCK commands do?
4. A programmer may spend a thousand hours to write a good computer game. If the programmer earns $15 per hour, how much does it cost to write the game program? If the game is sold on a "copy-protected" diskette for $30, do you think it is right for someone to "break" the protection system and make a copy for personal use? As a "back-up" in case the original fails? A few copies for friends? Many copies for sale to others?

Entering the Design Program

IN THIS SESSION YOU WILL:
• Enter the design program you began in Session 7.
• Save the finished program on the diskette.

Computer Work

Enter the pattern program you began in Session 7. If you need to, use line-number editing to make any changes needed to finish your design.

Choose a name for the program and put the name in a REM statement at the beginning. When you are satisfied with the design, save the program on the diskette. Use a file with the same name you gave to the program.

If you have extra lab time:

- Make improvements to your design program.
- Load program ROCKET and make improvements to it.
- Load program BLAST OFF. Change the PRINT statements in lines 220 through 420 so that the program tells the computer to launch something besides a rocket. To see these lines, type

    LIST 220, 420

    and press the (RETURN) key. (The same program can make a flower grow, for example. Try it.)

Part 1

Vocabulary Table

Here are the new BASIC words you studied in Part 1. The blank spaces are for words you will learn later.

BASIC Vocabulary (Shaded Areas Show Standard BASIC Words)

Commands		Statements			Functions
Program	Diskette	Action	Action	Control	
RUN	LOAD	——	——	——	—
LIST	SAVE	——	——	—	—
NEW	DELETE	PRINT	——	——	—
——	CATALOG	REM	——	—	—
——	LOCK	——	——	——	
	UNLOCK	——	——		
———		——	—	——	
———					
———		HOME			

New BASIC Words

CATALOG A command to show the names of all files on the diskette.

DELETE A command to delete a file from the diskette.

HOME A statement that tells the computer to clear the screen.

LIST A command to show all BASIC statements in the computer.

LOAD A command that tells the computer to move a copy of a file from the diskette into the computer.

LOCK A command you use to keep a file on the diskette from being erased accidentally.

NEW A command that tells the computer to erase all BASIC statements from the computer, but not from the diskette.

PRINT A statement that tells the computer to output letters and numbers.

REM A statement you use to put an explanatory **remark** or **comment** into a program. The computer ignores REM statements.

RUN A command that tells the computer to perform all BASIC statements in the computer.

SAVE A command that tells the computer to move a copy of a program from the computer to the diskette.

UNLOCK A command you use to cancel the LOCK command so that you can remove or change a file on the diskette.

New Ideas

BASIC A computer language invented in 1963 by John Kemeny and Thomas Kurtz. The letters stand for Beginners All-purpose Symbolic Instruction Code.

blank line A line number with no statement after it. Blank lines separate parts of a program and make it easier to read. In Applesoft BASIC, a colon must follow the line number of a blank line.

command A single word or phrase that tells the computer to do something with a program or file.

computer language A special set of words and grammar rules for writing instructions that a computer will follow.

cursor A symbol that appears on the output screen when the computer is ready for input.

diskette A small, flexible disk used to store information in magnetic form.

disk drive A unit the computer uses to input information from a diskette and output information to it.

file A collection of information. You give that collection a name and store it on a diskette, cassette tape, or other medium.

immediate mode A mode of operation in which the computer performs statements as soon as you enter them.

input The information a computer takes in.

I/O An abbreviation for *input/output,* which is the way a computer communicates with the outside.

keyboard A set of switches, like typewriter keys, you use to enter information into the computer.

lines The elements that make up a BASIC program. Every line has a line number followed by a statement.

line number A number that identifies a line in a BASIC program.

line-number editing A way to make changes in a program by changing the numbered lines of that program.

output The information a computer gives out.

processing Making changes in the information in a computer.

program A set of instructions, written in a *computer language,* that tells the computer how to perform a task.

program mode A mode of operation in which the computer performs statements only after the command RUN has been given.

screen A TV screen on which the computer displays *output.*

statement A single instruction written in a computer language.

syntax error A spelling, punctuation, or grammar mistake in a command or statement.

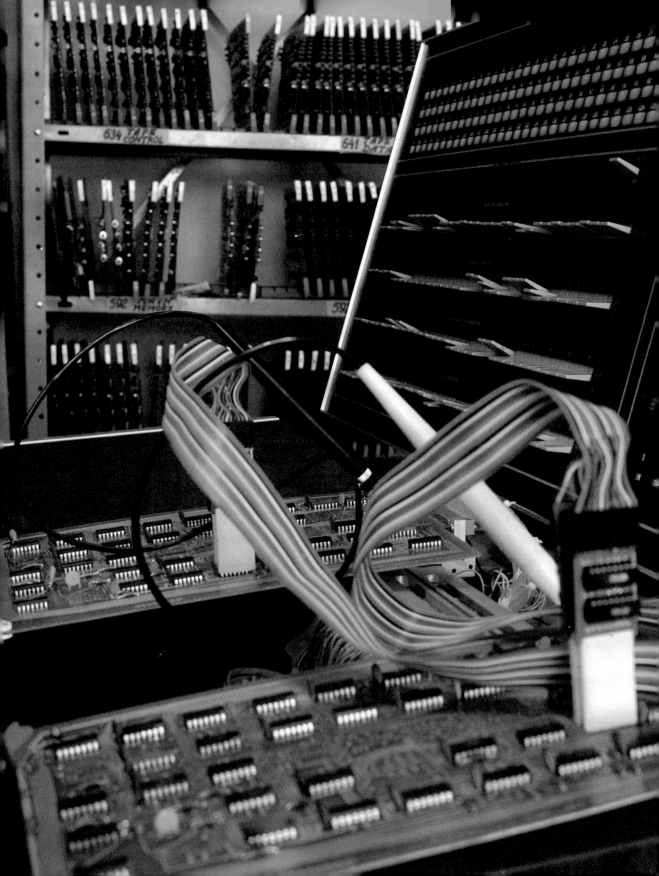

Part 2

How Programs Work

You have run programs stored on your diskette. You have written your own programs. You may be wondering how a computer carries out the steps of a program and how it "understands" words like LIST and RUN. In Part 2, you will begin to learn what goes on *inside* a computer.

Does it matter? People drive cars without knowing how a gasoline engine works. People use microwave ovens without understanding what microwaves are. People use electric drills without understanding how an electric motor works. Shouldn't the same be true of computers?

A working knowledge helps It always helps to understand how things work, especially when there are problems. If the highway is covered with snow, drivers have to put chains on their tires. Only two chains are needed, but which wheels should they go on? People who know only *rules* may remember this old one: "Put the chains on the back wheels." But the driver who knows *how chains work* knows that the purpose of the chains is to "dig in" when the engine turns the wheels. So the chains should go on the wheels that are connected to the engine. On older cars, those are the back wheels; but many newer cars have front-wheel drive, and the chains go on the front wheels. Drivers who know how things work won't end up "spinning their wheels."

Solving problems Much of your time at the computer will be spent dealing with unusual problems: The computer will refuse to accept input, and you will wonder why. It will produce strange output or no output, and you will wonder why. Your programs will contain errors ("bugs"), and you will wonder how to fix ("debug") them. To solve these problems, you will need to know more than rules. If you understand how a computer works, you won't "spin your wheels" needlessly.

A working model Of course, you don't need to be an electronics wizard; but you do need to know what the main parts of a computer are and how they work together. In Part 2, you will learn these things through a simplified model of a computer. After you see how the model works, you will know a lot about how every real computer works.

A Model of Your Computer

IN THIS SESSION YOU WILL:
- Learn that a computer *is* what it is programmed to *do*.
- Learn what hardware and software are.
- Learn the parts of a model computer.
- Use a model of a computer to explain how line editing works.

What Makes the Computer Run?

Suppose you wanted to make your computer into a machine that would print the message

```
RIGHT
ON!
```

whenever you typed the command RUN. You could do this by putting the following program into the computer:

```
10 PRINT "RIGHT"
20 PRINT "ON!"
```

The computer program   Computers can do only what they are told to do. A **computer program** is a list of statements that tells the computer what to do. Without a program, a computer can do nothing. That is the big difference between a computer and any other machine. A lawn mower can only cut grass. An elevator can only raise and lower weights. An electric mixer can only mix things. But a computer can do thousands of things. What it does depends on only two things:

1. **Its basic capabilities.** Can the computer draw pictures? Can it make sounds? Can it turn on your house lights? Does it contain a clock and a calendar?
2. **The program it is running.** What do the program statements tell the computer to do?

Hardware and software   To change the basic capabilities of a computer, you have to remove or add **parts**. These parts, usually electric circuits and mechanical devices, are called **hardware**. **Software** is the collection of programs that make a computer do a job. *It takes hardware and software to make a computer do anything.* You will not change the hardware in this course, but you will write software.

What Is a Computer? (Part 2)

In Session 3, you learned to describe a computer by what it could do: *Input* information, *process* it, and *output* the results. But there is another way to describe a computer. You can list its parts and say how they work together. In this session, you will study a model of a real computer.

Why use models? Using models is a powerful way to explain how things work. A model airplane helps explain how a real airplane works. Most science is the invention of models for things that really happen. When you understand how the model works, you learn a lot about the real thing.

Kinds of models Some models are objects, such as a plastic model of a human heart. Some models are mathematical: For example, the law of gravity is an equation that helps explain how an apple falls to the ground and how the moon goes around the earth. The model you will use is a picture. Here is what it looks like:

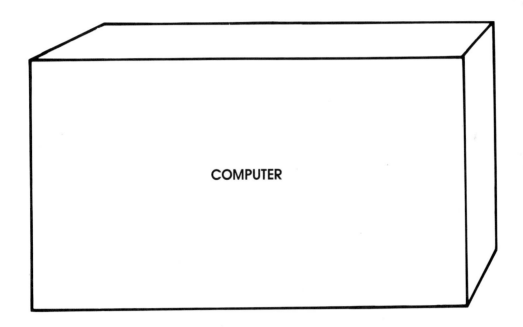

COMPUTER

This picture may not look very helpful, but it is a starting point. To most people, a computer is just a mysterious "black box" that can do things. Your job is to add parts to this picture and make it more like the real thing.

Input hardware Every computer has **input hardware** you use to put information into the computer. The keyboard and the disk drive are examples of input hardware. The keyboard gets information from your fingers. The disk drive gets information from diskettes.

The input slot Our model computer needs a part for input. Here it is:

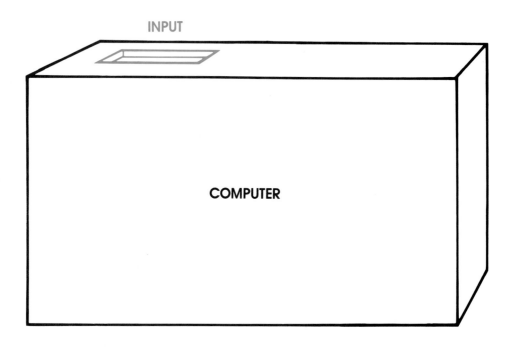

The computer's keyboard is input hardware. The monitor screen is output hardware.

Input hardware acts like a mail slot: Information gets dropped into the computer through the input slot.

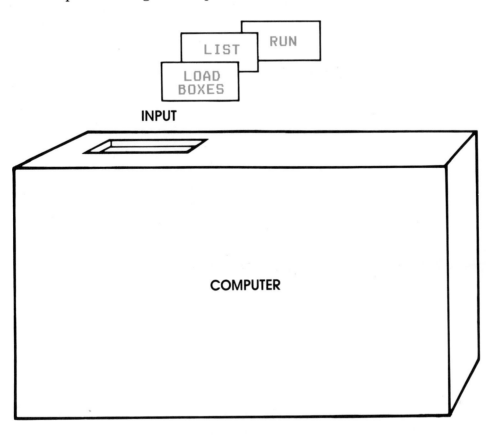

The figure above shows the LOAD BOXES, LIST, and RUN commands being dropped into the input slot.

Output hardware Every computer has **output hardware** for giving out information. The main piece of output hardware on your computer is the TV screen. The computer puts words and pictures there for you to read and look at. The disk drive is also an output device, as well as an input device. When you save a program, the disk drive puts information on a diskette.

The output scroll Our model computer needs a part for output. (To keep the model simple, we will leave out the disk drive.) Here is the new picture:

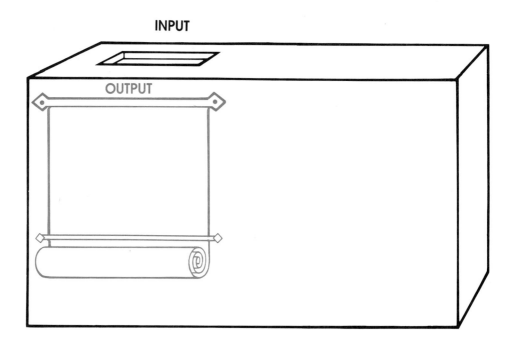

The output screen is like a scroll of paper. The computer writes on the flat part of the paper. When there is no room left, the computer turns the scroll up a little and writes on the bottom line. The scroll only goes up. You can think of the computer as tearing off the extra paper that comes out at the top and throwing it away.

Adding a Memory to the Model

Your model shows how information goes into and comes out of the computer. Next we will see where the information goes when it is *inside* the computer.

Memory hardware You entered line-numbered statements into your computer and later found you could LIST the statements and RUN them. The computer *remembered* your statements. Later still, you entered the NEW command and the computer *forgot* your statements. Every computer contains a **memory unit**. It stores all the information inside the computer.

The Apple II memory The memory in your computer is inside the case. If you took off the lid of your Apple II, you would see a flat green board with about a hundred little black rectangular blocks. The main memory is stored in 48 of these blocks. Inside each block, information is stored electrically in a tiny sliver of silicon called a **chip**. One memory chip in the Apple II holds about 200 English words, numbers, or other information.

The memory chalkboard Today, computers store information in electric circuits. Older computers used magnets. Whatever the method, any computer can put information into its memory, and it can erase its memory. Computer memory is like a chalkboard: It can be written on and erased. Let's add a memory chalkboard to our model.

Memory and the LIST command The picture shows the three parts of the computer just after the LIST command was dropped into the input slot. The LIST command tells the computer to read the program on the memory chalkboard and then to write it on the output scroll. The program on the chalkboard is this:

```
10 PRINT "RIGHT"
20 PRINT "ON!"
```

So the computer writes these same lines on the output scroll. That is why the picture above looks the way it does. You should think of the LIST command as your "window" into the program in memory. Of course, you cannot "see" inside the memory in a real computer. To find what is there, you must enter the LIST command and look at the output screen.

Using the Model: Line-Number Editing

You can use the model computer to understand what happens in the real computer when you edit a program. Here are "snapshots" of the output and memory as you input each new line.

The current state Here is how the output scroll and the memory chalkboard look before you start editing. The presence of the cursor tells you that the computer is ready for you to drop something into the input slot.

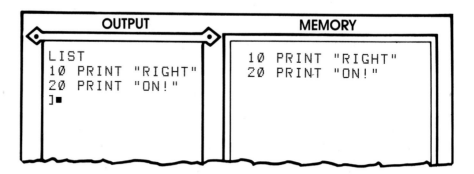

Inserting a new line Now, drop the line, 15 PRINT "LEFT", into the input slot. Here is the new state of the output and the memory. Notice that the statements in memory are in a different order than the ones on the output scroll. That is true because the computer keeps the program lines in numerical order in the memory.

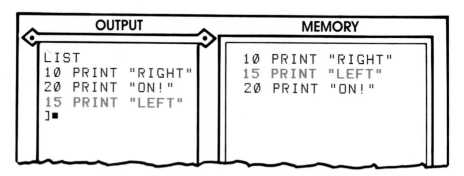

Changing a line Next, drop 20 PRINT "STOP" into the input slot. Here is the new state. The *old* line 20 is still on the output scroll, but only the *new* line 20 is in memory.

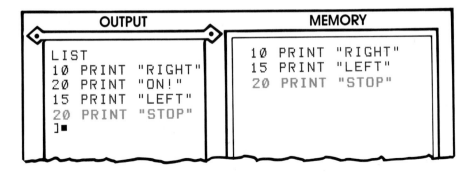

```
         OUTPUT                    MEMORY

LIST                      10  PRINT  "RIGHT"
10  PRINT  "RIGHT"        15  PRINT  "LEFT"
20  PRINT  "ON!"          20  PRINT  "STOP"
15  PRINT  "LEFT"
20  PRINT  "STOP"
]■
```

Deleting an old line Next, drop just the number 20 into the input slot. Notice that line 20 has disappeared in the new state of the memory.

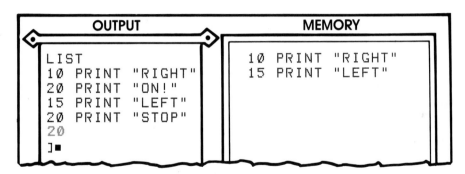

```
         OUTPUT                    MEMORY

LIST                      10  PRINT  "RIGHT"
10  PRINT  "RIGHT"        15  PRINT  "LEFT"
20  PRINT  "ON!"
15  PRINT  "LEFT"
20  PRINT  "STOP"
20
]■
```

Deleting everything Finally, drop the word NEW into the input slot. Now all the information in memory is erased. The output scroll has also turned up a line, and the LIST that used to be at the top of the screen is gone.

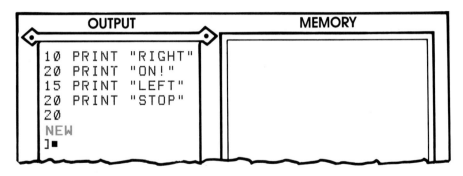

```
         OUTPUT                    MEMORY

10  PRINT  "RIGHT"
20  PRINT  "ON!"
15  PRINT  "LEFT"
20  PRINT  "STOP"
20
NEW
]■
```

1. What are the two things that determine what a computer can do?

2. What is software?

3. What is hardware?

4. What part of the model computer is the keyboard like?

5. You have just dropped the word HOME through the input slot. What does the model computer do to the output scroll?

6. What are the three parts in the model of a computer?

7. What is the purpose of each part in the model?

8. What will be in the memory of the computer after you enter these lines?

```
NEW
10 PRINT "FIRST"
20 PRINT "SECOND"
```

9. After entering the lines in question 8, you enter these lines.

```
30 PRINT "FIRST"
20 PRINT "THINGS"
```

What is in memory now?

10. After entering the lines in questions 8 and 9, you enter HOME and then the RUN command. What is on the output screen?

11. What will be in the memory of the computer after you enter these lines?

```
NEW
50 PRINT "A"
40 PRINT "B"
30 PRINT "C"
40 PRINT "D"
50 PRINT "E"
```

Designing Your Own HELLO Program

IN THIS SESSION YOU WILL:
- Learn what the HELLO program does.
- Improve the HELLO program.
- Make a HELLO program.
- Finish work on the design program started in Session 7.

Your Own HELLO Program

Start the computer exactly as you did in previous sessions. If your memory needs refreshing, turn to pages 6 and 7.

There is a special program on your diskette. Its name is HELLO. Let's look at it.

LOAD HELLO — Put it into memory.

RUN — That should look familiar.

LIST — Read the program.

You have probably guessed why the HELLO program is special. Every time you enter PR#6 to start a computer session, the computer automatically runs this program. The HELLO program tells the computer to print this message on your output screen:

SUCCESS!!!

WELCOME TO COMPUTER LITERACY

Many people like to make up their own HELLO program. Let's suppose your name is Juanita. You might like the first line of the HELLO message to say this:

JUANITA'S DISKETTE

The first step is to edit the program now showing on your screen. Just retype line 130 and use your own name instead of the name JUANITA.

LIST — Check for errors and fix any.

The next step is to save the new program in the file named HELLO. Do that now.

SAVE HELLO — Whoops! We have a problem.

The HELLO file is locked so you will not erase it by accident. You learned about locking and unlocking in Session 7. If you want to erase the old version and save the new one, you must unlock the diskette version. You probably remember how. If not, review Session 7.

Use the UNLOCK command and then the SAVE HELLO command to put the new version on your diskette.

The job is done. You now have a new HELLO program on your diskette. Let's see what happens when you start the computer with this diskette. Type PR#6 and press (RETURN). You should get your new message after the diskette stops spinning.

1. What is the purpose of the HELLO program on your diskette?
2. How do you put a different HELLO program on the diskette?

Improving the HELLO Program

You can make two simple improvements to your HELLO program. First, you can make it tell the computer to clear the screen before printing your message. All you need is a HOME statement at the beginning.

Add a HOME statement before the first PRINT statement in your new HELLO program. Save the new version. Then test it by typing PR#6.

This time your HELLO program should clear the screen first and then print your new greetings. But there is a problem you may not have noticed:

After typing PR#6, enter the LIST command. You have just found a new user trap: *The HELLO program stays in the memory of the computer after it is performed.* If you now start typing a new program, you will actually be adding lines to the HELLO program.

To avoid this user trap, you have to remember to type NEW every time you start using the computer. It would be easier if the HELLO program ended by erasing itself from memory. Here is how to tell the computer to do that:

Use the NEW command as a statement in the HELLO program. Give a line number big enough to make it the last statement in the program. Then save the new version with the name HELLO. To test it, type PR#6. After the greeting message appears, enter the LIST command.

Nothing should be listed. The NEW command at the end of your HELLO program has exactly the same effect as typing NEW on the keyboard: Memory is erased.

3. How can you make a program tell the computer to clear the screen before printing on it?
4. How can you make a program tell the computer to erase the program from memory?

If you have extra lab time:

- Make your HELLO program more interesting. (You might want to start with the design you made and saved in Session 8.) Be sure to lock HELLO when you are satisfied with it.
- Experiment some more with your design program. Try a completely new design.

Left: The first electronic computer had tubes and transformers inside.
Right: Today's computers have tiny silicon chips.

11 System Programs: LIST and NEW

IN • Add parts to the model of the computer.
THIS SESSION • Learn that the computer has system software built into it.
YOU WILL: • Learn how the LIST and NEW system programs work.

System Software

You have used the LIST command to tell the computer to print a list of all the BASIC statements in memory. Your RUN command told the computer to perform those statements. Your NEW command told it to erase them from memory. You may wonder how the computer "knows" to do all these things. Perhaps you think that this knowledge is somehow "wired into the computer's brain."

Dumb computers and smart people *There is no knowledge in any computer except what a human being put there.* Your computer knows about LIST, RUN, and NEW because someone wrote *programs* telling the computer exactly what steps to carry out for each command. These programs are part of the **system software** that comes with your computer and makes it understand BASIC commands.

All computers have system software.

ROM and RAM In the Apple II computer and many others, the LIST, RUN, and NEW programs are stored in **read-only memory** circuits, also called **ROM** (rhymes with Tom). These programs are in the computer whenever you turn the power on. The BASIC programs you write or load from the diskette are stored in **random-access memory**, also called **RAM** (rhymes with Pam). Whatever you store in RAM erases what information was there before. When you turn the power off, you lose all information in RAM.

The LIST Program

In this session, you will use the model computer to take a close look at the LIST program. It is a **system program** that tells the computer how to list a BASIC program.

The line pointer The model computer will need some new parts. First, it needs a **line pointer.** It points at a line of the BASIC program in the memory. In the picture, the line pointer is at line 1Ø, which has just been entered through the input slot.

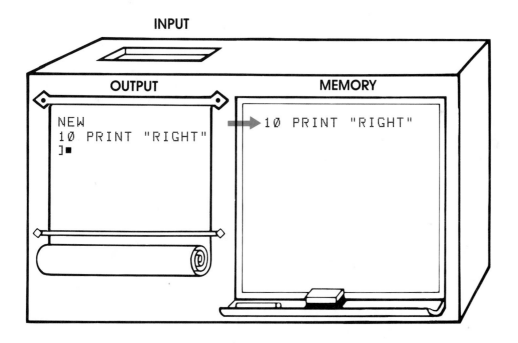

The current line In this session, we will see that the computer can move the line pointer from one line of a BASIC program to another line. Whatever line the pointer is at is called the **current line**. When the pointer moves, there is a new current line. You will soon see why the current line is important.

The LIST program This program is written not in BASIC, but in the **machine language** of the computer. You cannot use the LIST command to list machine-language programs. They are just long lists of 1s and 0s, called **binary code**, and make little sense to a person. So we have written the main steps of the LIST program in ordinary English. (Later, when you know more BASIC, you will rewrite parts in BASIC.)

The LIST Program

1. Move the line pointer to the first line of the BASIC program in the memory unit.

2. Repeat the following steps as long as the line pointer is pointing at a BASIC line.

2a. Read the current line, and write it on the output screen.

2b. Move the pointer to the next line of the program in the memory unit.

The control unit Next, the model needs a part that decides which step of the LIST program to do next. This new part is called the **control unit**. Here is a picture of the model after line 20 has been entered:

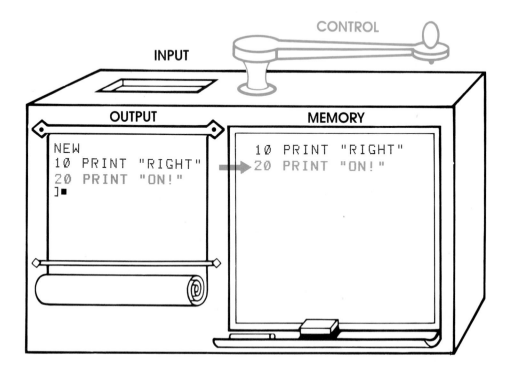

The control unit is shown as a big crank. Each turn of the crank carries out one step in whatever program is running and then moves the pointer to the next step.

Stepping through the LIST Program

Here is a picture of the model computer with its new parts. The program in the memory unit is the same one we put there in Session 9. The word HOME has just been dropped through the input slot.

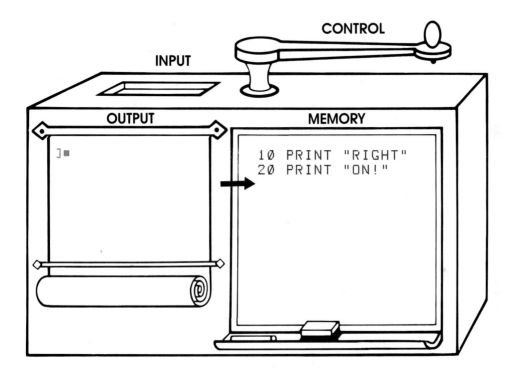

Next, we drop the LIST command through the slot. The computer prints LIST on the output scroll and starts running the LIST program. Here is what the first step says to do and what the output and memory units look like afterward.

1. **Move the pointer to the top.**
2. Repeat 2a and 2b until no lines are left:
   2a. Read the current line, and write it on the output.
   2b. Move the pointer down.

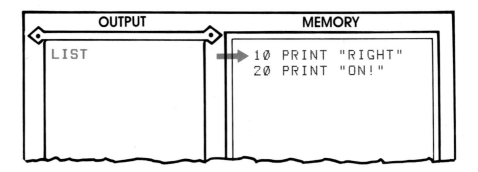

The word LIST is on the output screen. The cursor is missing because the computer is not ready for input now. It is busy processing the LIST program. Line 1Ø is the current line.

Step 2 of the LIST program says to do steps 2a and 2b until no lines are left. Here is step 2a and a picture of the computer afterward:

1. Move the pointer to the top.
2. Repeat 2a and 2b until no lines are left:
   2a. **Read the current line and write it on the output.**
   2b. Move the pointer down.

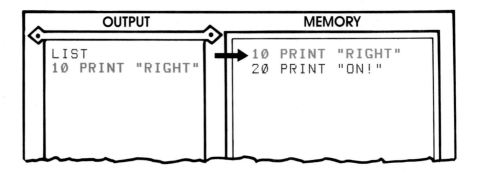

Next, the computer must do step 2b. Here is what step 2b says to do and what the computer looks like afterward:

1. Move the pointer to the top.
2. Repeat 2a and 2b until no lines are left:
   2a. Read the current line and write it on the output.
   2b. Move the pointer down.

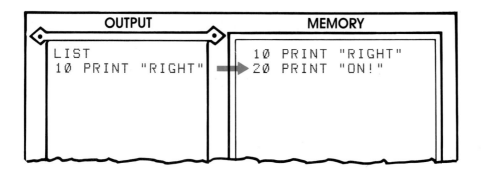

At this point, the computer must test whether the line pointer is pointing at a program line. If not, the LIST program says to stop. If so, it says to repeat steps 2a and 2b. Since the line pointer *is* pointing at a line, the computer must repeat step 2a of the LIST program. Line 20 is now the current line.

1. Move the pointer to the top.
2. Repeat 2a and 2b until no lines are left:
   2a. Read the current line and write it on the output.
   2b. Move the pointer down.

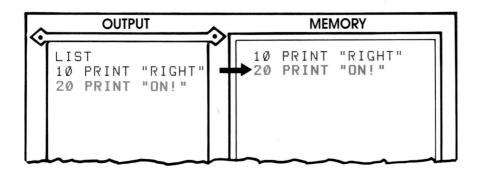

After step 2a, the computer must do step 2b of the LIST program. Here is the new state of the memory and output units.

1. Move the pointer to the top.
2. Repeat 2a and 2b until no lines are left:
   2a. Read the current line and write it on the output.
   2b. Move the pointer down.

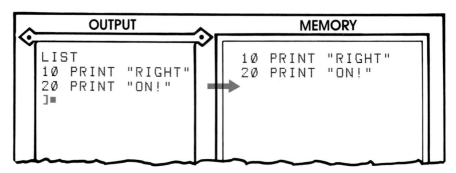

The LIST program says to stop now, because the line pointer is no longer pointing at a line of the BASIC program. The computer turns on the cursor, telling you that it is waiting for input.

The NEW Program

You have used the NEW command to erase the program in the memory unit. But remember that the computer must have a program somewhere to know how to do anything. You have just seen that when you typed LIST, you really told the computer to do the steps of the LIST program, which is part of the system software built into your computer. The NEW command also tells the computer to run a built-in program. Here are the steps of the NEW program:

The NEW Program

1. Move the line pointer to the first line of the BASIC program in the memory unit.
2. Repeat the following steps as long as the line pointer is pointing at a line.
   2a. Erase the current line.
   2b. Move the pointer to the next line of the program in the memory unit.

Again, it is the job of the control device to tell the computer which step of the NEW program to do next.

Stepping through the NEW Program

The NEW program is very much like the LIST program, so you should be able to put the NEW program through the model computer by yourself. Start with the model computer in the state shown in the picture on page 60, right after the LIST program ended. Then begin with step 1 of the NEW program, which says to put the pointer at line 10. Continue with step 2 of the NEW program, and so on.

QUESTIONS

1. Why does your computer need system software?
2. Why is RAM like a chalkboard and ROM like a page in a book?
3. What does the line pointer do?
4. What does the control unit do?
5. How does the computer know what LIST means?
6. What does the first step of the LIST program tell the computer to do?
7. Why is the cursor not on the screen while the LIST program is running?
8. When the LIST program is running, what happens when the line pointer moves past the last line in the memory unit?
9. Suppose there is no program in memory. What does the LIST program say to do?
10. How are the NEW and LIST programs similar in the way they work?
11. How are the NEW and LIST programs different in the way they work?
12. What is in the memory unit after the NEW program is run?
13. What is on the output display after the NEW program is run?
14. Suppose there is no program in memory. What does the NEW program tell the computer to do?
15. HOME does to the screen what NEW does to the memory. The computer does not clear the screen all at once. There is a step-by-step program. Can you write an English-language version of the HOME program? (Hint: You will have to add an "output line pointer" to the model.)

Block Editing and Output Control

IN • List parts of a program.
THIS SESSION • Delete parts of a program.
YOU WILL: • Control output speed.
• Stop and restart output to the screen.

More about the LIST Command

You have already used the LIST command to display a complete program. You can also use LIST to see a part of a program.

Follow the usual starting procedure with your diskette. Make sure the Applesoft prompt symbol (]) is at the left of the screen.

```
LOAD BLAST OFF
RUN
```
Move a copy of BLAST OFF from the diskette into the computer; see what it does.
```
LIST
```
We have a problem.

The program is too long to fit on your screen. It scrolls up the screen. When the scrolling stops, only the last part of the program is visible.

```
HOME
LIST 250, 420
```
Now, only those lines from 250 to 420 are listed.
```
HOME
LIST 610, 700
```
Look at a different set of lines.

Experiment with other line numbers in the LIST command. Try numbers that are not in the program. Try 0 for the first number. Try 9999 for the last number.

Find out whether you can list a single line of your program. Find what happens if the line you ask for is not there.

See whether you can use the LIST command to list the program backwards.

1. What would you type if you wanted to see lines 200 through 300 in a program?

2. Suppose a BASIC program has lines from 400 to 800 in steps of 10. What would happen if you typed LIST 525, 625?

3. If a BASIC program has lines from 30 to 60 in steps of 5, what would happen if you typed LIST 15, 42?
4. If a BASIC program has lines from 1000 to 3000 in steps of 100, what would happen if you typed LIST 300, 900?

Deleting Lines from a Program

You know how to erase a whole program from memory: Simply type NEW. You also know how to erase single lines from a program: Simply type the line number, press the (RETURN) key, and the line is gone. But suppose you want to erase a group of lines at the same time? You will learn how to do that in this section.

```
LOAD ROCKET
LIST
```
Start with a copy of program ROCKET.

```
DEL 150, 200
LIST
```
Lines 150 through 200 are erased from the computer's memory.

```
RUN
```
You have a short rocket now.

Experiment with other line numbers in the DEL command. If you delete everything, just load ROCKET again. Try 0 for the first number. Try 9999 for the last number.
    Find out whether you can use DEL with a single line number, as you can with LIST. Try DEL with no line number.

5. What is the purpose of the DEL command?
6. How would you delete lines 400 through 550 in a BASIC program?
7. How would you delete lines 400 through 550 in a BASIC program without using the DEL command?
8. If there were no NEW command, how could you use the DEL command for the same purpose?

Slowing the Output

You have probably noticed that the PRINT statements in a program tell the computer to print *very quickly* on your TV screen. For example, look at program HI THERE:

```
LOAD HI THERE
RUN
```
...and answer the question.

The whole screen filled very quickly. You may not always want that speed.

```
LIST
```
Look at HI THERE.

Again, the listing happened very fast. In this section, you will see how to slow things down. Let's add a new statement to your program.

```
135 SPEED= 100
LIST
```
Check the program.
```
RUN
```
...and answer the question.

Now the program is printing much more slowly. The SPEED= statement told the computer to change the output speed to 100. (Top speed is 255.) What do you think the speed is right now? Is it back at top speed, or is it still 100? Let's find out.

```
LIST
```
Note the speed.

The output speed was changed to 100 by the program, and it stayed that way. *Whenever you use a SPEED= statement in a program, you should set the output speed back to its original value before the program ends.* Here is how to do that:

```
170 SPEED= 255
LIST
```
Check the change.
```
RUN
```
...and answer the question.

Now let's see whether the program reset the output speed correctly.

```
LIST
```
The speed should be back to normal now.

You can also use the SPEED= statement in the immediate mode (without a line number). In other words, you can treat SPEED= as a command, such as LIST.

Experiment with the SPEED= statement in the immediate mode. See what happens when you list a program at different speeds.

Find out what happens when you try to break the speed limit (255). Is there a negative speed?

9. How can you control the speed at which the LIST program operates?

10. How can you control the speed of the PRINT statements in a program?

11. If a program changes the PRINT speed, what should it tell the computer to do before ending?

Stopping the Output

You have seen how to change the output speed. There may be times when you want to stop the output and look at it for a while before continuing. You will see how to do that next.

```
LOAD TURTLE TROT
```
Load a new program.
```
SPEED= 255
```
Set the top speed.
```
LIST
```
List TURTLE TROT.

This is a long program, and it whizzes up your screen so fast that you cannot read it. You could slow the output speed, of course, but then it would take a very long time to go through the whole listing.

There is another way: You can stop the output and then restart it. You use a "control key" to do this. *To type a control key, you must hold down the* (CONTROL) *key at the left end of the keyboard. While the* (CONTROL) *key is down, you must press one of the letter keys.* You will be using the (S) key in this section. We call this combination "control-S" and write it (CONTROL | S).

Now, let's use (CONTROL | S) to stop output to the screen. Do the next steps very quickly. If the listing comes to an end, enter the LIST command again.

```
LIST
```
Now, very quickly...
```
(CONTROL | S)
```
That stops output.
```
(CONTROL | S)
```
That restarts it.
```
(CONTROL | S)
```
That stops it again.

Now try pressing other keys on the keyboard. Any key restarts output.

(CONTROL | C), another control key, also stops things. It not only stops screen output, but also permanently stops whatever program the computer is running. Let's use (CONTROL | C) to stop the LIST program.

```
LIST
```
Now, very quickly...
```
(CONTROL | C)
```
That stops the LIST program. Notice that the cursor is back this time.
```
(CONTROL | C)
```
That did *not* restart it.

You stopped the LIST program before it finished listing all of TURTLE TROT. (CONTROL | C) does not restart the program it stopped.

12. What does (CONTROL | S) do?

13. What does (CONTROL | C) do?

If you have extra lab time: EXPLORE

- Find the smallest value allowed for the output speed.
- List program BLAST OFF and figure out what the SPEED= statement in line 610 does. Change it and see what happens.
- Rockets pick up speed as they leave the launch pad. Change the program BLAST OFF so that the rocket picks up speed as it rises on the screen.

Left: Once, editors wrote or typed their work. *Right:* Today, they use computers to store and change what they have written.

The RUN Program

IN • Learn how the RUN program tells the computer to carry out a BASIC program in the memory unit.
• Compare the RUN program to the LIST program.

Review

In Session 12, you learned how to use the LIST and DEL commands with parts of the program in the memory unit. You also learned how to control the output speed of the computer and how to start and stop the output.

Selective LIST command The LIST command tells the computer to list on the screen the whole program in the memory unit. You can list parts of the program by adding a **line-number range**. (Example: LIST 200, 300 tells the computer to list all program lines in the range 200 through 300. If there are no lines in that range, then nothing is printed on the output screen.) You can use the LIST command to display a single line. (Example: LIST 250 tells the computer to list line 250.)

Selective DEL command The NEW command tells the computer to erase the whole program in the memory unit. You can erase parts of the program by using the DEL command. (Example: DEL 200, 300 tells the computer to delete all lines in the range 200 through 300 from the program in the memory unit.) Unlike LIST, DEL used without a line-number range or with just one line number will produce an error message.

Controlling output speed With the SPEED= statement, you can control the speed at which characters are printed on the output screen. (Example: SPEED= 255 sets the highest output speed. SPEED= 0 sets the lowest.) When you turn on the computer, the speed is set to 255 automatically. If you change the output speed, it stays that way until you reset it.

Starting and stopping output You can temporarily stop the printing of characters on your screen by holding the (CONTROL) key down while pressing the (S) key. (This combination is called control-S.) You can start output again by pressing (CONTROL | S) or any other key. (CONTROL | S) acts like an on/off switch. (CONTROL | C), by contrast, stops the entire program, turns on the cursor, and waits for you to type a command.

The RUN Program

You saw in Session 11 that it took a program (called the LIST program) to tell the computer how to carry out the LIST command. It should be no surprise that the computer also needs a program to tell it how to carry out the RUN command. This program, called the RUN program, is part of the system software built into your computer. Here, in ordinary English, is what the RUN program tells the computer to do. (We will make a small improvement to this version in Session 25.)

The RUN Program (Initial Version)

1. Move the line pointer to the first line of the BASIC program in the memory unit.
2. Repeat the following steps as long as the line pointer is pointing at a BASIC line:
   2a. Perform the statement in the current line.
   2b. Move the pointer to the next line of the program in the memory unit.

The model computer Here is a picture of the model computer. The program you studied in Session 11 is in the memory unit. The LIST command has been dropped through the input slot, and the computer has just finished carrying out the steps of the LIST program. The RUN command is about to drop in next.

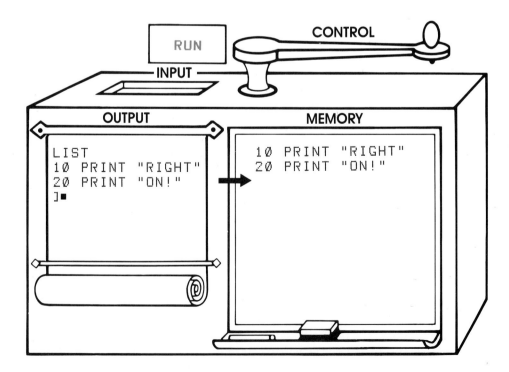

Stepping through the RUN Program

As you enter the RUN command, it tells the computer to start performing the steps of the RUN program. Here is what the first step says to do
and a picture of the model computer after the step is done:

1. **Move the pointer to the top.**
2. Repeat 2a and 2b until no lines are left:

   2a. Perform the statement in the current line.

   2b. Move the pointer down.

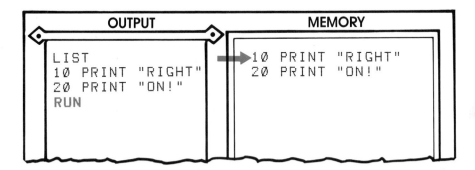

The word RUN is on the output screen. The cursor is missing, because
the computer is not ready for input now. It is busy processing the RUN
program. The computer just finished putting the line pointer at line 1Ø,
so that is the current line. Next, the computer must do step 2, which
says to do steps 2a and 2b. Here is what step 2a says to do:

1. Move the pointer to the top.
2. Repeat 2a and 2b until no lines are left:

   2a. **Perform the statement in the current line.**

   2b. Move the pointer down.

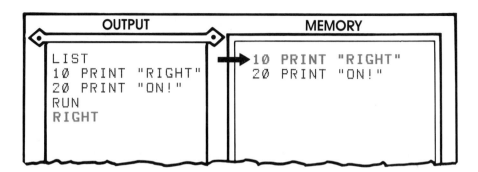

The computer has performed the PRINT "RIGHT" statement by printing RIGHT on the output scroll.

1. Move the pointer to the top.
2. Repeat 2a and 2b until no lines are left:

  2a. Perform the statement in the current line.

  2b. Move the pointer down.

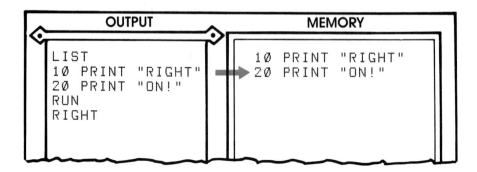

At this point, the computer must again test whether the line pointer is pointing at a BASIC line. It is, so step 2a must be repeated. Here is the step and the new picture:

1. Move the pointer to the top.
2. Repeat 2a and 2b until no lines are left:

  2a. Perform the statement in the current line.

  2b. Move the pointer down.

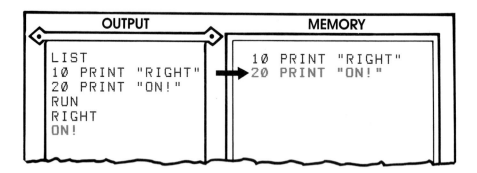

Line 20 is the new current line. The BASIC statement says to print ON! on the output unit, and the computer has done that. After step 2a, the computer must do step 2b of the RUN program:

1. Move the pointer to the top.
2. Repeat 2a and 2b until no lines are left:
   2a. Perform the statement in the current line.
   2b. Move the pointer down.

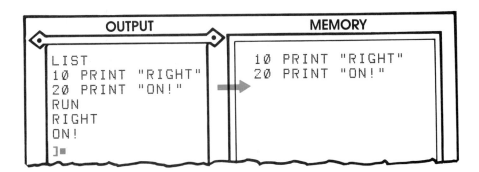

```
        OUTPUT                          MEMORY

LIST                            10  PRINT  "RIGHT"
10  PRINT  "RIGHT"              20  PRINT  "ON!"
20  PRINT  "ON!"
RUN
RIGHT
ON!
]■
```

The RUN program says to stop now, since the pointer no longer points at a line of the BASIC program. The computer turns on the cursor, telling you that it is again ready for input.

People control computers by writing and running programs.

Comparing the LIST and RUN Programs

The RUN program works almost the same way as the original version of the LIST program. The two programs are so much alike that it is worth comparing them.

The RUN Program (Initial Version)

1. Move the line pointer to the first line of the BASIC program in the memory unit.
2. Repeat the following steps as long as the line pointer is pointing at a BASIC line:
    - **2a.** Perform the statement in the current line.
    - **2b.** Move the pointer to the next line of the program in the memory unit.

The LIST Program

1. Move the line pointer to the first line of the BASIC program in the memory unit.
2. Repeat the following steps as long as the line pointer is pointing at a BASIC line:
    - **2a.** Read the current line, and write it on the output screen.
    - **2b.** Move the pointer to the next line of the program in the memory unit.

QUESTIONS

1. What is a line-number range, and how do you write one?
2. You cannot have a single line number after DEL. How, then, can you delete a single line from a program?
3. What happens when there are no program lines in the line-number range of a LIST command? Of a DEL command?
4. ⌊CONTROL S⌋ and ⌊CONTROL C⌋ interrupt program output in different ways. How are they different?
5. How should the LIST program (see above) be changed to make it work properly when a line-number range is given?
6. Why was the cursor not on the screen while the RUN program was running?

7. When the RUN program is running, what happens when the line pointer moves past the last program line in the memory unit?

8. Suppose there is no program in memory. What does the RUN program say to do?

9. Suppose someone took the memory chips containing the LIST, NEW, and RUN programs from your computer. Why would the computer no longer carry out the LIST, NEW, and RUN commands?

10. Which parts of the original LIST and RUN programs are identical?

11. What, in your own words, is the difference between the LIST program and the RUN program?

Programming Project

IN THIS SESSION YOU WILL:
- Plan a program with REM, HOME, PRINT, and SPEED= statements.
- Enter and debug the program.
- Use the INVERSE, FLASH, and NORMAL statements.
- Save the program on the diskette.

A New Project

Plan your own program that will use all the BASIC statements you have learned so far: REM, HOME, PRINT, and SPEED=. Enter it into the computer and debug it.

Experiment with three new statements: INVERSE, FLASH, and NORMAL. Try them first in the immediate mode (no line numbers) just before running or listing your new program. Then use them as statements inside your program.

Save your program on the diskette.

1. What do INVERSE, FLASH, and NORMAL tell the computer to do?

2. If you run a program that ends with a FLASH statement, what will happen when you list the program?

If you have extra lab time:

■ Load program HI THERE from your diskette. Add these two statements to it:

```
135 FLASH
165 NORMAL
```

List the program and see whether you can guess what it tells the computer to do. Now run it and see.

■ In the next hands-on session, you will learn about graphics. Load some of the graphics programs, such as SYMMETRY and BOXES, from the diskette. Run each one and then list it. Look for statements that tell the computer to plot points or draw lines.

Real Computers and Their History

Four Main Parts

You have spent a lot of time in Sessions 9, 11, and 13 with a simple model of a computer. Of course, real computers do not have mail slots, cranks, chalkboards, or scrolls of paper. But each part in the model has a counterpart in any real computer. Here is a diagram showing the four main parts of all computers:

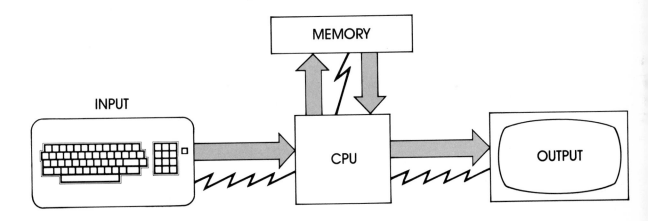

Central processing unit The middle box in the drawing is the central processing unit, or **CPU**. It actually has two parts, but they are usually combined into a single piece of hardware. One part (the control unit, or **CU**) controls the way all the parts work together. The other part (the arithmetic and logic unit, or **ALU**) does the actual processing of data. The lines between the CPU and the other parts show how two kinds of information flow between the parts.

Data paths The broad lines in the drawing show how pieces of information being processed (called **data**) flow between parts. The main path is from left to right. Data enters the computer through the input unit and goes to the CPU for processing. Processed data may go to the memory unit, come back, and finally go to the output unit and leave the computer.

Control paths The CPU is in charge of everything else; that is why the zigzag control paths in the drawing lead from the CPU to all other units. Like the conductor of an orchestra, the CPU beats time and keeps everything together. It signals the input unit when the computer is ready to receive data. It signals the memory unit when data is to be put there or taken out, and it tells what place in memory will be affected. It signals the output unit when data is coming.

The program Just as the musical score tells the players in an orchestra what to do, a program tells the computer what to do. The CPU reads the steps of the program and carries them out. The first computers ever designed or built had programs stored outside the computer, usually on many cards with holes punched in different locations. The computer would read one instruction at a time and carry it out. Since 1949, however, the program has been stored in the memory unit along with the data to be processed. The speed and power of modern computers depend on this fact.

This is part of Charles Babbage's mechanical computer.

What Computers Are Made Of

Today all computers are electronic. They need electrical power to operate. The main parts are wires and switches. You might guess that all computers must be electronic, but that is not true.

A steam-powered computer In 1833 Charles Babbage, an English mathematician, designed the first programmable computer. Although never completed, his computer would have contained only brass wheels and other mechanical parts. Programs were coded and punched into large, thick cards strung together like the cards that tell an automatic loom what pattern to weave. Babbage planned to use the power of a steam engine to turn the wheels of his computer, the "Analytical Engine," and step it through a program.

Air-powered computers People have designed and built complete computers based on the flow of air through thin pipes. The power comes from a pump that pushes air into the pipes and keeps it flowing. In many ways, a flow of air in a pipe is like the flow of electricity in a wire: Both the air and electricity move in a circuit. The pump in an air circuit is like the battery in an electric circuit.

Why electricity? There are two main reasons why practical computers today use electricity: speed and cost. Electric signals are very fast: They travel through wires at nearly the speed of light. Also, because many millions of microscopic electric circuits can be made in a single operation, they are cheap to build. Electronic computers, therefore, can be very fast, very small, and very inexpensive.

This photo shows the ENIAC, the first electronic computer, in operation.

Smaller and Smaller

As people learn how to put more and more electric circuits into less and less space, computers get smaller and smaller.

ENIAC The first electronic computer was the ENIAC (Electronic Numerical Integrator and Automatic Computer), built in 1946 at the University of Pennsylvania. It filled a room the size of a two-bedroom house. The electrical power it used would supply about 150 homes today. Almost all the power went into heating the 80,000 vacuum tubes used in the electronic circuits.

ENIAC hardware ENIAC's memory could hold 20 10-digit numbers. One rack of vacuum tubes, about the size of your disk drive, could store one digit of a number. The CPU could do about 300 multiplications in a second. The input unit was a set of electric switches. For output, ENIAC turned lights on and off in a coded fashion.

As vacuum tubes were replaced by transistors and then by chips, computers became smaller and smaller.

Software ENIAC's tiny memory could store nothing but data. To create a program, someone had to connect many hundreds of wires from one electric plug to another. Creating a simple program took many weeks. Every new program meant rewiring the panel. But without those program wires, ENIAC could do nothing. With each rewiring, it could do a different task. That ability to be programmed is what made ENIAC a true computer.

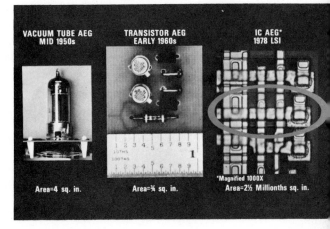

VACUUM TUBE AEG MID 1950s
Area=4 sq. in.

TRANSISTOR AEG EARLY 1960s
Area=¾ sq. in.

IC AEG* 1978 LSI
*Magnified 1000X
Area=2½ Millionths sq. in.

Improved hardware ENIAC proved that an electronic computer could work. During the next 15 years, input, processor, memory, and output hardware changed rapidly and dramatically. By 1960, the tiny, low-power transistor replaced the vacuum tube, and the CPU and memory suddenly became smaller, faster, cooler, more reliable, and much cheaper to build. Keyboards began to be used for input, TV screens for output, and magnetic disks for storing programs and data outside the computer.

Improved software The panel of programming wires quickly disappeared after the first ENIAC machine. Programs began to be punched into cards and entered into the computer through an input device called a card reader. The first programs were nothing but lists of 1s and 0s, a **binary** code that the machine understood. The biggest step forward was the writing of programs called **language processors**. They told the computer how to translate from a **programming language**, easy for people to learn, into the binary language of the machine. During this period FOR-TRAN, BASIC, COBOL, and many other programming languages were invented.

A single laser disk can store an entire set of encyclopedias.

Computers on chips By 1970, people had learned how to put thousands of transistors on one silicon chip smaller than your fingernail. A memory unit holding several hundred pieces of data could be put in a package smaller than a postage stamp. An entire CPU could be put on two or three chips. These **microprocessors** were tiny, cheap, and very reliable. The first **microcomputer** appeared in 1976. Nearly all the electric circuits in that microcomputer were on chips.

Cheaper and Cheaper

New products are always more expensive at first. Then, as people learn better ways to build them, the price drops. The first television sets (poor-quality, black-and-white models with small screens) cost the equivalent of about $2000 today. Within 10 years, a much-improved TV set cost just over $100, and the price has not changed much since then. That may seem like a big change, but it is tiny compared to the change in computer prices. If TV prices were like computer prices, the $2000 TV set of 1950 would have cost $56 in 1960, $1.60 in 1970, and 5 cents in 1980.

Price revolution In all recorded history, no new invention has become so cheap so fast. For more than 20 years, the price of computers has fallen about 50 percent every two years. Experts believe that this trend will continue for at least 10 years. The table shows what this change means to buyers. The table shows what you could have bought for the money you would have had to spend on a computer with the same capabilities as the one you're using now.

Year	Value of a Computer
1960	Rembrandt masterpiece
1965	50-foot yacht
1970	Three-bedroom house
1975	Family car
1980	Motorcycle
1985	Color TV set
1990	Telephone

Personal computers In less than half a lifetime, the computer will have changed from a luxury to a common household appliance. And the quality is better: Today's personal computer can store in memory 1000 times what ENIAC could store, can process data 100 times faster, is far easier to program, and uses less power than a light bulb.

QUESTIONS

1. What are the names of the four main parts of any computer?
2. What are two purposes of the CPU in a computer?
3. Computers need not be electronic. What other kinds of parts can a computer be built from?
4. Who designed the first programmable computer, and when?
5. Why is the ENIAC computer important?
6. How big was the memory of ENIAC?
7. What is a language processor, and why is it important?
8. What is a microprocessor, and why is it an improvement over older CPUs?
9. A large business computer costs $40,000 today. If the experts are right, how much will a similar computer cost two years from now? Four years from now?
10. Soon, anyone who can afford a TV set will be able to afford a computer. Does that mean that they will buy a computer? Explain your answer.

Part 2

REVIEW

Vocabulary Table

The BASIC words you have studied so far are shown in the table. The words printed in color were introduced in Part 2.

BASIC Vocabulary (Shaded Areas Show Standard BASIC Words)

Commands		Statements			Functions
Program	Diskette	Action	Action	Control	
RUN	LOAD	————	SPEED=	————	————
LIST	SAVE	———	FLASH	————	————
NEW	DELETE	PRINT	INVERSE	——	———
DEL	CATALOG	REM	NORMAL	——	———
———	LOCK	———	———	——	
———	UNLOCK	———	———	——	
—————			——		
—————		HOME			

New BASIC Words

DEL An Applesoft BASIC command that tells the computer to erase lines from the program in memory.

FLASH An Applesoft BASIC statement that tells the computer to make characters blink on and off when output to the screen.

INVERSE An Applesoft BASIC statement that tells the computer to make characters appear black against a white background when output to the screen.

NORMAL An Applesoft BASIC statement that tells the computer to cancel INVERSE and FLASH.

SPEED= An Applesoft BASIC statement that tells the computer what speed to use for printing characters on the screen. The fastest speed is 255 and the slowest is 0.

New Ideas

ALU See arithmetic and logic unit.

arithmetic and logic unit (ALU) A hardware device that performs all the computer's elementary operations, such as adding and comparing data.

central processing unit (CPU) A hardware device that combines arithmetic, logic, and control devices.

chip A small piece of silicon that contains thousands of electric circuits. Modern computers are constructed from such chips.

80 How Programs Work

control characters Special characters generated by holding the (CONTROL) key down while pressing another key. See (CONTROL S) and (CONTROL C).

control unit (CU) The part of the central processing unit that steps the computer through a program, one instruction at a time.

CU See *control unit*.

CPU See *central processing unit*.

(CONTROL C) In Applesoft BASIC, a control character that stops a running program.

(CONTROL S) In Applesoft BASIC, a control character that stops and restarts output to the screen.

current line The program line that is to be performed or listed next.

ENIAC The first completely electronic computer, built in 1946.

hardware The electric circuits and mechanical devices in a computer.

HELLO program A special program on the Apple diskette. When you turn on the computer or type PR#6, the HELLO program is loaded into memory and performed.

input hardware Hardware used to put information into the computer.

input slot The input hardware of the model computer.

line pointer A part of the model computer. It corresponds to information in the memory of the real computer that tells which program line is to be performed or listed next.

LIST program A built-in program that tells the computer to print the lines of the BASIC program in memory on the screen.

memory chalkboard Part of the model computer. It corresponds to the memory hardware in a real computer.

memory hardware The part of a computer in which the processor can rapidly store and recall data and program instructions.

model computer A model that helps people understand how a real computer works.

NEW program A built-in program that tells the computer to erase the BASIC program from memory.

output hardware Any hardware on which the computer displays information. The TV screen is an example of output hardware.

output scroll Part of the model computer. It corresponds to the output hardware in a real computer.

RAM See *random-access memory*.

random-access memory Memory hardware that temporarily stores the programs and data that you enter into the computer.

read-only memory Memory hardware that permanently stores built-in programs and data.

ROM See *read-only memory*.

RUN program A built-in program that tells the computer to perform the BASIC program in memory.

software The collection of programs that the computer uses to perform a task.

Part  3

Computer Graphics

Computer graphics is very popular today. The main output of electronic games, which are actually computers, is graphics. Scientists use computer graphics to plot graphs of data. Artists use the computer to experiment with graphic designs. Textile designers use color graphic displays to try patterns for fabrics without having to weave each one. Architects and city planners use computer graphics to experiment with building plans and to draw maps.

Graphics   *Graphics* is the arranging of shapes, colors, and symbols on a flat surface. (*Graphics* is usually a singular word, by the way, like *mathematics* and *economics*.) Graphics is used to design posters, advertising layouts, signs, maps, wall charts, package labels, book and record jackets, and countless other things you see every day.

Mechanics of graphics   Creating a graphic design means deciding which symbols, colors, and shapes to use and deciding how to arrange them on the page, poster, or chart. Often the designer starts by making pencil sketches. Later, the designer may make paper cutouts of parts of the design and then try different arrangements on the page. The designer also may experiment with parts of different colors or sizes.

Computer graphics   You can carry out every step of graphic design on a computer. The TV screen is your drawing board. You can choose points, lines, geometric shapes, letters, and numbers. You can experiment with different arrangements, different colors, and different sizes. *Computer graphics, then, is graphic design done on a computer.*

Apple graphics   In Part 3 of this course, you will learn how to tell the Apple II computer to draw shapes and colors on your TV screen. You will learn five new statements. In the hands-on sessions, you will create your own graphic designs.

Introduction to Graphics

IN THIS SESSION YOU WILL:
- Use both the text mode and the graphics display mode.
- Select the color you will use in the computer drawing.
- Use the PLOT statement to draw points on the screen.
- Use the VLIN and HLIN statements to draw lines on the screen.

Drawing on the Screen

In this session, you will use new statements to tell your computer to draw in color on the screen. (If there is no color display for your computer, the colors show up as different textures and shades of gray.)

CAUTION: The new statements in this session are part of Applesoft BASIC, but they are *not* part of Standard BASIC. Most other computers also have graphics statements, but they are different from the ones you will use here.

Plotting Points

Follow the usual starting procedure with your diskette.

Let's start with a few small experiments. See what happens when you type the following phrases:

```
NEW
HOME
```
That should be familiar.
```
GR
```
This is something new.

Note what is on the screen and where the cursor is now. GR lets you enter graphics mode, which means you are ready to draw. Now let's draw something.

```
PLOT 20, 20
PLOT 0, 0
```
Nothing seems to be happening, except that PLOT 20, 20 disappeared.
```
COLOR= 2
PLOT 20, 20
```
Now you should have a small blue spot of light in the middle of your screen.

```
PLOT 0, 0
```
_____ Now there is another spot at the upper left.
```
COLOR= 0
PLOT 20, 20
```
_____ The first spot disappeared. What did
`COLOR= 0` do?
```
PLOT 0, 0
```
_____ Now the other spot is gone.
```
COLOR= 15
PLOT 0, 0
```
_____ The spot is back again, but now it is white.

The `PLOT` statement tells the computer to draw a spot. The `COLOR=` statement lets you pick a color for that spot. (`COLOR= 0` is black.) You should think of `COLOR=` as a single word. You have used a statement like this before—the `SPEED=` statement you learned in Session 12.

1. What does the `GR` statement tell the computer to do?
2. What is the purpose of the `COLOR=` statement?
3. What does the `PLOT` statement tell the computer to do?

Exploring the Screen

Now, let's see how the numbers in the `PLOT` statement work.

```
PLOT 1, 0
PLOT 2, 0
PLOT 3, 0
PLOT 10, 0
PLOT 20, 0
PLOT 30, 0
```
_____ The six new points are all in a horizontal
row.

```
COLOR= 4
PLOT 22, 0
PLOT 22, 1
PLOT 22, 2
PLOT 22, 20
PLOT 22, 30
```
_____ Changing the second number moves the
spot down the screen.

Find the numbers that mark the boundaries of the left and right edges of the graphics screen. Now find the top and the bottom boundaries. What happens when you try to plot a point that is not inside the boundaries?

What happens when you type HOME? Now type GR again. What is the color after you type GR?

Type PLOT 30, 20 but do not press (RETURN) yet. Put your finger on the screen where you think the computer will draw the spot. Then press (RETURN) and find out if you were right.

4. What does the first number in the PLOT statement tell the computer?
5. What does the second number in the PLOT statement tell the computer?
6. What statement tells the computer to plot a point at the upper left corner of the screen? At the lower right corner?
7. How do you tell the computer to erase the graphics screen? The text screen?

The Text and Graphics Screens

When you type GR, the computer erases the top part of the screen, where the PLOT statements draw spots of light. After that, the HOME command erases only the bottom four lines, where your statements appear when you type them. Let's see how we can return the screen to the way it was before you typed GR.

TEXT
_____

HOME
_____

That was a big change. You should see many @ symbols.
HOME told the computer to erase the whole screen this time.

The computer is back in its normal display mode.

The GR statement tells the computer to put the screen in the **graphics display mode**. In that mode, the PLOT statement turns on spots of light in the upper part of the screen. The TEXT statement returns the screen back to the normal, or **text display mode**.

8. If you see text on the main portion of the screen, how do you switch to the graphics display mode?
9. If you see graphics on the screen, how do you switch to the text display mode?

Drawing Lines

You have learned how to plot points on the screen while it is in the graphics mode. You could draw lines by using many PLOT statements. However, there is an easier way.

Set graphics display mode. Set the color number to 12. Then do these experiments with two new statements.

```
HLIN 0, 39 AT 0
```
Draw a horizontal line across the top of the screen.

```
HLIN 0, 39 AT 39
```
Draw one across the bottom.

```
HLIN 10, 30 AT 20
```
Draw a shorter horizontal line across the center of the screen.

```
VLIN 0, 39 AT 0
```
Draw a vertical line down the left of the screen.

```
VLIN 0, 39 AT 39
```
Draw one down the right.

```
VLIN 10, 30 AT 20
```
Draw a shorter vertical line down the center of the screen.

10. How would you draw a horizontal line from column 15 to column 22 at row 17?
11. What will VLIN 2, 8 AT 14 do?

If you have extra lab time:

- Use the COLOR= statement followed by different numbers and see what happens.
- Set text (normal) mode. Find out what the PLOT, HLIN, and VLIN statements do in text mode.
- See if HLIN and VLIN can draw lines "backwards"; that is, from a greater column or row number to a lesser one.
- Load TURTLE TROT into your computer. List lines 2600 through 2999. Find out what they tell the computer to do.
- Load and run BOXES, SYMMETRY, and QUILT. They are good examples of graphics programs.

How Graphics Works

IN
THIS SESSION
YOU WILL:
- Recognize that computer graphics requires special hardware and software.
- Learn how to locate points on a surface.
- Learn the Applesoft BASIC coordinate system for graphics.
- Review Applesoft BASIC graphics statements.
- Create a design and write a program to draw it.

Graphics Hardware and Software

Computer graphics is graphic design done on a computer. Like any other computer task, computer graphics requires input, processing, and output. There is nothing special about the computer processor used for graphics. But special graphics software is necessary, and special graphics input or output hardware may be needed.

The TV screen is the most common graphics output hardware.

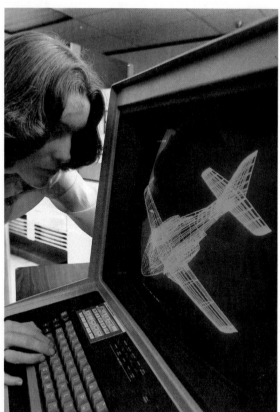

Graphics output hardware Most computer graphics output appears on a TV screen under computer control. There are other **graphics output units**, however. One of these is the **X-Y plotter**. It has one or more pens, and the computer can tell the plotter to raise or lower a pen and to move the pen from one place to another. When the pen is down, it touches and draws on a sheet of paper. Another output unit is a **film recorder**. The computer draws the picture on a tube similar to a TV screen, and a camera takes a photograph of the screen.

Graphics input hardware A **graphics input unit** allows a designer to enter shapes directly into a computer. A **graphics tablet** is an example of this kind of input hardware. The user draws with an electronic pen, and the tablet tells the computer which points the pen passes over.

Graphics statements Computer graphics, like all computer work, requires both hardware and software. In graphics work, the software tells the computer how to choose a point on the screen or page and draw something there. Nearly all small computers have such **graphics statements** in their versions of BASIC.

The graphics tablet is a graphics input unit.

This drafting plotter is a graphics output unit.

Locating Points

A person who wants the computer to draw a picture must have a way to tell the computer where on the screen to place each point or line. Let's see how to do this.

Points on a line   We'll start with something simple. How do you tell someone where your house is? If you live in a city, you probably tell how to find your street. Then you give your house number. If you think of the street as one long line, the house numbers tell the location of all houses on the line. In the same way, the numbers on the mileposts on interstate highways tell the location of points along the highway. Streets and highways are like the **number lines** you studied in math classes. *By giving a single number, you can locate any point on the line.*

Points on a surface   To tell a computer to draw something, you have to be able to locate points on a *surface,* not a *line.* How do you do that? You cannot locate a point on a surface with just one number. However, there are many different ways to locate points on a surface with two numbers.

Latitude and longitude   If you want to say where Chicago is located, you can give its latitude (42 degrees north of the equator) and its longitude (88 degrees west of Greenwich, England). There is only one place on the earth with those latitude and longitude numbers.

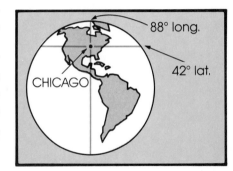

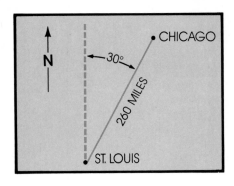

Direction and distance If you were a pilot flying from St. Louis to Chicago, you would locate Chicago in a different way. You would say that your plane must head in a direction 30 degrees east of the north direction and the plane must travel 260 miles. Starting from St. Louis, you would arrive at only one place on the earth if you traveled that number of miles and went in that direction.

East/west and north/south If you were standing in the middle of Chicago and someone asked you to give directions for getting to the post office, you might say, "Go 4 blocks east and 3 blocks north." From your starting point, those two numbers tell the location of only one place in the city.

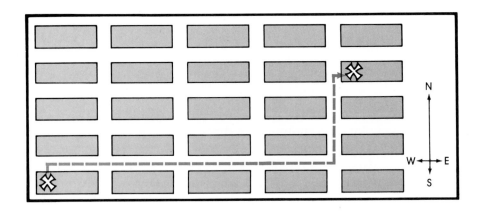

Two numbers needed There are many other ways to locate points on a surface. *No matter how you do it, though, you will discover that it always takes two numbers.* That is why we say that a surface has *two dimensions.* A line has only one dimension, since you need only one number to locate a point on a line.

Applesoft BASIC Coordinates

You have to tell the computer how to locate points on the two-dimensional TV screen. In your computer work in Session 16, you found out how to use Applesoft BASIC statements to do that job.

Horizontal and vertical coordinates The picture on a TV screen is made up of a large number of horizontal lines. The computer locates a point on one of those lines by telling the horizontal distance along the line and the vertical distance to the line. Nearly all computer graphics hardware and software use this method. These distances are called **Cartesian coordinates**. The horizontal coordinate is called the

abscissa or the **X coordinate**. The vertical coordinate is called the **ordinate** or the **Y coordinate**.

The origin The two coordinates tell the distance from a point called the **origin**. In Applesoft BASIC, the top left corner of the screen is the origin. In other words, the X coordinate of a point tells how far the point is from the *left* edge of the screen. The Y coordinate tells how far the point is from the *top* of the screen. (This is different from the origin usually used in drawing graphs. That origin is usually at the bottom left.)

The size of the screen You found in Session 16 that there are 40 different horizontal locations across the screen and 40 different vertical locations. These locations are numbered from 0 to 39. In addition, there is a **text area** at the bottom of the screen. The drawing shows a picture of the screen coordinate system and the X and Y coordinates of a point.

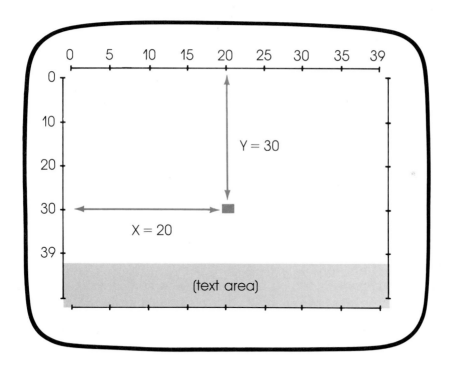

Applesoft BASIC Graphics Statements

We turn now to the statements you used in Session 16 to tell the computer to put dots and lines on the screen.

The GR and TEXT statements You used the GR statement to tell the computer to set *graphics mode* and make it possible for the other graphics statements to work correctly. To get back to *text mode,* you used the

TEXT statement. GR tells the computer to clear the graphics screen, but TEXT does *not* clear the text screen. GR also tells the computer to set the color to zero (black).

The PLOT statement You used the PLOT statement to tell the computer to draw rectangular dots on the screen. The first number in the statement is the X coordinate and the second number is the Y coordinate.

The COLOR= statement You used the COLOR= statement to tell the computer what colors to use on the screen. Different numbers after the COLOR= statement produce different colors. If you have a black-and-white TV set, instead of colors you see different shades of gray, with or without stripes. The table tells what each color number means.

COLOR=	color TV	black-and-white TV
0	black	black
1	magenta	dark stripe
2	dark blue	dark stripe
3	lavender	light stripe
4	dark green	dark stripe
5	gray	gray
6	medium blue	light stripe
7	light blue	light stripe
8	brown	dark stripe
9	orange	light stripe
10	gray	gray
11	pink	light stripe
12	green	light stripe
13	yellow	light stripe
14	aqua	light stripe
15	white	white

A graphics program In Session 16, you saw how to combine the PLOT and COLOR= statements to draw colored dots on the screen. Here is a program containing these statements:

```
10 REM--PROGRAM COLOR DOTS
20 COLOR= 1
30 PLOT 30, 10
40 COLOR= 13
50 PLOT 15, 20
60 COLOR= 15
70 PLOT 5, 30
```

It tells the computer to put a magenta (bluish red) dot, a yellow dot, and a white dot on the screen, as shown in the drawing on the next page.

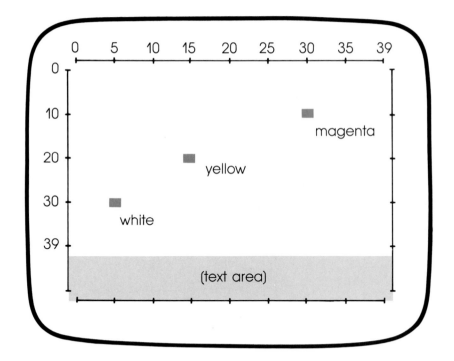

The HLIN and VLIN statements   You learned you could use the HL I N and VL I N statements to draw horizontal lines and vertical lines. The lines are made up of a series of rectangles like the ones produced by the PL0T statement. The first two numbers of each statement tell the ends of the line, and the third number tells the computer where to put the line. For example, the program

```
10 REM--PROGRAM COLOR LINES
20 COLOR= 11
30 HLIN 5, 30 AT 20
40 COLOR= 2
50 VLIN 10, 30 AT 15
```

tells the computer to draw what you see on the next page.

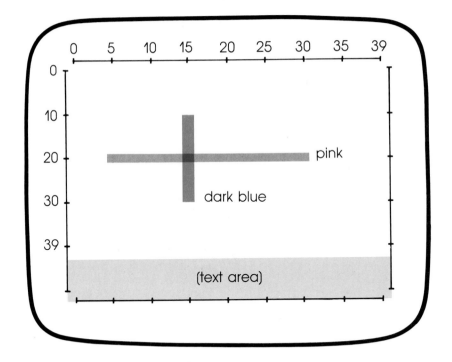

Designing Your Own Picture

You now have all the tools necessary to draw pictures on your Apple computer. Spend the rest of your time in this session creating a design of your own. It is a good idea to begin your design on a sheet of graph paper or a special printed form. Number the columns from 0 to 39 across the top and down one side. *If you are using graph paper, use two squares side by side to stand for one of the rectangular dots on the Apple screen.* Sketch the drawing in light pencil. If you have crayons or colored pens, fill in the boxes with the colors you need for your design.

After you finish the design, write on paper an Applesoft BASIC program that will tell the computer how to draw your design and color it. **Save your work so that you can enter the program into the computer in Session 18.**

1. What is computer graphics?
2. Name two graphics output units.
3. In addition to graphics hardware, what does a computer need to draw graphics?

4. Name two different ways of locating a place on a map.

5. Why do we say that a line is one-dimensional and a surface is two-dimensional?

6. How many numbers are necessary to locate a point on your TV screen?

7. What are the X and Y coordinates of the four corners of the screen?

8. Where, in words, is the point with X coordinate equal to 39 and Y coordinate equal to 20?

9. What do the GR and TEXT statements tell the computer to do?

10. What do the two numbers in a PLOT statement tell the computer?

11. What does the third number in a VLIN statement tell the computer?

18 Graphics Project—1

IN • Improve the HELLO program.
THIS SESSION • Work on your graphics design program.
YOU WILL:

A Change to the HELLO Program

Your main purpose in this session and Session 20 is to enter your graphics design program into the computer and get it to work properly. Before doing that, though, make a simple improvement to your HELLO program.

You would like the HELLO program to clear the whole screen as soon as you start the computer with your diskette. But if the last person to use the computer left the screen in graphics mode, your present HELLO program would clear only the bottom four lines.

Start the computer in the usual way with your diskette. Then do these experiments.

```
GR
```
This sets graphics mode and clears the top of the screen.

```
COLOR= 14
VLIN 0, 39 AT 20
```
This draws an aqua line down the middle of the graphics screen.

```
PR#6
```
Now, start the computer again.

You should have seen your HELLO program output quickly scrolling by on the bottom four lines of the screen. To make the program do what you want, you must make it start by setting text mode. Here is how:

```
LOAD HELLO
LIST
```
Load the program into the computer and look at it.

```
5 TEXT
```
This should put a TEXT statement *before* the HOME statement.

```
UNLOCK HELLO
SAVE HELLO
LOCK HELLO
```
Put the new version on diskette.

Next, see whether HELLO works correctly now. To check it, first set graphics mode and then do the start-up process. Here goes:

```
GR
```
Set graphics mode.
```
PR#6
```
Start the computer with your diskette.

This time, the computer should have set text mode and then cleared the entire screen before performing the rest of the HELLO program. *It is a good idea to start every program with a* TEXT *statement, followed by a* HOME *statement, so that the screen will be in text mode and will be blank.*

1. Why do you need both a TEXT statement and then a HOME statement to clear the screen?
2. Suppose that your HELLO program used only the graphics screen. How should the program begin in order to set graphics mode and clear the entire screen?

Entering Your Graphics Program

Spend the rest of your time on this session entering the program you wrote at the end of Session 17. Run the program and make any changes necessary. Before leaving, save your program on diskette with the name DESIGN. You will have more time to work on the program during Session 20.

Getting a Printed Listing

If you have a printer connected to your computer, you can use it to print a listing of your program. (Make sure the printer is switched on and the "on-line" light is glowing.) Here are the steps.

```
LOAD DESIGN
POKE 33, 30
```
This will keep long lines from being broken.
```
PR#1
LIST
```
This connects the printer and starts the listing.
```
PR#0
TEXT
```
This disconnects the printer and restores normal screen output.

Computers for Art and Entertainment

Graphics and Sound for Pleasure

In the last three sessions, you learned how to tell the computer to draw points and lines in color on the TV screen. The Apple II computer does not have special BASIC statements for sound output, but other personal computers do. Graphics and sound have practical applications, but they also have entertainment value.

Eye and ear pleasure Many of the things we do for pleasure or amusement involve looking and listening. We go to movies, look at pictures and paintings, and listen to music. Since computers can be told to draw pictures and make sounds, many artists, musicians, and entertainers are beginning to use the computer as a new creative tool.

Computers are used to design and animate movie characters.

Skills needed The computer does not make works of art or music by itself, any more than it plays chess by itself. A person must tell it what pictures to draw and what sounds to make. To put a computer to an artistic use, a person needs both artistic creativity and programming skill. All the graphic and musical ideas come from a person, who must then express the ideas in a form the computer can understand.

Many details You are beginning to discover how much detailed work goes into the program for even a very simple picture. The PLOT, HLIN, and VLIN statements force you to think carefully about your picture. In Part 4, however, you will learn how to hide these details in packages of statements that, for example, have the computer draw a border around the screen or fill in a whole rectangle in a solid color.

For complex graphics work, such as the examples in this session, you would want many such packages.

Video arcade games contain microcomputers and use a variety of input devices.

Video Games

The most popular creative use of computer graphics and sound is in video games. The games are controlled by microcomputers.

The game designer The people who create a game must tell the computer everything about it: the rules of the game, the inputs to expect from the player, all the pictures to draw, and all the sounds to make. They write this information into a program, and the program is then stored permanently in a read-only-memory (ROM) chip in the game computer.

Graphics resolution Most video games draw pictures with finer detail than you can with the PLOT statement. Pictures with more detail have higher **resolution**. The PLOT statement works at a low resolution, equal to 40 different positions across and 40 down the screen. Most video games have a resolution of about 250 by 250 different positions. There is a higher-resolution graphics mode on the Apple II. If you become interested in graphics, you should read the Applesoft manuals for more information.

Art

For more than 25 years, artists have used computer programs and graphics output devices to draw pictures or experiment with designs.

High-resolution plotters Some artists use computers with plotters that write with very fine pens on large sheets or rolls of paper. Some plotters can draw points and lines in more than 10,000 by 10,000 positions. They also can use many different sizes of pen and colors of ink.

This repetitive design was drawn by a computer on a high-resolution plotter.

Repetitive designs As you will soon learn, one of the easiest things to tell a computer to do is to repeat what it just did, possibly with small variations. For this reason, much computer art has repetitive designs. It is far easier to tell the computer to draw a straight line, rotate it a little, draw it again, etc., than it is to tell the computer to draw a human face.

Video art Artists have become interested in using color TV to create pictures.

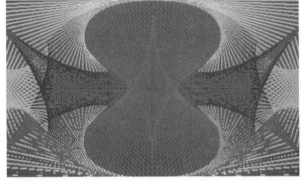

Resolution is still limited to about 700 by 700 positions, but TV allows artists to "draw" solid areas of color on a screen. And animation and sound are possible with TV.

Making Movies by Computer

By putting a movie camera in front of a television screen, an artist can make a motion picture of computer graphics. The computer draws each frame of the movie, and the camera takes a picture and then moves the film forward, ready to take the next frame.

Science fiction films The next time you go to a science fiction film, read the credits. Often the special effects were created by computer graphics. It is easier and cheaper to create some pictures with computer programs than to build expensive sets and props.

Camera control Computers are used in movies in another way. Filmmakers often build very small model sets. A whole city block can be put on a tabletop. In the past, people used to photograph the city by moving a camera carefully over the model. Today, the camera can be mounted on a mechanical arm controlled by a computer. Then a computer program tells the arm how to move and turn, for example, the way a helicopter would.

Movie robots Recently, filmmakers have built small models of prehistoric animals. They cover mechanical arms and legs with a skin that looks like the animal. A computer controls the motion of the animal, and a computer-controlled camera records the picture.

Computers in the Theater

Computers are used in modern theaters. No, the computers do not move actors on the stage, but they do other things.

Lighting control A big part of any play is lighting. You may think that the lights just come on when the curtain rises and go off when it comes down. Actually, lights are coming on, getting brighter, getting dimmer, and going off throughout the play. Sometimes a lighting effect will occur suddenly and sometimes slowly, but at each performance the effects must be the same.

Programmed lighting An easy way to control lighting is to store the instructions for each lighting change in the memory of a computer. Then the operator has the computer change the lights when the actors get to the right place in the play. The computer remembers what it is supposed to do.

Computer Music

In many ways, a sheet of music is like a computer program: It tells the players what to do and when to do it. Musicians discovered the computer long ago.

Computer sounds In the early days of computers, someone brought an AM radio into the computer room. The speaker suddenly started to make sounds at different pitches. The radio was picking up the electrical noises from the computer. It did not take long for someone to write programs to control those noises and make music out of them.

Modern music systems Today there are computer-based music systems. A piano-style keyboard is the input device. Computer memory stores the notes and the time intervals between notes. The processor can modify the notes, add harmonics, change the rhythm, change the speed, and do many other things, always under program control. The output goes to a tape recorder or a stereo system.

Computer graphics helps artists and animators visualize and change their work.

Computers and Creativity

As you learn more about computers, keep in mind that they can be used for many different things. We must decide how to make them do the things we want them to do.

QUESTIONS

1. Is computer art human art or is it machine made? Explain your answer.
2. To use a computer to create art, a person needs programming skill. What else does that person need?
3. What does a video-game designer have to tell the computer?
4. A computer system claims to have 100 by 100 graphics resolution. What does that mean?
5. What kind of graphic designs are easiest for the computer?
6. How are computers used in making movies?
7. How can computers be used in the theater?
8. What input and output devices are used to make computer music?

Graphics Project—2

IN	• Finish work on the graphics design program.
THIS SESSION	• Explore the SUBPICTURES program.
YOU WILL:	

More Work on DESIGN

At the end of Session 18, you saved your graphics design program in a file named DESIGN. Start the computer as usual with your diskette. Then check the catalog to make certain that DESIGN is there. If so, load it into the computer.

Spend about 20 minutes making changes and improvements to DESIGN, but leave 20 minutes at the end of this session to explore a new program, SUBPICTURES.

Before starting SUBPICTURES, be sure to save your finished graphics program under the name DESIGN.

Exploring the SUBPICTURES Program

Your diskette has a graphics program in a file named SUBPICTURES. Nearly all the statements in SUBPICTURES should be familiar to you now. Load program SUBPICTURES from your diskette. Delete line 135. Run the program.

If all went well, you should be looking at a very simple picture. It has a gray border around the graphics screen. In the center is a gray plus sign. Now, let's look at the program listing. Set text mode and clear the screen. List the program.

You should now be looking at all but the first line of program SUB-PICTURES. Don't worry about the missing line: It is just a REM statement with the title.

There are three statements here that you have not studied yet: END, GOSUB, and RETURN. Part 4 of this course is about these important statements, but it's not too soon to get some experience with them.

You have probably noticed that the SUBPICTURES program is divided into four main parts. The first part goes from line 100 (a REM statement) to line 140 (an END statement). The second part also starts with a REM statement (line 200), but it ends with a RETURN statement (line 240). The third part is like the second: It starts with a REM (line 400) and ends with a RETURN (line 450). The fourth part also starts (line 600) and ends (line 630) like the second and third parts.

Notice that many lines have two colons (:) between the line number and the BASIC statement. The colons indent the statements and make it easier for you to read the program. The computer ignores the colons when you run the program.

1. What do lines 210 through 230 tell the computer to do?
2. What do lines 410 through 440 tell the computer to do?
3. What do lines 610 and 620 tell the computer to do?

If you have extra lab time:

- Delete line 120. Run the program and see what happens.
- Delete lines 120 and 130. Run the program and see what happens.
- Add these lines:

```
130  GOSUB 600
131  COLOR= 0
132  GOSUB 600
133  COLOR= 7
134  GOSUB 600
135  COLOR= 0
136  GOSUB 600
137  COLOR= 7
138  GOSUB 600
```

Now run the program several times and see what happens. (The picture changes quickly, so look closely.)

- Most of the other programs on your diskette have the same form as program SUBPICTURES. List BOXES, SYMMETRY, and QUILT, and find the parts in each.

Vocabulary Table

Words printed in color were introduced in this part.

BASIC Vocabulary (Shaded Areas Show Standard BASIC Words)

Commands		Statements			Functions
Program	Diskette	Action	Action	Control	
RUN	LOAD	————	SPEED=	————	———
LIST	SAVE	———	FLASH	————	———
NEW	DELETE	PRINT	INVERSE	——	———
DEL	CATALOG	REM	NORMAL	——	———
———	LOCK	PLOT	COLOR=	——	———
———	UNLOCK	HLIN	TEXT	——	———
————		VLIN	GR	——	
————		HOME			
————					

New BASIC Words

COLOR= In Applesoft BASIC, a statement that lets you choose which color the computer will use while displaying information on the graphics screen.

GR In Applesoft BASIC, a statement that tells the computer to set graphics display mode.

HLIN In Applesoft BASIC, a statement used to draw a horizontal line on the graphics screen.

PLOT In Applesoft BASIC, a statement used to plot points on the graphics screen.

TEXT In Applesoft BASIC, a statement that tells the computer to set text display mode.

VLIN In Applesoft BASIC, a statement used to draw a vertical line on the graphics screen.

New Ideas

computer graphics Graphic design done on a computer. See *graphics*.

graphics The art of arranging shapes, lines, colors, and symbols on a flat surface.

graphics display mode A mode of operation that allows the computer to print graphics on a special (graphics) screen.

graphics input hardware Hardware used to put graphics information in the computer. An example is the graphics tablet.

graphics output hardware Hardware on which the computer displays graphics. Examples are a TV screen, an X-Y plotter, and a film recorder.

graphics resolution A measure of the detail in which graphics can be drawn by output hardware. High resolution gives greater detail.

graphics screen A TV screen that displays graphics information.

text display mode A mode of operation that allows the computer to print letters and numbers on the regular (text) screen.

text screen A TV screen that displays letters and numbers.

X coordinate The horizontal distance to a point.

Y coordinate The vertical distance to a point.

Right: Designers once drew and redrew their work with pens and drawing tools. *Below:* Today, computer design systems make designing faster and easier.

Part

Software Tools: Subroutines

Each statement in a program can tell the computer to do only simple things. Yet a complex program is built with these simple statements.

Tools and tasks Think about the tools a carpenter uses to build a house. With only a saw, a measuring tape, and a hammer, a person can cut lumber, place it correctly, and nail it together to make a simple house. But you cannot imagine how the finished house will look just by looking at the carpenter's tools.

Programming tools Statements in a programming language are like the carpenter's tools. When you first look at the few statements and the simple things they can do, you probably cannot imagine the many and complex programs you can build with those few tools. Still, everyone who has written a complex program has solved his or her problems with a few fundamental statements.

Using tools to build tools If you have a job to do, the first thing to do with your simple tools is to build special tools. The house carpenter who has only a saw, tape measure, and hammer starts by building special construction tools: a sawhorse to hold lumber off the ground for sawing, pointed stakes to mark off the ground, braces to hold up walls while they are being built, a ladder to reach high places, and so on.

Reusing tools When the house is finished, the carpenter does not throw away the sawhorses and ladders but takes them to the next job and uses them there. The carpenter is familiar with these tools and knows how they work. Good software tools are reusable too. You build them the first time to do a single job. But if you build good software tools, you will be able to use them again and again in other programs.

Subroutines are software tools Every programming language gives you a way to create useful tools by combining a group of statements into a single package. In BASIC, the package is called a **subroutine**. In this part you will learn about subroutines. You will see how the GOSUB, RETURN, and END statements work. Finally, you will see how to use subroutines to make complex programs simple.

Packaging Statements

IN	• Read programs that contain subroutines.
THIS SESSION	• Learn the form of a main routine.
YOU WILL:	• Learn the form of a subroutine.
	• Learn what GOSUB, RETURN, and END tell the computer to do.

Review

You have used only 13 BASIC statements so far. The table shows each kind of statement and its purpose.

Statement	Purpose
PRINT	Send information to the screen
REM	Put a remark in a program
HOME	Clear the screen
SPEED=	Set printing speed
INVERSE	Set inverse print mode
FLASH	Set flash print mode
NORMAL	Set normal print mode
COLOR=	Set a color
GR	Set graphics mode
PLOT	Plot a point
HLIN	Draw a horizontal line
VLIN	Draw a vertical line
TEXT	Set text mode

Standard statements The first two statements in the table, PRINT and REM, are called Standard BASIC statements: They are found in every version of BASIC. The rest are found only in Applesoft BASIC. The last six statements apply to graphics, as you learned in Part 3.

Simple actions Each of the 13 statements you have learned so far tells the computer to perform a single, simple action. PRINT tells the computer to print characters on the output screen, PLOT tells it to draw a point on the graphics screen, HOME tells it to clear the text screen, and so on.

Complex actions Most computer programs make the computer carry out very long and complex actions. For example, TURTLE TROT somehow tells the computer to use colored letters to make a bold title. It also tells the computer to draw two pictures of turtles in two different colors and then to make the turtles move. The first time you looked at

TURTLE TROT, perhaps you guessed that the program had a special statement that told the computer to draw big letters, another statement to draw turtles, and another one that told it to make them move. If so, you guessed wrong. The person who made the TURTLE TROT program created these complex actions by combining simple BASIC statements.

Building new actions In this session, you will learn the tools in BASIC that will help you combine a group of simple statements into a single package. You will also learn how BASIC allows you to tell the computer to perform the whole package, just as if it were one statement.

A Program with Subroutines

In Session 20, you loaded a program named SUBPICTURES from your diskette. When you ran the program, the computer drew a gray border around the graphics screen and then drew a gray plus sign inside it. The listing of SUBPICTURES looked like this:

```
100 REM--PROGRAM SUBPICTURES
110:: GOSUB 200: REM--SET UP
120:: GOSUB 400: REM--BORDER
130:: GOSUB 600: REM--PLUS
140 END
190:
200 REM--SUB SET UP
210:: HOME
220:: GR
230:: COLOR= 5
240 RETURN
390:
400 REM--SUB BORDER
410:: HLIN 0,39 AT 0
420:: HLIN 0,39 AT 39
430:: VLIN 0,39 AT 0
440:: VLIN 0,39 AT 39
450 RETURN
590:
600 REM--SUB PLUS
610:: HLIN 15,25 AT 20
620:: VLIN 10,30 AT 20
630 RETURN
```

Form of the program You can see at a glance that the program is divided into four blocks. Blank lines (lines with only a colon after the line number) in 190, 390, and 590 separate the blocks from one another. Each block in this program is called a **routine**. All four routines have a similar form.

Form of the routines Each routine starts with a REM statement that tells a reader what the purpose of the routine is. The statements of each routine are indented to make it clear that the statements are part of that routine. These indented statements make up the **body** of the routine. (In Applesoft BASIC, you have to use colons after the line number to indent a line.) Finally, each routine ends with an unindented statement, either an END or a RETURN statement.

Blank lines and indentions   The computer ignores blank lines, indentions, and REM statements when the program is run. But that does not mean you should leave them out. They make the program much easier to read. Soon you will be working with complicated programs that would be very difficult to read if they were not written this way.

Two Kinds of Routines

You can see from the listing of program SUBPICTURES that the program has two different kinds of routines. One ends with an END statement, and the other ends with a RETURN statement.

The main routine   The first block at the top of the program is called the **main routine**.

```
100 REM--PROGRAM SUBPICTURES
110:: GOSUB 200: REM--SET UP
120:: GOSUB 400: REM--BORDER
130:: GOSUB 600: REM--PLUS
140 END
```

The main routine starts with a REM statement in line 100, which tells the purpose of the program. The body of the main routine contains three examples of a statement (GOSUB) you have not studied yet. Each GOSUB statement is followed by a colon and a REM that helps explain its meaning. The routine ends with another new statement (END) in line 140. The END statement tells the computer to stop performing the program. We will come back to the meaning of the GOSUB statement soon. *The main routine must have an* END *statement.*

First subroutine   Each of the three remaining blocks is called a **subroutine**. The listing of the first subroutine looks like this:

```
200 REM--SUB SET UP
210:: HOME
220:: GR
230:: COLOR= 5
240 RETURN
```

The REM statement explains the purpose of the subroutine. Three familiar statements make up the body of the subroutine. The RETURN statement tells the computer that there are no more statements in the subroutine; so the computer *returns* to the main routine. *Every subroutine must have a* RETURN *statement.*

Second subroutine The second subroutine has the same form as the first, but its body is different. Here is the listing:

```
400 REM--SUB BORDER
410:: HLIN 0,39 AT 0
420:: HLIN 0,39 AT 39
430:: VLIN 0,39 AT 0
440:: VLIN 0,39 AT 39
450 RETURN
```

You can see that the four statements of the body tell the computer to draw lines at the top, bottom, left, and right edges of the screen.

Third subroutine The last subroutine in SUBPICTURES also has the same form as the other two, but a different body.

```
600 REM--SUB PLUS
610:: HLIN 15,25 AT 20
620:: VLIN 10,30 AT 20
630 RETURN
```

The two statements of the body tell the computer to draw a large plus sign in the middle of the screen.

How Program SUBPICTURES Works

Now that you are familiar with all the parts of the SUBPICTURES program, you are ready to see how it works. Each subroutine contains statements (instructions) for doing a task. But how does the main routine tell the computer to *perform* the task in a subroutine?

The GOSUB statement The GOSUB statement in the main routine tells the computer to go to a subroutine and perform the statements there. The number after the word GOSUB tells the computer which subroutine to perform. The number must match the line number of the first statement in the subroutine. For example, GOSUB 200 tells the computer to go to line 200 and perform the statements in the subroutine that begins on that line.

How does GOSUB work? There is a very simple way to picture how the GOSUB statement works: Imagine that it tells the computer to *substitute* the body of the subroutine for the GOSUB statement. For example, in line 110

```
110:: GOSUB 200: REM--SET UP
```

the computer replaces GOSUB 200 with these three statements:

```
HOME
GR
COLOR= 5
```

After performing these three statements, the computer continues with line 120 of the main routine.

More to come This explanation of the GOSUB statement is accurate as long as the main routine and the subroutines are written *correctly*. In Sessions 26 and 27, you will learn how common errors happen and how the computer responds to those errors.

Subroutines and Complex Actions

No single BASIC statement tells your computer to draw a border around the graphics screen or a plus sign in the center. But program SUBPICTURES has subroutines that tell the computer how to do those things. Once a subroutine has been written, a *single* GOSUB statement tells the computer to perform *all* the statements in the body of the subroutine, no matter how long and complex it is.

A simple main routine In program SUBPICTURES, the body of the main routine is simple and easy to read. Here is the main routine:

```
100 REM--PROGRAM SUBPICTURES
110:: GOSUB 200: REM--SET UP
120:: GOSUB 400: REM--BORDER
130:: GOSUB 600: REM--PLUS
140 END
```

Each one of its three statements is a GOSUB. The trailing remark after each GOSUB tells what the subroutine does:

1. First, set up the computer for graphic display.
2. Next, draw the border around the screen.
3. Finally, draw the plus sign at the center of the screen.

Later you will see that you use this kind of verbal description when you begin writing *any* program.

Subroutines hide details When carpenters build ladders, they pay careful attention to the details of the design of the tool. But when the carpenters or other people use the ladder, they usually forget all those details. They just put the tool to work. Subroutines are built and put to work much in the same way. When you build a subroutine, you must pay attention to the details of how it works. Later, when you and others start using the subroutine, you can usually ignore the details. You should think of the subroutine as just one more action that your computer can do.

1. What action does the HLIN statement tell the computer to perform?

2. Do any of the statements in the table on page 108 tell the computer to draw a border around the graphics screen? If so, which? If not, what statements would have to be combined to do that job?

3. What are the blocks of program SUBPICTURES on page 109 called?

4. What statements appear on the last lines of the routines in SUBPICTURES?

5. Which lines form the body of the last routine in SUB-PICTURES?

6. Why are blank lines and indents used in program SUBPIC-TURES?

7. What is the difference between the form of the main routine and the form of a subroutine?

8. The REM statement in line 400 of program SUBPICTURES on page 109 says SUB BORDER. Why do you think the writer used those two words?

9. When the computer performs line 120 of program SUBPIC-TURES, what four statements does it substitute for the GOSUB 400 statement?

10. When the computer performs line 130 of program SUBPIC-TURES, what two statements does it substitute for the GOSUB 600 statement?

11. How do subroutines allow you to add new actions to the ones already present in BASIC?

12. How do subroutines make the main routine simple and easy to read?

13. When is it important to think about *how* a subroutine *works*?

14. When is it important to know *what* a subroutine *does*?

Reading and Changing Programs with Subroutines

IN THIS SESSION YOU WILL:
- Read programs that contain subroutines.
- Find out what happens when you delete GOSUB statements from the main routine.
- Find out what happens when you add GOSUB statements to the main routine.
- Trace the use of subroutines in complicated programs.

Program BLAST OFF

In Session 21, you learned how statements can be grouped into packages called subroutines. A GOSUB statement in the main routine tells the computer to perform a subroutine. In this session, you will study programs with subroutines.

Start the computer in the usual way with your diskette. Load program BLAST OFF from your diskette. Run it. Then list lines 100 through 130.

Look at the statements indented inside the main routine. Line 110 contains GOSUB 200 and the remark ROCKET. The subroutine beginning at line 200 draws the rocket. Line 120 contains GOSUB 600 and the remark LAUNCH. The part of the program that moves the rocket up and off the screen begins at line 600.

List lines 200 through 430. There are too many lines to fit on the screen at the same time, so you must list them in blocks.

Subroutine ROCKET is almost the same as the program ROCKET that you have run several times. The main difference is that the statements of program ROCKET have been packaged into a subroutine in program BLAST OFF. The statement GOSUB 200 tells the computer to print the picture of a rocket.

List lines 600 through 890. Again, you will have to list the lines in blocks.

The LAUNCH subroutine consists of many PRINT statements and two SPEED= statements. The first SPEED= statement slows down the rate at which the computer performs the PRINT statements, so the rocket appears to move off the screen at a speed slower than normal print speed. The second SPEED= statement resets top speed.

```
RUN
```
The rocket is launched as you have seen before.

```
110
120
```
Delete the GOSUBs in lines 110 and 120.

```
LIST 100, 130
```
This is the main routine.

```
RUN
```
Nothing happens. (You will fix this soon.)

1. What statement tells the computer to perform a subroutine?
2. If the body of the main routine contains no statements, what will happen when the program is run?

Immediate Mode

The version of BLAST OFF now in your computer has no GOSUB statements. But it does have all the statements of the rocket and launch subroutines. You can use the immediate mode to tell the computer to perform a subroutine. Just type the GOSUB statement without a line number.

```
GOSUB 200: REM--ROCKET
```
There is the rocket.

```
HOME
```
Erase it.

```
GOSUB 200
```
There it is again. The REM statement was not necessary.

```
GOSUB 600
```
Blast off!

Once a subroutine is in the memory, you can use the immediate mode to tell the computer to perform the subroutine.

3. What does the statement GOSUB 200 tell the computer to do? Explain in your own words.
4. You saw that the REM after the GOSUB was not necessary. Why do you think the writer put a REM after each GOSUB statement?

Extra GOSUB Statements

Next, let's see what happens when you start putting GOSUB statements back into the main routine.

```
110:: GOSUB 200: REM--ROCKET
LIST 100, 130
```
Now the GOSUB to the rocket subroutine is back.

```
RUN
```
The rocket is on the screen, but there is no launch.

```
120:: GOSUB 600: REM--LAUNCH
LIST 100, 130
```

The GOSUB to the launch subroutine is back.
The program is back to normal.

```
RUN
```

```
122:: GOSUB 200: REM--ROCKET
124:: GOSUB 600: REM--LAUNCH
LIST 100, 130
```

Another rocket GOSUB and launch GOSUB have been added.
Now two rockets blast off.

```
RUN
```

```
126:: GOSUB 200: REM--ROCKET
128:: GOSUB 600: REM--LAUNCH
LIST 100, 300
```

Still another rocket and launch.

```
RUN
```

Now three rockets blast off.

5. Why does the program now draw and launch three rockets? Explain in your own words.

6. What determines the order in which the computer performs subroutines?

Reading Program BOXES

Most of the programs on your diskette are written in the form of a main routine and a few subroutines. Now you will learn to read programs and to identify all the routines.

   Load program BOXES. List the main routine (lines 100 through 180). Use the GOSUB statements as a guide to tell you where each subroutine is located. Then list each one and study the statements in the body.

   There are a few new statements in this program, but don't worry about them now. The main idea here is the form of the program.

7. What lines of program BOXES contain the main routine?

8. Which subroutine actually draws the boxes?

If you have extra lab time:

- Find the main routine in program SYMMETRY. List each subroutine separately.

- Find the main routine and all the subroutines in program QUILT. Notice that subroutine REPEAT has a GOSUB statement to another subroutine, PATTERN.

Top-Down Programming

IN	• Review the way subroutines work.
THIS SESSION	• Learn the structure of main routines and subroutines.
YOU WILL:	• Use top-down design to plan a new program.
	• Write the subroutines needed to carry out a main routine.

Review

In Sessions 21 and 22, you saw how complex programs are built from groups of statements called *subroutines*. Each subroutine used simple BASIC statements to define a complex action. You learned that the GOSUB statement tells the computer to perform a subroutine. You used the GOSUB statement inside the main routine of a program. You also used GOSUB in the immediate mode, and you saw that the body of one subroutine could contain a GOSUB to another subroutine.

Defining new actions *The important thing about subroutines is that they give you a way to define new actions for the computer to carry out.* You learned in Session 21 that there is no BASIC statement that tells the computer to draw a border around the graphics screen. But you can define that action by adding these statements to your program:

```
400 REM--SUB BORDER
410:: HLIN 0, 39 AT 0
420:: HLIN 0, 39 AT 39
430:: VLIN 0, 39 AT 0
440:: VLIN 0, 39 AT 39
450 RETURN
```

Then, whenever you need to have a border, all you have to do is put a GOSUB 400 statement into your program.

Performing new actions You removed the GOSUB statements in the BLAST OFF program and then ran it. The computer did nothing. Then you added extra GOSUB statements, and the computer drew several rockets and launched them. GOSUB *is the statement that tells the computer to perform the action defined in the subroutine.* If there is no GOSUB statement in the main routine, the computer will not perform the subroutine. If there are two identical GOSUB statements in the main routine, the computer will perform the subroutine twice.

Structure of a Well-Written Program

A well-written computer program is like a well-written English composition. Both should be easy to read.

It takes planning to design a good computer program. A software team spends many hours on the plan before they start programming.

Structure of a composition The first few sentences should explain what the whole composition is about. Major ideas should be put in separate paragraphs. Each paragraph should have a topic sentence. Blank lines should separate one paragraph from the next.

Structure of a program The routines of a well-written program are like the paragraphs of an English composition. The main routine tells what the whole program is going to do. Each subroutine should have a name that gives the reader an idea of what it will do. Subroutines should be separated from one another by blank lines.

Rules of good structure Your English teacher checks your spelling and punctuation. The computer checks your programs in the same way. Your English teacher also helps you organize your ideas and write them more clearly. Unfortunately, the computer does not help you organize your programs so they are clear and easy to read. The computer will run hard-to-read programs (such as program SPAGHETTI on your diskette) without complaint. So it is up to you to learn a few rules that will make your programs easy to write, read, and change.

Standard program outline The best way to start both an English composition and a program is with an outline. Nearly every program you will see in this course has this outline form:

I. Main routine
II. First subroutine
III. Second subroutine
IV. Third subroutine
    etc.

Outline of main routine Every program that contains subroutines should begin with a main routine. It is usually short. It gives a complete picture of the whole program, but it leaves out the details. No matter what the program does, the structure of the main routine should be the same. Here is an outline:

```
___  REM--PROGRAM name of program
___
___
___     body of main routine
___     (mostly GOSUB statements)
___
___
___  END
```

The blank lines show where line numbers will go. The first statement in the main routine should be a REM statement giving the name of the program. The last statement *must* be an END statement. The REM statement opens the main routine, and the END statement closes it. The body of the main routine tells which subroutines are to be performed and in what order.

Outline of subroutine The details of a program appear in the subroutines. All subroutines have the same form, regardless of what they do. Here is an outline:

```
___  REM--SUB subroutine name
___
___
___       body of subroutine
___
___
___  RETURN
```

Every subroutine should begin with a REM statement that names the action the subroutine defines. Every subroutine *must* end with a RETURN statement. The REM statement opens the subroutine, and the RETURN statement closes it. The body of the subroutine contains the statements that define the action of the subroutine. You saw in program QUILT that subroutines can contain GOSUBS to other subroutines. This is an example of one tool using another.

Indentions and blank lines It is a good idea to indent the body of each routine. Indentions make it clear where the body begins and ends. Blank lines between routines make it clear where one routine ends and the next one begins. As you know, you must use colons in Applesoft BASIC to indent and create blank lines.

Breaking the rules Some of the rules given above are required by the computer. There *must* be an END statement or a STOP statement between the main routing and the first subroutine. There *must* be a RETURN statement at the end of every subroutine. (In Session 26, you will see what happens if you break these rules.) By contrast, the computer ignores blank lines, indentions, and REM statements. They have only one purpose: to make programs easy to read.

Top-Down Design of a Program

Let's use the outlines you have learned to help you design a new program.

A name in lights Suppose you have three classmates named Ana, Nan, and Ann, all of whom want to see their names in lights. You decide to write a program to do just that. The program will have a subroutine to print a big N and another one to print a big A. With these two subroutines, the program can spell all three names.

Start at top It is easy to get bogged down in details when you are trying to solve a problem. (How can I make the computer print a big N? A big A?) It is almost always better to ignore these details at first. Start with the main routine and figure out what it must tell the computer to do. If there are no BASIC statements that tell the computer to do what you want it to do, use a GOSUB statement instead.

Main routine outline Here is an outline of the main routine, written partly in English and partly in BASIC:

```
100 REM--PROGRAM NAMES
110::  clear screen
120::  print a big N
130::  print a big A
140::  print a big N
150 END
```

Convert to BASIC You can tell the computer to perform line 110 with a single BASIC statement, HOME. To perform line 120, the computer will need several PRINT statements that make a letter like this one:

```
&.&.        &.&.
&.&.&.&.     &.&.
&.&. &.&.  &.&.
&.&.    &.&.&.&.
&.&.        &.&.
```

Let's not worry about those details now. Instead, we will "bury" them in a BIG N subroutine, which can be written after we finish the main routine. Here is the completed main routine, plus an outline of the subroutines.

```
100 REM--PROGRAM NAMES
110::  HOME
120::  GOSUB 400: REM--BIG N
130::  GOSUB 600: REM--BIG A
140::  GOSUB 400: REM--BIG N
150 END
390:
400 REM--SUB BIG N
---
---        print big N
---
500 RETURN
590:
600 REM--SUB BIG A
---
---        print big A
---
700 RETURN
```

Top-down design The method you have been using to solve this problem is called *top-down* programming. Here are the steps you used:

1. Write an English-language version of the body of the main routine.

2. Convert into BASIC each English phrase that you can express by one or two BASIC statements.

3. If you cannot convert the English phrase into one or two BASIC statements, convert it to a GOSUB statement.

4. After you convert all the English phrases in the main routine, repeat this whole process for each subroutine named in step 3.

Top-down programming has two good effects: It makes you think about what the whole program is supposed to do, and it keeps you from getting bogged down in details.

Writing the subroutines We'll leave it to you to design the BIG A and BIG N subroutines out of PRINT statements. You will be entering your solution to this problem into the computer in Session 24, so save your work.

QUESTIONS

1. What part of a program tells the computer how to carry out a new action?

2. What tells the computer to perform a subroutine?

3. Suppose that a program contains two subroutines. What determines the order in which the computer performs the subroutines?

4. What goes at the top of a main routine?

5. What goes at the bottom of a main routine?

6. Why must the body of the main routine contain GOSUB statements if the program has subroutines?

7. What is the purpose of the RETURN statement?

8. Why should the body of a routine be indented?

9. What is the purpose of blank lines in a program?

10. In your own words, what does top-down programming mean?

11. Why is top-down programming helpful?

Practice with Subroutines

IN
THIS SESSION
YOU WILL:
• Enter program NAMES into the computer.
• Vary the main routine in program NAMES.
• Use FLASH, INVERSE, and NORMAL to control the printing mode.

Entering Program NAMES

In Session 23, you wrote two subroutines to print big letters on the screen. The subroutines were called BIG N and BIG A. The main routine of NAMES used these subroutines to put Nan's name on your screen. The program outline looked like this:

```
100 REM--PROGRAM NAMES
110:: HOME
120:: GOSUB 400: REM--BIG N
130:: GOSUB 600: REM--BIG A
140:: GOSUB 400: REM--BIG N
150 END
390:
400 REM--SUB BIG N
---
---     print big N
---
500 RETURN
590:
600 REM--SUB BIG A
---
---     print big A
---
700 RETURN
```

At the end of Session 23, we asked you to write the bodies of the two subroutines. They can be built out of PRINT statements. For example, the big A might look like this:

```
   00000
  00   00
  0000000
  00   00
 000   000
```

Enter the complete program NAMES into the computer now. If you did not write the subroutine bodies in Session 23, do so now. Run the program a few times and make any improvements you like. Remember, you can get a blank line before each big letter by putting an "empty" PRINT statement (one without anything after the word PRINT) as the first statement in the subroutine body.

Changing the Main Routine

Now that you have two new subroutines, you can use them in different ways. All you have to do is use a GOSUB 400 when you want a big *N* and a GOSUB 600 when you want a big *A*.

Type GOSUB 400 and GOSUB 600 a few times in the immediate mode.

Now, change the main routine to make program NAMES print Ann's name in big letters. Change it again to print Ana's name.

1. What tells the computer *which* letter to print first, which to print second, and so on?

2. What tells the computer *how* to print a big *A?*

Changing the Printing Mode

In Session 12, you learned how to use the SPEED= statement to control the speed at which characters are printed on the screen. Let's review the SPEED= statement.

Use the SPEED= statement in the immediate mode to change the printing speed. Now run program NAMES.

In Session 14, you learned about FLASH, INVERSE, and NORMAL statements. Use each one in the immediate mode just before running NAMES.

SPEED=, INVERSE, FLASH, and NORMAL are Applesoft BASIC statements. You can use them in programs as well as in the immediate mode. They are not available in Standard BASIC, however.

3. What statement would you put into the program NAMES to make the big letters on the screen flash? Where should the statement go?

4. Suppose you want the first letter of Nan's name to flash, the second letter to be normal, and the third letter to be in inverse video mode. What lines would you add to the program NAMES?

5. What statement would you add to the end of the program in question 4 to make sure the printing mode returns to normal before the program stops?

If you have extra lab time:

- Use FLASH, INVERSE, and NORMAL statements in the program NAMES to make the results more interesting. When you are satisfied with your program, save it on your diskette as program NAMES. You will use this program in future sessions.

- Unlock your HELLO program so that you can make changes in it. Change the HELLO program so that it uses INVERSE and FLASH. Be sure to put a NORMAL statement at the end of the program. When you are satisfied, save the new version of the HELLO program and lock it.

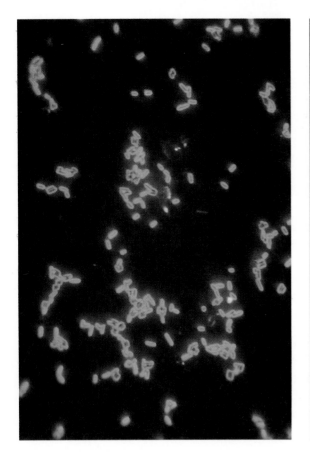
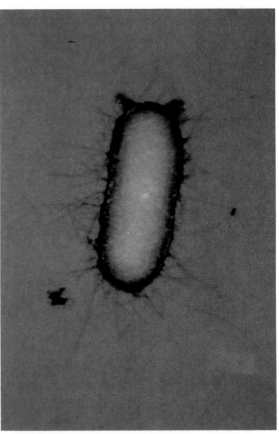

Left: These E. Coli bacteria are magnified under a traditional optical microscope. Right: A single bacterium of the same type appears larger when an electron microscope is used. Colors are added by a computer programmed to exaggerate contrasts.

How GOSUB and RETURN Work

- Add a return address stack to the model computer.
- Use the model computer to explain how subroutines work.
- Improve the RUN program.

Review

In Sessions 21 through 24, you learned how to use subroutines in programs. You did not have to know exactly *how* subroutines worked.

More is needed The idea that the subroutine body *replaces* the GOSUB statement is a good one. It gives you a feeling for what is taking place. Nevertheless, this idea alone does not explain everything about subroutines. Later, you might need to know exactly how the computer performs subroutines, especially if the computer will not do what you want it to do.

Why details matter If you always follow the rules for writing programs with subroutines, you won't need to think about how the computer actually performs the GOSUB and RETURN statements. But suppose you forget to put an END statement after the main routine, forget the RETURN statement, or use the wrong line number in the GOSUB. *The result is very confusing if you don't have a good mental picture of what is going on inside the computer.*

A Better Model Computer

In Sessions 11 and 13, you learned that a computer model can help you understand how the real computer works. The model can also give you a much better idea of how the computer performs subroutines.

Simple example Let's start with a simple program that uses a subroutine correctly. The program does nothing useful, but it shows how the computer performs a GOSUB and a RETURN statement. There is a main routine and one subroutine.

```
10 PRINT "ONE"
15 GOSUB 60
20 PRINT "THREE"
50 END
55:
60 REM--SUB TWO
65:: PRINT "TWO"
70 RETURN
```

As before, we will use the computer model to explain how the real computer performs this program. Here is the model after you enter the program and drop the words HOME and RUN into the input slot. Remember, this input tells the computer to clear the screen and then perform the RUN program: It starts by putting the line pointer at the first BASIC line, line 10:

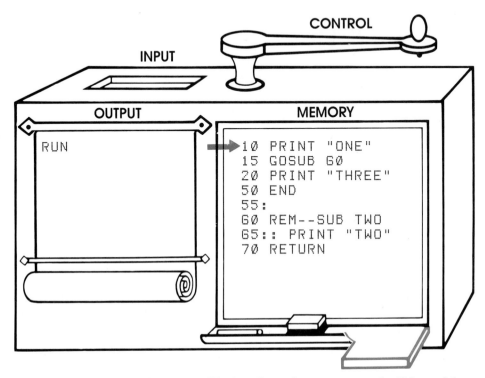

A new memory feature Notice that the memory chalkboard has something new at the lower right corner. It is a small shelf. The shelf can hold a stack of cards, which we will call the **return address stack**. The computer model has a supply of blank cards. It can write numbers on the cards and put them on the return address stack. You will soon see why the model needs this stack.

Perform PRINT and move pointer The RUN program says to perform the PRINT statement in line 10 and then move the pointer down to line 15. Here is how the output scroll and the memory chalkboard look after that.

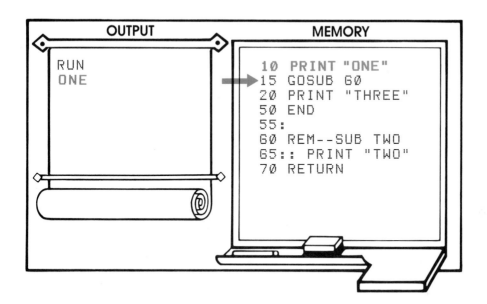

Perform GOSUB The RUN program now says to perform the GOSUB statement. How does the computer perform a GOSUB? Here are the rules:

The computer's rules for performing the GOSUB statement

1. On a blank card, write the line number of the statement after the GOSUB statement. Put the card on the top of the return address stack.

2. Move the line pointer to the line number that matches the number after the word GOSUB.

The *statement* after the GOSUB statement is in line 20, so step 1 tells the computer to write 20 on the card. The *number* after the word GOSUB is 60, so step 2 tells the computer to move the line pointer to line 60. Here is the picture of the computer after the GOSUB statement is performed.

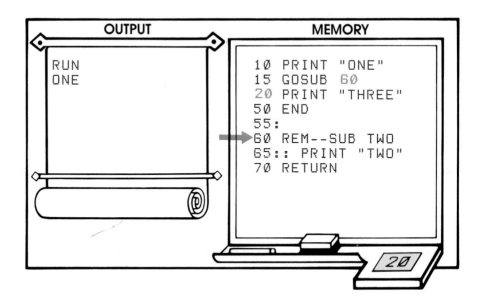

Notice that the return address stack now has a card with the number 20 written on it. Notice also that the line pointer is at line 60.

Perform REM and PRINT Now it is time to perform line 60. It is a REM statement, so the computer skips it. The computer moves the line pointer down to line 65 and performs the PRINT statement. It tells the computer to print TWO on the output scroll. Then the computer moves the line pointer down to line 70. Here is the picture at that time.

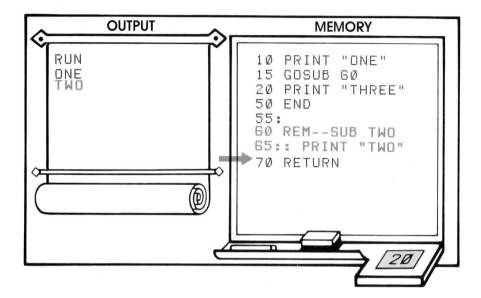

Perform the RETURN Now the computer must perform the RETURN statement. Here are the rules.

The computer's rules for performing the RETURN statement

1. Remove the top card from the return address stack.
2. Read the number on the card, move the line pointer to that line number, and throw the card away.

Here is the picture of the computer after it performs the RETURN statement.

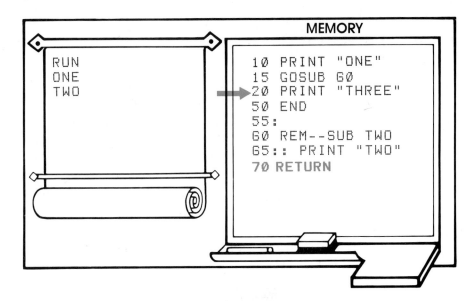

Notice that the return address stack is now empty. The RETURN statement told the computer to remove the card and move the pointer to line 20, the number that was written on the card.

Perform PRINT Now the computer must perform the PRINT statement in line 20 and then move the pointer down to line 50. Here is the picture after that.

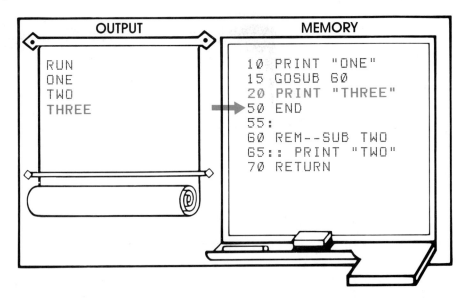

The output scroll has THREE on it, and the line pointer is at line 50.

Perform END Next, the computer must perform the END statement in line 50. Here are the rules.

> **The computer's rules for performing the END statement**
>
> **1.** Stop the RUN program.
> **2.** Put the cursor back on the screen.

Here is the model of the computer after it performs the END statement.

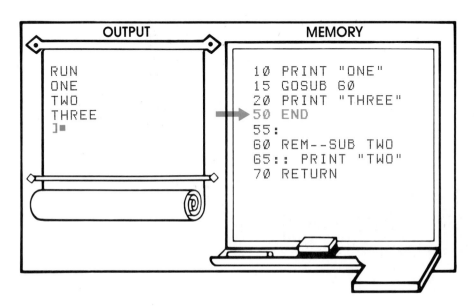

```
        OUTPUT                        MEMORY

    RUN                     10  PRINT "ONE"
    ONE                     15  GOSUB 60
    TWO                     20  PRINT "THREE"
    THREE            ➡      50  END
    ]■                      55:
                            60  REM--SUB TWO
                            65:: PRINT "TWO"
                            70  RETURN
```

Return address stack The return address stack is the key idea. You should note very carefully how the GOSUB and the RETURN statements use this stack. The GOSUB tells the computer to put a card on the stack. The RETURN tells the computer to take one off. The GOSUB tells the computer to write a line number on the card before putting it on the stack. The RETURN tells the computer to remove the top card on the stack and to move the line pointer to the line number written on the card.

Improving the RUN Program

The initial version of the RUN program is not quite correct. It needs to be changed slightly to explain how subroutines work. Before subroutines were introduced, the RUN program told the computer to move the line pointer through the program *in line-number order*. After the BASIC statement in a line was performed, the RUN program told the computer to move the line pointer to the next line in the program. With subroutines, however, the line pointer does not go automatically to the next line. As you have seen, GOSUB and RETURN tell the computer to move the line pointer to different points in the program.

Initial RUN program   Here is the initial version of the RUN program:

> ### The RUN Program (Initial Version)
>
> **1.** Move the line pointer to the first line of the BASIC program in the memory unit.
>
> **2.** Repeat the following steps as long as the line pointer is pointing at a BASIC line.
>
> **2a.** Perform the statement in the current line.
>
> **2b.** Move the pointer to the next line of the program in the memory unit.

The problem lies in step 2b. Suppose the line pointer is pointing at line 15, which says GOSUB 60. Step 2a says to perform the GOSUB. That puts the line pointer at line 60. Now comes the problem: Step 2b says to move the pointer down to the next line *after* 60. *So the computer would never perform line* 60.

Improved RUN program   We need a better RUN program. Here is an improved version with a new step 2b:

> ### The RUN Program (Improved Version)
>
> **1.** Move the line pointer to the first line of the BASIC program in the memory unit.
>
> **2.** Repeat the following steps as long as the line pointer is pointing at a BASIC line.
>
> **2a.** Perform the statement in the current line.
>
> **2b.** If step 2a just moved the line pointer, leave the pointer there; if not, move the pointer to the next line of the program in the memory unit.

Subroutines treated correctly   If there is a GOSUB statement at step 2a, the computer moves the line pointer to the beginning of the subroutine. Because the line pointer *was* moved in step 2a, *step 2b says to leave the line pointer exactly where the GOSUB put it.* Similarly, a RETURN statement at step 2a tells the computer to move the line pointer to the line number written on the top card on the return address stack. Again, the line pointer *was* moved in step 2a, so step 2b says to leave the pointer exactly where the RETURN put it.

Line pointer jumps Statements that tell the computer to move the line pointer or stop the program are called **control statements**. The other statements are called **action statements**. When the computer finishes performing an action statement, it always goes to the next statement in the listing. That is not true of control statements, such as GOSUB, RETURN, and END. You will learn about other control statements in Part 6. The improved version of the RUN program will handle these new statements properly.

Why worry about details? You may feel that this little detail in the RUN program is not worth all the attention we gave it. After all, the first version of the RUN program was pretty good. If somebody gave *you* those rules, you would know what to do when something new came along, such as the GOSUB statement. A person would use *judgment* and would *adapt* the rules.

Computers are fussy Computers do not use judgment. They cannot adapt. They carry out instructions exactly as written. They are fussy about details. When you write programs for a computer, you must be just as fussy about getting the details right. Don't rely on the machine to show intelligence or judgment. It has neither.

QUESTIONS

1. What statement should end a main routine?
2. What statement should begin a subroutine?
3. What statement should end a subroutine?
4. What statement tells the computer to perform a subroutine?
5. What does a GOSUB statement, such as GOSUB 100, tell the computer to do? Explain in your own words.
6. How does the RETURN statement tell the computer to move the line pointer?
7. You now know two ways that the RUN program is stopped. What are they?
8. Why did the RUN program need to be updated? Explain in your own words.
9. Which BASIC statements you have studied move the line pointer?
10. How does the computer use the return address stack?

Exploring Subroutine Bugs

IN	• Study the missing END statement bug.
THIS SESSION	• Study the missing RETURN statement bug.
YOU WILL:	• Study GOSUB bugs.

Programs with Subroutine Errors

If you always followed the proper rules for writing subroutines, there would be no need to worry about "buggy" programs—programs with errors. But, sooner or later, you will forget to put an END statement at the end of the main routine or will leave out the RETURN at the end of a subroutine. Mistakes like these sometimes produce error messages and sometimes not. Let's look at these often surprising situations.

Start the computer in the usual way with your diskette.

The "Missing END Bug"

The purpose of the END *statement is to stop the* RUN *program.* One of the most common bugs in programs with subroutines happens when you leave out the END statement. We will use the program you studied in Session 25 to see what happens because of the "missing END bug."

```
10 PRINT "ONE"
15 GOSUB 60
20 PRINT "THREE"
50 END
55:
60 REM--SUB TWO
65:: PRINT "TWO"
70 RETURN
```
Enter the program.
```
RUN
```
Check the program.

The program is working correctly if you see ONE, TWO, and THREE down the left side of the screen. Correct any errors in your program before going on. Now comes the bug:

```
50
```
Delete the END statement.
```
LIST
```
Make sure it's gone.
```
RUN
```
Run the program.

By removing the END statement, you put an error in the program. You see ONE, TWO, and THREE as before, but now there is an *extra* TWO and a message that says ?RETURN WITHOUT GOSUB ERROR IN 70. Why did this happen? In Session 27, you will study this same problem and see exactly why it happened. For now, just note that a missing END statement is a serious bug in a program.

1. What is the purpose of the END statement?
2. If the END statement is missing, what will happen?

The "Missing RETURN Bug"

Another common bug is forgetting to put a RETURN statement at the end of a subroutine. Let's look at this bug next.

Put the END statement back at line 50. Run the program and check it. Then list it. You should see this listing on your screen:

```
10 PRINT "ONE"
15 GOSUB 60
20 PRINT "THREE"
50 END
55:
60 REM--SUB TWO
65:: PRINT "TWO"
70 RETURN
```

Now, let's put the missing RETURN bug into the program.

70 ⎯⎯⎯⎯⎯⎯⎯⎯⎯⎯⎯⎯⎯⎯⎯ Delete the RETURN statement.

RUN ⎯⎯⎯⎯⎯⎯⎯⎯⎯⎯⎯⎯⎯⎯ Look at the results.

This bug produced very interesting results. ONE and TWO are printed on the screen, but THREE is missing. But what is most interesting is that *there was no error message*. The program is not working properly; yet you would get no clue if you simply ran the program and looked at the results.

Another kind of missing RETURN bug can show up if there is more than one subroutine in a program. **Put the RETURN statement back in line 70. Then add the new lines shown here:**

```
10 PRINT "ONE"
15 GOSUB 60
20 PRINT "THREE"
25 GOSUB 80
50 END
55:
60 REM--SUB TWO
65:: PRINT "TWO"
70 RETURN
75:
80 REM--SUB FOUR
85:: PRINT "FOUR"
90 RETURN
```

Read your listing carefully and fix any errors before going on. Then run the program.

This program should have no bugs; it is correct if you saw ONE, TWO, THREE, and FOUR down the left side of the screen. Now let's put in a bug.

70 _____ Delete the RETURN statement in line 70.

RUN _____ See what happens.

This time, you got ONE, TWO, FOUR, THREE, and FOUR, *and there was no error message.* Now, the program certainly *is* buggy.

3. What is the purpose of the RETURN statement?
4. What happens if the computer performs a subroutine that has no RETURN statement at the end?
5. Will a missing RETURN statement always cause an error message?
6. What will the computer do if you accidentally put two RETURN statements at the end of a subroutine?

GOSUB Bugs

If a GOSUB is missing or if there is an incorrect line number used with GOSUB, bugs will show up in programs.

Put the RETURN statement back at line 70. Check the program. Now remove the GOSUB statement at line 15. Run the program.

This time you see ONE, THREE, and FOUR on the screen. You probably knew what would happen. TWO is missing because the GOSUB to the subroutine that prints TWO is missing. The computer will not perform a subroutine just because it is in the program; there must be a GOSUB to that subroutine.

7. What is the purpose of a GOSUB statement?
8. What happens if a GOSUB statement is missing?
9. Will a missing GOSUB statement cause an error message?

Bugs in Nested Subroutines

Now, let's look at program bugs that can show up when a subroutine contains a GOSUB to yet *another* subroutine. We'll need a new program for that.

```
NEW
```
Clear out the old program.

```
10 GOSUB 50
15 END
20:
50 REM--SUB 1
55:: GOSUB 75
60:: PRINT "THERE"
65 RETURN
70:
75 REM--SUB 2
80:: PRINT "HI"
85 RETURN
```
Enter the new program.

```
RUN
```
Check the results.

If you see HI and THERE on the screen, the program is working correctly. Notice that SUB 1, the first subroutine, contains a GOSUB to SUB 2, the second subroutine. We say that SUB 2 is **nested** in SUB 1. Now let's look at the same kinds of bugs that you have already seen.

```
15
```
Take out the END statement.

```
RUN
```
See what happened.

Here is what you should see on the screen:

```
HI
THERE
HI
THERE
?RETURN WITHOUT GOSUB ERROR IN 65
```

```
15 END
```
Put back the END statement.
```
65
```
Take out the first RETURN statement.
```
RUN
```
Check what happens.

This time the screen shows HI, THERE, and HI. There was no error message.

```
65 RETURN
```
Put the first RETURN statement back.
```
85
```
Take out the second RETURN statement.
```
RUN
```
What happened?

The screen shows HI but not THERE. There was no error message.
These results are typical of what can happen if you make mistakes while writing subroutines. In the next session, you will see exactly how and why each of the bugs happened.

10. What is a nested subroutine?
11. What would happen if you put the subroutines at the top of a program and the main routine at the bottom?

A Subroutine with a GOSUB to Itself

The final bug you will see leads to a completely different error, one that seems very mysterious. You will solve the mystery in Session 27.

```
NEW
```
Clear out the old program.
```
10 REM--SUB 1
20:: PRINT "AGAIN AND"
30 RETURN
```
Enter the new program.
```
GOSUB 10
```
Perform the subroutine in the immediate mode.

So far, nothing new has taken place. The PRINT statement inside the subroutine told the computer to print AGAIN AND on the screen. Now for something new.

```
25:: GOSUB 10
LIST
```
Inspect the new version.

This new version of the subroutine raises an interesting question. Can a subroutine contain a GOSUB to *itself*? There is one way to find out.

Again, perform the subroutine in the immediate mode.

The new GOSUB *inside* the subroutine completely changes the instructions it gives the computer. Now, instead of a single AGAIN AND, you see a whole series of these words, with the message ?OUT OF MEMORY ERROR IN 20. This is the first time you have seen this error message. What do you think it has to do with subroutines? You will answer that question in Session 27.

If you have extra lab time:

- Program BLAST OFF has two subroutines. See what happens when you deliberately put subroutine bugs into the program.
- Add a GOSUB 100 statement to the end of your ROCKET program and run it. Change the GOSUB 100 to a GOSUB 120 and run it again.
- Find a nested subroutine in program QUILT. See how many nested subroutines you can find in LITTLE TROT.

The Model Computer and Subroutine Bugs

Review

In Session 26, you experimented with "buggy" programs that contained subroutines. You saw what can happen when an END statement is missing, when a RETURN statement is not where it is supposed to be, and when a GOSUB statement is missing. Sometimes the computer detects an error and alerts you with an error message, but not always. The buggy results are often hard to understand. Why do bugs produce such strange results?

The model computer is just what we need to answer all the questions about buggy programs with subroutines.

The "Missing END Bug"

Here is the program you studied first in Session 26, but without the END statement in line 50.

```
10 PRINT "ONE"
15 GOSUB 60
20 PRINT "THREE"
55:
60 REM--SUB TWO
65:: PRINT "TWO"
70 RETURN
```

Let's look at the model computer *after* lines 10, 15, and 20 have all been performed. Here is the picture.

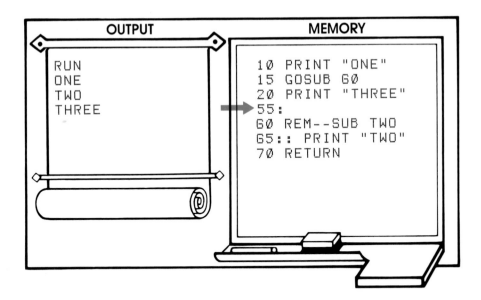

```
          OUTPUT                      MEMORY

        RUN                    10  PRINT  "ONE"
        ONE                    15  GOSUB  60
        TWO                    20  PRINT  "THREE"
        THREE            ───▶  55:
                               60  REM--SUB  TWO
                               65::  PRINT  "TWO"
                               70  RETURN
```

Here is what has happened so far: Line 10 told the computer to print ONE on the output scroll. Line 15 told the computer to put a card with 20 written on it on the return address stack. The computer then moved the line pointer to line 60. The computer ignored the REM statement and moved the pointer to line 65.

Perform the subroutine Line 65 told the computer to print TWO on the output. Line 70 told the computer to take the card from the return address stack and move the pointer to line 20, the number on the card. Line 20 then told the computer to print THREE on the screen. The computer then moved the pointer down a line, to line 55. The picture above shows how the computer model looks at that point.

Keep-performing statements This time, there is no END statement. The RUN program keeps going. The computer performs line 55. That is a blank statement. It is like a REM: Both tell the computer to do nothing. Next, the computer moves the line pointer down a line to line 60.

Perform subroutine again *The line pointer "falls into the subroutine" by accident.* Line 60 is a REM, so the computer does nothing and then moves the line pointer down to line 65. It is a PRINT statement, so the computer prints TWO on the scroll and moves the pointer down again.

Perform the RETURN   The pointer now points at the RETURN state-ment. Here is the picture.

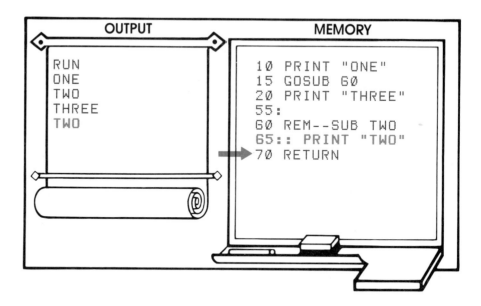

Notice two things now. First, there is an extra TWO on the output. (You just saw how it got there.) Second, there is no card on the return address stack.

Error message   *This is the point at which the computer first dis-covers the bug in your program.* By the rules for performing the RETURN statement, the computer is supposed to remove the top card from the return address stack. But there is no card there. What return address do you think the computer should use? The computer has no way of telling, so it stops the RUN program and prints the ?RETURN WITHOUT GOSUB ERROR message.

A weakness in BASIC   The real error in your program was the miss-ing END statement. It would have been more helpful to get an error message as soon as the line pointer "fell into the subroutine," but the computer waited until it reached the RETURN statement before it gave the error message. If the subroutine is a long one, you wait a long time for that error message. Unfortunately, in BASIC there is no way for the computer to tell whether the line pointer entered the subroutine by accident or on purpose. Most other computer languages make it impos-sible to perform subroutines by accident. Watch out for this bug.

The "Missing RETURN Bug"

Another common subroutine bug is forgetting the RETURN statement at the end of a subroutine. Here is a program like the one you have been studying, except that the RETURN statement is missing this time.

```
10 PRINT "ONE"
15 GOSUB 60
20 PRINT "THREE"
50 END
55:
60 REM--SUB TWO
65:: PRINT "TWO"
```

Let's look at the computer model *after* the computer has performed lines 10 and 15. Here is the picture.

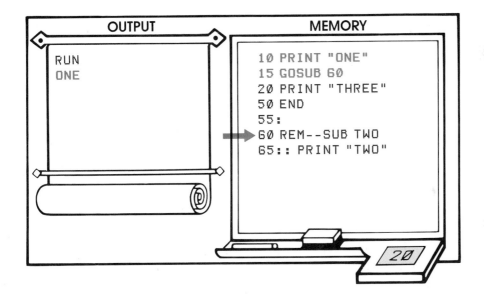

Here is what happened: Line 10 told the computer to print ONE on the output scroll. Line 15 told the computer to put a card with 20 written on it on the return address stack. The computer then moved the line pointer to line 60.

Perform the subroutine   Line 60 is a REM statement, so the computer just moves the pointer down a line. Line 65 tells the computer to print TWO on the output.

Move the pointer down and stop   Now the computer follows the rules of the RUN program and moves the pointer down a line. *Since there are no BASIC statements after line 65 now, the* RUN *program tells the computer to stop.* Here is the computer model at that final point.

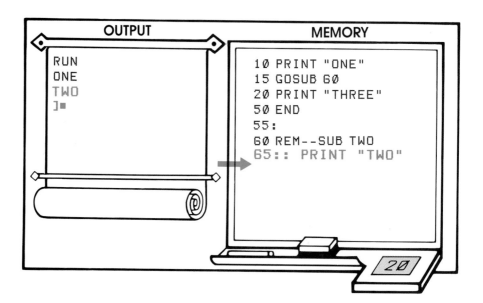

Notice that the return address card is still on the stack. But there was no RETURN statement to tell the computer to use it. In some versions of BASIC, the computer will notice the extra card on the stack and will print a message, such as GOSUB WITHOUT RETURN, after the program ends.

The "double whammy" The worst subroutine bug occurs when you have two subroutines in a row and you leave out the first RETURN statement. Here is an example. This is the *correct* program.

```
10 PRINT "ONE"
15 GOSUB 60
20 PRINT "THREE"
25 GOSUB 80
50 END
55:
60 REM--SUB TWO
65:: PRINT "TWO"
70 RETURN
75:
80 REM--SUB FOUR
85:: PRINT "FOUR"
90 RETURN
```

You ran this program in Session 26 and saw it produce the following output:

```
ONE
TWO
THREE
FOUR
```

The buggy program Now, suppose that by accident you leave out the RETURN in line 70. The program now looks like this:

```
10 PRINT "ONE"
15 GOSUB 60
20 PRINT "THREE"
25 GOSUB 80
50 END
55:
60 REM--SUB TWO
65:: PRINT "TWO"
75:
80 REM--SUB FOUR
85:: PRINT "FOUR"
90 RETURN
```

You ran this buggy program in Session 26 and saw this output:

```
ONE
TWO
FOUR
THREE
FOUR
```

Where do you think the extra FOUR came from? Why didn't the computer find your error? *The answer is that the computer never sees an error.* Your GOSUB 60 statement says to perform the subroutine starting in line 60. But the computer sees no RETURN statement until line 90. *To the computer, subroutine TWO runs all the way from line 60 to line 90.* So it prints TWO *and* FOUR on the screen. Then line 20 prints THREE. Finally, line 25 performs the subroutine in lines 80 to 90, which prints FOUR.

Avoiding bugs   The surest way to avoid these bugs is to pay careful attention to the form of your program. *Put blank statements between the main program and the subroutines.* The blanks make it easy to see whether there is an END statement. *Indent the body of each subroutine.* Indentions will make it easy to match the opening REM of each subroutine with its closing RETURN statement.

One Subroutine Performs Another

You have seen how to use a subroutine to create a new action. The GOSUB statement tells the computer to perform the new action. All the GOSUB statements so far in this session have been in the main program. But in Session 26, you saw that it is possible to use a GOSUB statement inside the body of a *subroutine*. (This is called a nested GOSUB.)

Sample program   Here is the program you ran in Session 26 to demonstrate nested GOSUBs. It contains two subroutines.

```
10 GOSUB 50
15 END
20:
50 REM--SUB 1
55:: GOSUB 75
60:: PRINT "THERE"
65 RETURN
70:
75 REM--SUB 2
80:: PRINT "HI"
85 RETURN
```

The main routine is in lines 10 and 15. The GOSUB in line 10 tells the computer to perform the first subroutine, which is in lines 50 to 65. Line 55, *in the body of the subroutine*, is a GOSUB. Line 55 tells the computer to perform the second subroutine, in lines 75 to 85. How do you think the computer performs this program? What will appear on the output screen?

The model computer The best way to answer these questions is to see how the model computer would run the program. Here is the initial state of the output scroll and the memory chalkboard.

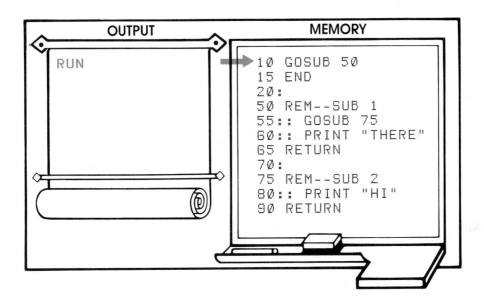

Perform GOSUB The computer starts by performing line 10, the first GOSUB statement. It tells the computer to write 15 (why?) on a card and put it on the return address stack. Then it tells the computer to move the line pointer to line 50 (why?). Here is the new state.

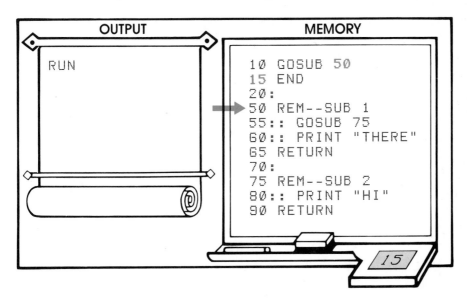

Notice the card on the return address stack.

Drop pointer, perform GOSUB Line 5Ø is a REM statement, so the computer just moves the pointer down to the next line, line 55. It is another GOSUB statement. Following the rules for a GOSUB, the computer writes 6Ø, the next line number, on a card and puts the card on the *top* of the return address stack. Then the computer moves the line pointer to line 75 (why?). Here is the picture after the computer performs the second GOSUB.

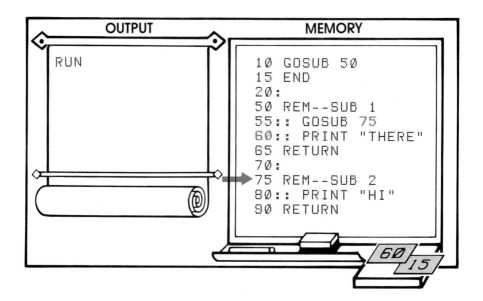

Notice that there are *two* cards on the return address stack. The top one has 6Ø written on it, and the bottom one has 15 written on it.

Drop pointer, perform PRINT Line 75 is another REM, so the computer drops the pointer down a line to line 8Ø. It is a PRINT statement, so the computer prints HI on the output scroll. Then the computer moves the pointer down to line 9Ø, the RETURN statement in the *second* subroutine. Here is the picture just before the RETURN is performed.

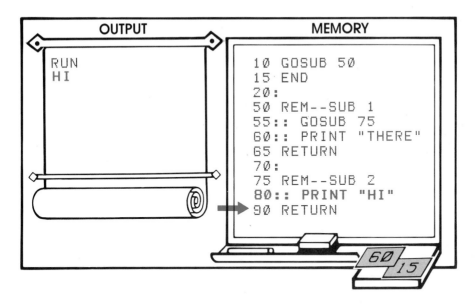

Perform RETURN Now it is time to perform the RETURN in line 90. Remember the rules. The computer must take the card from the *top* of the return address stack. It has 60 written on it. Then the computer must move the line pointer to that line. Here is the picture *after* the RETURN is performed.

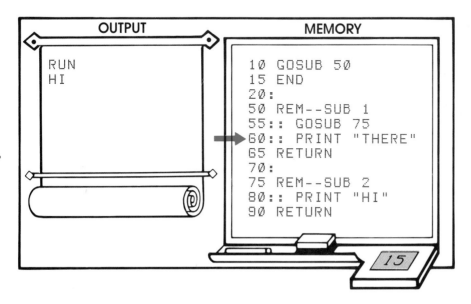

Notice that only one card is left on the return address stack. The number on it is 15.

Perform PRINT and move pointer Now the computer must perform line 6Ø, which says to print THERE on the scroll. After that, the computer drops the line pointer down to line 65, the RETURN statement for the *first* subroutine. Here is the picture just before the computer performs the RETURN.

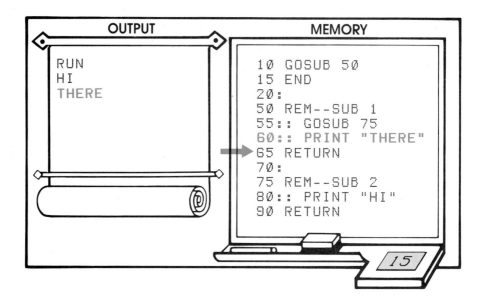

Perform RETURN The computer's rules for doing the RETURN are the same as before. It must remove the top (and only) card from the return address stack. Then it must move the line pointer to the line number written on the card. It is line 15. On the next page is the picture *after* it performs the RETURN.

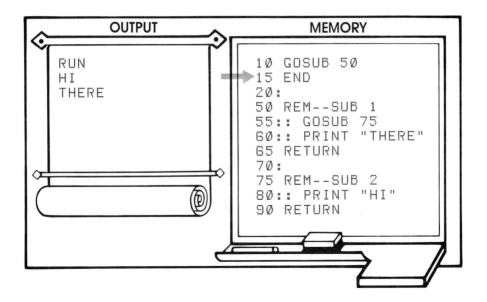

```
       OUTPUT                          MEMORY

   RUN                        10 GOSUB 50
   HI                         15 END
   THERE                      20 :
                              50 REM--SUB 1
                              55 :: GOSUB 75
                              60 :: PRINT "THERE"
                              65 RETURN
                              70 :
                              75 REM--SUB 2
                              80 :: PRINT "HI"
                              90 RETURN
```

Notice that the return address stack is now empty and the line pointer is back at the line after the first GOSUB statement.

Perform END Finally, the computer performs line 15, which says to stop the RUN program.

Matching GOSUBs with RETURNs This example shows you how the computer is able to put each RETURN statement together with the correct GOSUB. The secret is in the return address stack. If the computer performs five different GOSUB statements, followed by five different RETURN statements, the return address stack tells the computer how to match the GOSUBs and RETURNs correctly. The first RETURN the computer performs automatically goes with the last GOSUB it performed. The second RETURN goes with the next-to-last GOSUB, and so on.

A Subroutine That Has a GOSUB to Itself

Now we can explain the last exercise you did in Session 26. Here is the program:

```
10 REM--SUB 1
20 :: PRINT "AGAIN AND"
25 :: GOSUB 10
30 RETURN
```

When you ran this program in the immediate mode with GOSUB 10, the computer moved the line pointer to the beginning of the program. The computer ignored the REM statement and moved the pointer to line 20, the PRINT statement. Line 20 told the computer to print AGAIN AND on the screen. When the line pointer reached line 25, the computer put the number of the *next* statement (30 in this case) on the return address stack. But the statement in line 25, GOSUB 10, moved the line pointer back to line 10, and the whole process started again.

Stack overflow Each time the computer performed the subroutine, *another* line number 30 was put on the return address stack. Since the computer line pointer never reaches the RETURN statement, the computer *did not remove any numbers from the return address stack.*

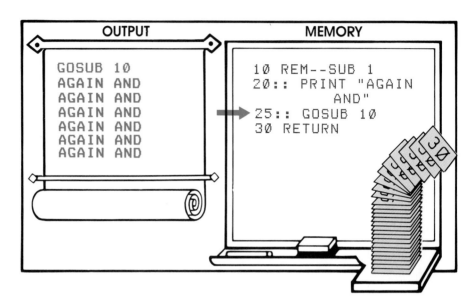

The stack can hold only so many numbers. If the stack is full and the computer tries to put another number on the stack, it stops the RUN program and prints ?OUT OF MEMORY ERROR IN LINE 25 saying that the (stack) memory is full.

QUESTIONS

1. If you leave out the END statement at the end of the main routine, the line pointer "falls into a subroutine." What makes the line pointer move down from the main program into the subroutine?

2. Here is a program with a missing END statement:

```
10 PRINT "GOOD"
15 GOSUB 30
25:
30 REM--SUB 1
35:: PRINT "NEWS"
40 RETURN
```

What will appear on the output screen after the program is run?

3. In the program on page 145, why did the computer treat subroutine FOUR as part of subroutine TWO when you left out the RETURN statement in line 70?

4. How can you best avoid subroutine bugs?

5. A program ends and there is still a card on the return address stack. How could that happen?

6. What does the computer do if it tries to perform a RETURN statement when the return address stack is empty?

7. A program contains two subroutines. The main routine contains a GOSUB to the first subroutine. When the program is run, the computer performs *both* subroutines. What bug made this happen?

8. The computer performs five GOSUB statements and then two RETURN statements. How many cards are on the return address stack?

9. Here is a program with two subroutines.

```
10 PRINT "START"
15 GOSUB 55
20 GOSUB 35
25 END
30 :
35 REM--SUB 1
40 :: PRINT "ONE"
45 RETURN
50 :
55 REM--SUB 2
60 :: PRINT "TWO"
65 :: GOSUB 35
70 RETURN
```

Write a list of line numbers in the order that the computer performs them.

Reading Complex Programs

28

IN	• Read a long program on your diskette.
THIS SESSION	• Use the main routine as a guide to the subroutines.
YOU WILL:	• Look for details in each of the subroutines.
	• Write an outline of the program.

A Long Program

In Session 22, you learned how to read programs that contain a main routine and a set of subroutines. You used the main routine the way you would use the table of contents in a book: The main routine gives you the main ideas and also tells you where to look for the details. All the programs you looked at in Session 22 were fairly short. Now look at a very long program: LITTLE TROT. You have probably run this program before, but it is a good idea now to review the way it works. **Load LITTLE TROT from your diskette and run it one or two times.**

1. In your own words, what are the *main* things that LITTLE TROT tells the computer to do? Make a list of them.

The Main Routine

Like most programs on the diskette, LITTLE TROT is written in top-down style. But it is a lot longer than most others. **Find the main routine and list it on your screen.**

2. What lines contain the main routine of LITTLE TROT?
3. Look at the REM statements in the body of the main routine. What are the main things that LITTLE TROT tells the computer to do?

The First Subroutine

The first statement in the body of the main routine is GOSUB 400. The trailing REM says that this subroutine is named DEFINITIONS. **Find this subroutine, and list it on your screen.**

Notice that the subroutine contains three statements you have not seen before: READ, DATA, and LET. Skip these details for now. Your goal is to find the parts of the program and see how they work together. The REM statements in this subroutine are more important for that purpose.

4. Look at the REM statements. What lines in the program would you have to understand if you wanted to change the colors of the turtles?

5. Suppose you wanted to rewrite the program to work on a computer that has a graphics screen with 64 horizontal positions instead of 40. What lines would you have to understand?

The Second Subroutine

Now let's move on to the next subroutine mentioned in the main routine. List the main routine again. Use it to find the START RACE subroutine. List it.

As before, the best thing to do when you first look at a subroutine is to look for the main ideas and avoid details. The REM statements inside START RACE tell you what those main ideas are.

6. In your own words, what do you think this subroutine tells the computer to do?

7. Suppose you deleted line 610. Look at the trailing REM statement. What do you think would happen if you ran the program without line 610?

Looking Deeper

Line 610 in subroutine START RACE is a GOSUB to another subroutine. In long programs, the work of a single subroutine is often very large. It makes sense to divide the task and put the small details in other subroutines. Use line 610 as a guide and find subroutine BACKGROUND. List it.

8. What do you think subroutine BACKGROUND tells the computer to do? Explain in your own words.

9. The task of this subroutine is also large. What details did the writer put into other subroutines?

The Lowest Level

The last line of the body of subroutine BACKGROUND is a GOSUB to subroutine TITLE. In Session 16, you looked at the statements in TITLE, so they may be familiar to you. Find subroutine TITLE, list it, and read the lines in it. All the statements should be familiar to you this time.

10. What does subroutine TITLE tell the computer to do?

11. Why do we say this subroutine is "at the lowest level"? (Hint: Look for GOSUB statements inside TITLE.)

Outlining the Program

A good way to get a clear idea of a long program is to outline it. The headings in the outline are the GOSUBs in the main routine. If a subroutine contains GOSUBs, they become *subheadings* in the outline. A partial outline of program LITTLE TROT begins like this:

```
GOSUB 400: REM--DEFINITIONS

GOSUB 600: REM--START RACE

    GOSUB 2200: REM--BACKGROUND

        GOSUB 2400: REM--BOX
        GOSUB 2600: REM--TITLE

    GOSUB 800: REM--DRAW
```

Write a complete outline of program LITTLE TROT. Indent to make your outline easy to read. You will need about 10 minutes to write the outline.

Another Version of the Program

The writer of program LITTLE TROT was very careful to make the program easy to read, easy to understand, and easy to change. Not all programs are written this way. Some writers care more about making programs short or making them run fast than they do about readability. Program SPAGHETTI on your diskette is an example. It does everything LITTLE TROT does, but it is faster and shorter.

Load SPAGHETTI from the diskette. Run it a few times. List it by 100-line groups. Try to read it and understand how it works.

12. Which version of the program, LITTLE TROT or SPAGHETTI, do you like better? Explain your answer.

13. If you had to make improvements in the program, which version would you prefer to work with, and why?

If you have extra lab time:

- Programs LITTLE TROT and SPAGHETTI both tell the computer to print the title TURTLE TROT on the screen. Change program LITTLE TROT so that the title becomes TURTLE TRIP.

- Now change program SPAGHETTI so that the title becomes TURTLE TRIP.

Subroutines: Tools for Thinking

IN THIS SESSION YOU WILL:
- Review the idea of levels of detail in a program.
- Learn that newspaper stories, English compositions, and cookbook recipes are structured by level of detail.
- Study the structure of an everyday activity.
- Learn what spaghetti programming is.

Solving Complex Problems

In Sessions 25 through 27, you learned many details about the GOSUB and RETURN statements and how they work. These details are important, but you should also keep in mind why these statements are valuable: They allow you to break down a complex program into simpler subroutines.

Divide and conquer In Session 28, you saw how a program writer handled a long, complex problem by using subroutines. The main, or top-level, part of program LITTLE TROT has only six lines. The main program says to do these things:

1. Define some numbers for later use.
2. Put turtles at the starting gate.
3. Run the race.
4. Show the winner.
5. Set text mode.
6. Clear the screen.

At the top level, this program is very simple. The English sentences say what the computer must do first, second, third, and so on. It is clear that if the computer did those things, we would see a turtle race.

Levels of detail The description in the main routine, however, is not very specific. How does the computer "run the race" or "show the winner"? The top-level version of the program is simple because the writer hides the details somewhere else. You can find what "run the race" means by reading the subroutine listing and seeing what it says.

More details If the job of a subroutine is also complex, then the writer can simplify it the same way: by hiding details in other, lower-level subroutines. The lower the level of the subroutine, the more details one finds there. The bottom level is pure detail: There are no GOSUBs to other routines.

Level Structure

In a computer program, it is easy to tell the level of any part. The main routine is the top level. The GOSUBs in the main routine are the second level. The GOSUBs of the second level refer to GOSUBs at the third level, and so on. You saw in Session 28 that you could make an accurate outline of the level structure of a program just by reading the listing.

Newspaper stories Other things besides computer programs have this same level structure. Nearly all newspaper reports are written in top-down style. The headline is the title. Two or three sentences in the first paragraph say in just a few words what the news is. The next two or three paragraphs give details about the first sentence. The next few paragraphs give details about the second sentence. In a long report, later paragraphs tell the story in even greater detail.

English compositions When you outline a paper that you are going to write, you use top-down methods. The main headings are the top-level version of the paper. The subheadings give details about what the headings mean. Lower-level subheadings give even more detailed information.

Recipes Most recipes are also written in top-down style. Beginning cooks discover this fact quickly. In just a few sentences, the recipe tells what ingredients to use and how to use them. First, they read the top-level version of the recipe: In cookbooks for beginners, detailed instructions follow. In advanced cookbooks, the writer assumes you already know what "drawn butter," "blanched carrots," and "sauce vinaigrette" are. If you need more details, you must go to the index and look up each "subroutine."

Levels of Meaning

The reason level structures show up so often in writing and thinking is that most activities are organized into levels. For example, if we asked you to tell what you do before going to school or work, you might say, "I get up. I have breakfast. Then I catch the bus." That description is correct, but it leaves out the details. It is a top-level description.

The getting-up subroutine Suppose we asked you what getting up means. You might say, "I get out of bed, do bathroom chores, make the bed, and go downstairs." That is a lower-level description of getting up. But we could ask for even more details.

The getting-out-of-bed subroutine Suppose we asked next what getting out of bed means. You might answer, "I turn off the alarm, throw back the covers, and put on my slippers." That answer is a low-level description of your morning activities. That is not the end of what you know, though. We could ask you how you turn off your alarm.

More subroutines To answer each question, you have to recall tiny details that you do not think about often. But the information is in your memory. With a little effort you can answer questions in more and more detail. Each answer is like a subroutine at a lower level.

Choosing the right level Suppose you are trying to understand something, or solve a problem, or help someone learn a new skill. The work goes best if you pay attention to the idea of levels of knowledge. If a friend asked you what you did this morning, would you begin your answer by saying you used your left hand to squeeze toothpaste onto the toothbrush in your right hand? This would confuse your friend. It is too much detail at the beginning. But if you said "I got up," your friend would probably feel that you were not telling very much. Yet both answers are true.

Top-down thinking It is important to pay attention to these levels of detail when you are writing for the computer (or writing in English or just thinking about things). As a rule, it is a good idea to put off the details and begin with the main ideas. Once the main ideas seem right, go down a level and start filling in the details. If the details are complex, you may want to put them off even further. This top-down approach to thinking about things lets you divide very complex problems into small pieces that are usually easier to handle.

Spaghetti thinking If instead you plunge into the problem and put one program statement (or English sentence or idea) after the other without planning, the result will be like a tangled mess of spaghetti. It will be hard to see any pattern or purpose. People will not understand what you write and think, even when it is correct. In the world of computing, this approach is called **spaghetti programming**. But if you look carefully, you can find examples of spaghetti writing and spaghetti thinking all around you.

QUESTIONS

1. How can you find the level structure of a BASIC program?
2. Can you find the level structure of a newspaper story? Clip one from the paper and draw a box around the top-level part. Find details later in the story for each sentence in the box.
3. Can you find the level structure of a recipe? Clip one from the newspaper and draw a box around the top-level part. Then look for detailed explanations.
4. Could a beginner use the recipe from question 3? Or would a beginner need more? If so, what details are left out?
5. How would you describe some everyday task at the top level? At lower levels?
6. What is spaghetti programming? What is wrong with it?

Part 4

Vocabulary Table

Words printed in color were introduced in this part.

BASIC Vocabulary (Shaded Areas Show Standard BASIC Words)

Commands		Statements			Functions
Program	Diskette	Action	Action	Control	
RUN	LOAD	____	SPEED=	GOSUB	____
LIST	SAVE	____	FLASH	RETURN	____
NEW	DELETE	PRINT	INVERSE	END	____
DEL	CATALOG	REM	NORMAL	____	____
____	LOCK	PLOT	COLOR=	____	____
____	UNLOCK	HLIN	TEXT	____	
____		VLIN	GR	____	
____		HOME			

New BASIC Words

END A statement that tells the computer to stop performing the program.

GOSUB A statement that tells the computer to perform a subroutine.

RETURN A statement that ends a sub-routine. RETURN tells the computer to return to the statement after the GOSUB statement that told the computer to perform the subroutine.

New Ideas

action statement A statement that tells the computer to perform some action. After performing an action statement, the computer goes to the next statement in the program listing.

body The statements inside a main routine or a subroutine.

control statement A statement that tells the computer to move the line pointer or stop the program.

main routine The program block at the beginning of a BASIC program. The body of the main routine is mainly GOSUB statements to subroutines.

nested subroutine A subroutine reached by a GOSUB statement in another sub-routine.

subroutine A block of statements that defines a new action. The action is performed by a GOSUB statement.

return address stack   A part of the memory of the computer. The stack contains line numbers needed to perform the RETURN statements.

top-down design   A way of structuring computer programs. The purpose of the program is defined generally in the main routine, and subroutines fill in missing details.

Above: Once, we only used the telephone to talk to other people. *Right:* Today, we can use it to "talk" to a computer.

Part 5

Naming Things: Data and Variables

You are now about halfway through this course. You have learned all the important BASIC statements that control *output*. The PRINT statement tells the computer to print characters on the text screen. SPEED=, FLASH, INVERSE, and NORMAL tell it to print the characters at different speeds or in different modes. PLOT, HLIN, VLIN, and COLOR= tell it to draw colored dots or lines on the graphics screen.

Input and processing Besides output, a computer can do input and processing. *Every computer language can tell the computer to perform input, processing, and output.* Part 5 of this course introduces BASIC statements for input and processing. The INPUT statement tells the computer to stop and wait for you to type words or numbers. The LET statement tells it what to do with those words or numbers.

Data In the world of computers, a word or a number is called a piece of **data**. The INPUT statement tells the computer to wait for you to enter data. The LET statement tells it how to process the data. The PRINT and PLOT statements tell the computer to output data.

A new problem Suppose you want to write a program that tells the computer to do two things: Ask the user for a piece of data, and then print the same piece of data on the screen. You know that PRINT "HOT" tells the computer to print HOT on the screen. But how can you write a PRINT statement that tells it to print *whatever* word you type?

Names for data The answer is important. *Every programming language lets you give names to the pieces of data in a program.* For example, suppose you use the name WORD$ to stand for whatever piece of data you want to enter. When you tell the computer to PRINT WORD$, the computer prints the piece of data that WORD$ stands for.

Variables Data that have names are called **variables**. Part 5 of this course will show you how variables work and how to use them in INPUT, LET, PRINT, and other statements.

Similar Subroutines

IN • Use the TAB feature of the PRINT statement.
THIS SESSION • Put TAB into your big-letter subroutines in program NAMES.
YOU WILL: • Find out why it is helpful to vary the way a subroutine works without having to write a new subroutine for each variation.

Using TAB in a PRINT Statement

So far, whenever you have used a PRINT statement, the computer has started its output at the left edge of the screen. In this section, you will find out how to tell the computer to start output at other places.

Start the computer with your diskette in the usual way. Then proceed with the following activities.

```
10 HOME
20 PRINT "---->"
RUN
```

Your program prints an arrow at the left of the screen.

```
30 PRINT TAB (5); "---->"
```

Be sure to use a semicolon after TAB (5), *not* a comma.

```
LIST
```

Check the program.

```
RUN
```

Notice where the second arrow is.

Add three more PRINT statements that tell the computer to print the arrow in columns 10, 20, and 35. Run the program.

Next, put a HOME statement ahead of each PRINT statement. Can you guess what that change in the program will make the computer do? Run the program and see whether you are right.

Finally, put a SPEED= statement at the beginning to slow down the arrow. Be sure to reset the top speed (255) at the end of the program.

1. How can you tell the computer to print an X in column 23 of the screen?

2. What does TAB (5) in a PRINT statement tell the computer to do?

More Facts about TAB

You have seen that TAB followed by a number in parentheses changes the way the PRINT statement works. Now you will learn some new facts about the TAB statement.

```
HOME
NEW
```
Erase screen and memory.

```
PRINT "X"
PRINT TAB (1); "X"
```
Now you know where TAB position 1 is.

```
PRINT TAB (40); "X"
PRINT TAB (41); "X"
```
Look carefully. TAB position 41 is not the same as TAB position 1.

```
PRINT TAB (1); "X"
PRINT TAB (41); "X"
PRINT TAB (81); "X"
```
See the difference.

3. Where on the screen is TAB position 1?
4. What is the TAB number of the right-hand column on your screen?
5. How is TAB (41) different from TAB (1)?

Using TAB in Your NAMES Program

In Session 24, you wrote and saved on your diskette a program called NAMES. It contains two subroutines, BIG N and BIG A, made up of several PRINT statements that tell the computer to draw big letters on the screen. By changing the main routine, you made the program print Ana, Nan, and Ann's names in big letters. Here is how one person's program looked when it was run:

```
****
**   **
******
**   **
***   ***

***   ***
*** **
******
** ***
***   ***

***   ***
*** **
******
** ***
***   ***
```

Load your program NAMES now. Run it. If necessary, change the main routine to print Ann's name in big letters.

Now for a change: Suppose you want to print Ann's name like this:

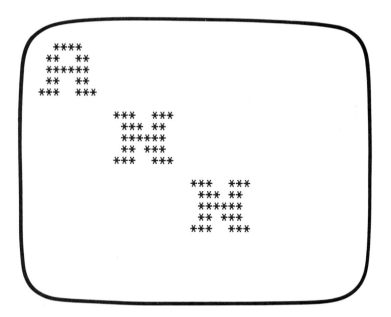

You have just learned how to use TAB in a PRINT statement to change where on the screen the computer starts to print.

Add TAB (11) to the PRINT statements in the BIG N subroutine in your NAMES program. Run the program. Find out whether the program put Ann's name diagonally on the screen, as shown above. Save this version of program NAMES on your diskette.

6. Why does the program start both *N*s in column 11?

7. Would you solve your problem if you changed the TAB of BIG N from 11 to 21?

Making Another Subroutine

Changing TAB from 11 to 21 would not solve the problem: The computer would not print Ann's name diagonally. TAB (11) is right for the first big *N*, but it is wrong for the second *N*. You need a TAB (21) for the second big *N*.

There is no way to write TAB (11) *and* TAB (21) at the same time. There is a solution to your problem, but it means a lot more typing. Your program could have two different subroutines for the big *N*: one with TAB (11) in the PRINT statements and the other with TAB (21). To make the second subroutine, you would have to copy *all* the statements in BIG N and change TAB (11) to TAB (21) in every PRINT statement.

It does not seem right that such a small change should take so much typing. You may be thinking that there must be an easier way to solve your problem. There is. You will learn about it in the next session.

8. How does a second BIG N subroutine solve the problem of printing Ann's name diagonally?

9. What new subroutines would you have to add to program NAMES to make it print Ana's name diagonally? Nan's name?

If you have extra lab time:

- Write a program that uses three subroutines to draw three different boxes on the graphics screen. One subroutine should draw a box around the border of the screen. (Program SUBPICTURES has a subroutine that draws such a box.) Another subroutine should draw a smaller box 8 units in from all the borders. The third should draw a still smaller box 16 units in from the borders. Notice how similar the three subroutines are. How many subroutines would you need if you wanted a program that drew 20 different boxes nested inside one another?

- Load program BOXES from your diskette into the computer. Run the program. List the program and study the subroutine that draws a box. The program drew many boxes, but it has *only one* BOX subroutine. You will learn how it works in the next few sessions.

Why Variables Are Needed

IN THIS SESSION YOU WILL:
- Review the TAB feature of the PRINT statement.
- Find out what a variable is.
- Use a variable in the BIG N subroutine.

Review of TAB

In your computer work in Session 30, you found out about the TAB feature of the PRINT statement. You used TAB in your NAMES program to tell the computer to start printing the big letters in different columns of the screen.

Text-screen size Your Apple II computer can print characters in 40 columns across the text screen. You learned in Session 30 that TAB (1) tells the computer to print the next character in the first column from the left. TAB (40) tells it that the next character should go in the last column from the left. *The columns are numbered differently on the graphics screen; there the first column is zero and the last column is 39.*

Lines wider than screen You also learned in Session 30 that you can use numbers above 40 with TAB. Column 40 is the last available position on the screen. But the computer can handle print lines that are wider than the screen. When the computer prints such a long line, it puts the first 40 characters on one line, the next 40 on the next line, and so on. We say these long lines are **folded** on the screen. So TAB (41) refers to position 41 in the **print line**, not the screen. After the computer folds a line, position 41 appears on the screen one line below and in column 1.

Maximum print line The longest print line allowed on the Apple II computer is 255 characters long. For this reason, you can follow the TAB statement with numbers from 1 to 255. These long lines may not seem very useful on your small screen, but they are important in programs that send their output to a **printer**, which may print characters in 80 or 132 or even more columns.

TAB errors You will get an ?ILLEGAL QUANTITY ERROR message when you use -1 or 256 as TAB positions. All negative numbers are illegal TAB positions. So is 256 or any larger number.

Using TAB

In Session 30, you added a TAB (11) to the PRINT statements in your BIG N subroutine in program NAMES. The program looked like this:

```
100 REM--PROGRAM NAMES
110:: HOME
120:: GOSUB 600: REM--BIG A
130:: GOSUB 400: REM--BIG N
140:: GOSUB 400: REM--BIG N
150 END
390:
400 REM--SUB BIG N
410:: PRINT
420:: PRINT TAB (11); "***   ***"
430:: PRINT TAB (11); " *** **"
440:: PRINT TAB (11); " ******"
450:: PRINT TAB (11); " ** ***"
460:: PRINT TAB (11); "***   ***"
500 RETURN
590:
600 REM--SUB BIG A
610:: PRINT
620:: PRINT "  ****"
630:: PRINT " **   **"
640:: PRINT " ******"
650:: PRINT " **   **"
660:: PRINT "***   ***"
700 RETURN
```

Output When you ran this version of NAMES, the output screen looked like this, with each of the big *N*s beginning in column 11:

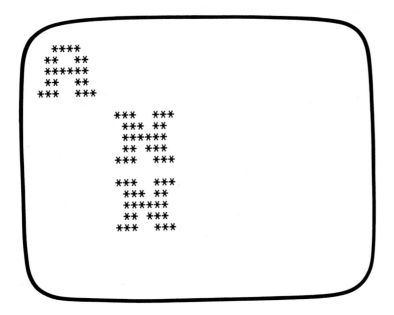

A new problem You were trying to make the program print Ann's name along a diagonal line. The first big N was in the right place, but you wanted to have the second one start in column 21. To do that, you could write a new subroutine. It would be exactly like the BIG N subroutine, except that you would substitute TAB (21) for TAB (11). Your new subroutine would look like this:

```
800 REM--SUB BIG N AT 21
810:: PRINT
820:: PRINT TAB (21); "***   ***"
830:: PRINT TAB (21); " *** **"
840:: PRINT TAB (21); " ******"
850:: PRINT TAB (21); " ** ***"
860:: PRINT TAB (21); "***   ***"
900 RETURN
```

The Need to Vary Things

To put a big letter in *any* column of the screen, you would need 30 or more *different* subroutines. You are probably thinking that there must be a better way. There is.

Small changes The two BIG N subroutines you need are almost identical. The only difference is the TAB number in each one. A very small change makes one subroutine become the other. This fact is a signal to you: *As a general rule, whenever you see two big blocks of statements that are almost identical, it means that there is a simpler way to write the program.*

Putting things off The problem with your two BIG N subroutines is that each one is tied down to its own TAB position. The first one is bound to print in column 11, and the second one is bound to print in column 21. Life would be much simpler if you could write a single subroutine that was not tied down to any one TAB position. Then, you could give the TAB position in the main routine and GOSUB to the subroutine.

Names for things You would not tie down your subroutine if you had a way to write something that could *stand for* the TAB position without actually *being* the position. In other words, you need a *name* that stands for 11 or 21 *or any other column on the screen*. The name, for example, might be COLUMN. Then you could write a single BIG N subroutine similar to this:

```
400 REM--SUB BIG N
410:: PRINT
420:: PRINT TAB (COLUMN); "***   ***"
430:: PRINT TAB (COLUMN); " *** **"
440:: PRINT TAB (COLUMN); " ******"
450:: PRINT TAB (COLUMN); " ** ***"
460:: PRINT TAB (COLUMN); "***   ***"
500 RETURN
```

Things for names Now the subroutine is no longer bound to print in any one column. Instead, the main routine tells what the name COLUMN stands for. Here, in a mixture of BASIC and English, is how you could write the main routine:

```
100 REM--PROGRAM NAMES
110:: HOME
120:: GOSUB 600: REM--BIG A
125:: let COLUMN stand for 11
130:: GOSUB 400: REM--BIG N
135:: let COLUMN stand for 21
140:: GOSUB 400: REM--BIG N
150 END
```

How it works Line 125 tells the computer what COLUMN stands for. Line 130 tells the computer to perform the BIG N subroutine. Inside the subroutine, the computer substitutes the number 11 for the name COLUMN wherever the name appears. Then line 135 tells the computer to forget the old meaning of COLUMN and to give it a new meaning. Line 140 tells the computer to perform BIG N again. This time, the computer substitutes the number 21 for the name COLUMN.

Data and variables In the world of computers, numbers such as 11 and 21 are examples of **data**. All programming languages allow you to use names such as COLUMN to stand for data. In the example above, the thing COLUMN stood for varied: first it was 11, and then it was 21. That is why a piece of data that has a name is called a **variable**. In the example above, COLUMN is a variable. On the other hand, 11 always equals the number 11. So 11 is called a **constant**.

Variables in real life The idea of variables and constants is not limited to computer programs. You use these ideas all the time in everyday situations. Suppose you are explaining the rules of softball to a friend. You might begin by saying, "The pitcher throws the ball to the catcher, and the batter tries to hit the ball." In a real game, however, Susan might throw the ball to Jeff, while Amy tries to hit the ball. You used the word *pitcher* to stand for whoever was doing the pitching. In other words, *pitcher* is a name that stands for the person doing the pitching. Susan is always Susan, and Amy is always Amy: They are constants. But the pitcher can be anyone: The pitcher is a variable.

Why variables are needed Imagine how difficult it would be to describe the rules of softball (or any other rules) if you could not use variables. You would have to say, "Susan throws the ball to Jeff." If Charles relieves Susan as pitcher, the rule would have to change to "Charles throws the ball to Jeff." You would need a different set of rules for every combination of people and positions on the the team. If you dislike the idea of writing 30 or 50 BIG N subroutines, you probably hate the thought of explaining 6,402,373,705,728,000 different sets of rules for softball.

Variables in BASIC BASIC, like every other programming language, gives you a way to use names to stand for actual data. In other words, BASIC lets you use both constants and variables. TAB (21) uses a constant, and TAB (COLUMN) uses a variable.

Looking ahead In Session 32, you will explore the way variables and constants work in BASIC. You will find that there is more than one type of data. Also, you will learn a new statement that tells the computer what the name of a variable stands for.

QUESTIONS

1. Suppose you tell the computer to print a line of 100 X's. What will the computer do?

2. What is the TAB position of the left edge of the screen? The right edge? What is the TAB position of the longest print line?

3. Using only constants for the TAB position, you needed two BIG N subroutines to print Ann's name along a diagonal line. Why couldn't you use the same subroutine for both big Ns?

4. What is the difference between a variable and a constant?

5. Why is it better to use a variable than a constant in your BIG N subroutine? Explain in your own words.

6. What is the purpose of line 125 in the main routine on page 171.

7. The United States Constitution says that the president is the commander-in-chief of the army. Is *president* a variable or a constant? What about *army?*

Exploring Variables  32

- Use variable names in PRINT statements.
- Use LET statements to say what variable names stand for.
- Use numeric variables and string variables.
- Discover common errors in using variables.

The LET Statement

In Session 31, you learned that it was possible to give a name to a piece of data. Let's start this session by exploring this idea on the computer.
Start the computer with your diskette as usual. Then begin the following activities.

`HOME` `NEW`	Erase screen and memory.
`PRINT 1984`	You should see 1984 under PRINT.
`PRINT YEAR`	Notice the 0. This is something new.
`LET YEAR = 1984`	This is also new. Watch carefully.
`PRINT YEAR`	There is no 0 this time.
`LET YEAR = 2001` `PRINT YEAR`	You should see 2001 under PRINT.
`LET YEAR = 1492` `PRINT YEAR`	The same PRINT statement does different things.
`PRINT YEAR`	The computer remembers what YEAR last stood for.
`NEW` `PRINT YEAR`	Now it has forgotten.

1. What do you think the statement LET YEAR = 2001 tells the computer? Explain in your own words.
2. You used the statement PRINT YEAR six times, and each time the computer printed something different. Why?
3. What did YEAR stand for after you entered the NEW command?

Another Type of Data

You just explored the use of a variable. The name of the variable was YEAR. You used the LET statement to specify what data YEAR stood for. The data were all *numbers*. There is another type of data in BASIC.

```
PRINT DAY
```
Another 0 should not surprise you.

```
PRINT DAY$
```
Be sure to use a dollar sign ($). Only a blank line was printed.

```
LET DAY$ = "MONDAY"
```
Be sure to use quotation marks.

```
PRINT DAY$
```
Note what was printed.

```
LET DAY$ = "BIRTHDAY"
PRINT DAY$
```
Note the new output.

```
NEW
PRINT DAY$
```
DAY$ no longer stands for BIRTHDAY.

Like YEAR, DAY$ is a name that stands for a piece of data. But this time the data are not numbers. Instead, they are English words. This type of data is called **string** data because a word is just a string of characters. DAY$ is the name of a **string variable**. "MONDAY" and "TUESDAY" are **string constants**. YEAR is the name of a **numeric variable**; 1984, 2001, 1492, and 0 are **numeric constants**.

4. What does the statement LET DAY$ = "BIRTHDAY" tell the computer? Explain in your own words.

5. What does a string variable stand for after you enter the NEW command?

6. What does a numeric variable stand for after you enter the NEW command?

Data-Type Errors

Now is a good time to see what happens when you accidentally use a string where you should use a number, or vice versa.

```
LET YEAR = 1984
```
That should be OK.

```
LET YEAR = "LEAPYEAR"
```
That is not allowed.

```
LET YEAR$ = "LEAPYEAR"
```
That's better.

```
LET YEAR$ = 1984
```
That won't do.

```
LET YEAR$ = "1984"
```
But that is OK.

YEAR is a numeric-variable name, and 1984 is a numeric constant. YEAR$ (pronounced "year-string") is a string-variable name, and "LEAPYEAR" is a string constant.

7. When did the computer print the message ?TYPE MISMATCH ERROR?

8. How do you think the computer tells the difference between a numeric-variable name and a string-variable name?

9. How do you think the computer tells the difference between a numeric constant and a string constant?

Name Errors

We have been using the names YEAR, YEAR$, DAY, and DAY$. You may have wondered how much freedom you have in picking names. Let's see.

```
NEW
LET YEAR = 2001
```
That says what YEAR stands for.

```
PRINT YEAR
```
No surprises here.

```
PRINT YEARN
PRINT YES
PRINT YE
```
Something strange is happening.

```
PRINT Y
```
Now you get 0 again.

You told the computer that YEAR stands for 2001. But it seems as if you also told it that YEARN, YES, and YE stand for 2001 too. The reason is simple: *In Applesoft BASIC, the computer looks at only the first two letters of a variable name.* All these names have the same first two letters, so the computer thinks they are the same name. But YE and Y do *not* have the same first two letters, so the computer treats them as different names. You never told the computer what Y stands for, so it assumed 0.

To avoid confusion, in the future our variable names will contain only one or two characters (plus $ for string variables). Do you think we can use *any* two characters? Let's see.

```
LET A = 5
LET AB = 10
LET A2 = 15
```
The computer accepts these names.

```
LET 2A = 20
LET A+ = 25
LET A? = 30
```
These names are illegal.

Names must start with a letter of the alphabet. After that, there can be letters or numbers (plus a dollar sign for strings). Other characters in names are illegal. Those are the main rules, but there are some exceptions on the next page.

```
LET AT = 1
LET CAT = 2
LET OGRE = 3
LET GR = 4
```

The computer does not accept these.

These names all start with a letter and contain letters, so they follow the rules above. But the computer complains. The reason is that the words AT and GR are part of Applesoft BASIC. (You used GR to set graphics mode, and you used AT in the HLIN and VLIN statements.) Notice also that AT is part of CAT and that GR is part of OGRE. *You cannot use an Applesoft BASIC word as any part of a variable name.*

10. Why are each of the names 2X, X*, and GREAT illegal?
11. Why is it a good idea to limit variable names in Applesoft BASIC to one or two characters?

If you have extra lab time:

■ Load program BOXES from your diskette. Identify all variable names. What statements tell the computer what the names stand for? What does subroutine BOX tell the computer to do with the variables?

■ Load program HI THERE from your diskette. It contains one string-variable name. What is it? There is no LET statement. Can you figure out how the computer knows what data the string variable stands for?

How Variables Work

IN THIS SESSION YOU WILL:
- Learn what is meant by the type, name, and value of a variable.
- Learn the spelling rules for constants and for names of variables.
- Learn what the LET statement means.
- Use the model computer to explain how the LET and PRINT statements work with variables.
- Recognize that a variable is a place in the memory of the computer.

Review

Your experiments with the computer introduced you to variables. You used a LET statement to give a name, such as YEAR, to a piece of data, such as 1984. After that, the computer dealt with that piece of data simply by using its name. *This is the most important idea in computer languages.*

Data types You found that BASIC lets you deal with two different types of data: *numbers* and *strings* of characters. Most other programming languages allow these two data types, and some allow additional types.

Constants You learned spelling rules for each type of constant. You wrote numeric constants the same way you write a number on a sheet of paper. You put string constants inside quotation marks. For example, 1984, 1492, and 2001 are numeric constants, while "1984", "JUNE", and "---->" are string constants.

Variable names You had to use a different kind of name for each type of data: Names of string variables end with a dollar sign ($), but names of numeric variables cannot end with $. When you used the wrong kind of name, the computer printed the following message: ?TYPE MISMATCH ERROR.

Problems with Variable Names

You learned that variable names must begin with a letter of the alphabet. Other characters in the name must be either letters or numbers. In Applesoft BASIC, the computer pays attention only to the first two characters (and the final $, if present). JACK and JANE and JA all refer to the same variable; so it is wise to use names with only one or two characters.

BASIC keywords The few dozen words that make up the BASIC language are called **keywords**. You learned the computer will not accept variable names that contain keywords, such as GR and AT. There are seven two-letter keywords in Applesoft BASIC:

```
AT    FN    GR    IF    ON    OR    TO
```

Since many English words contain at least one of these keywords, it is best to use short variable names. There are no one-letter keywords, so one-letter variable names never cause trouble.

Variables and Assignment

You used the LET statement to tell the computer what data a variable name stands for. When you typed

```
LET YEAR = 1984
PRINT YEAR
```

the result was the same as when you typed

```
PRINT 1984
```

The LET statement told the computer what the name YEAR stood for. PRINT YEAR told the computer to print what YEAR stood for.

Everyday LET statements Think again about the way we describe a softball game. When we explain the rules, we use *variables*: the pitcher, the catcher, the batter, and so on. But before the game can begin, we have to say who the pitcher is, who the catcher is, and so on. The captain of a team says, "Susan, you are our pitcher." Using the grammar of BASIC, you would say that sentence this way:

```
LET  pitcher = Susan
```

Value and assignment People often use two special words when they talk about variables. They say that the LET statement tells the computer "to **assign** a **value** to a variable." For example, LET YEAR = 1984 tells the computer to assign the *value* 1984 to the variable named YEAR. *The value of a variable is the piece of data that the name stands for.* We often call the LET statement the **assignment statement** because it assigns, or gives, a value to a variable. (In softball, the captain assigns Susan to the job of pitcher. The value of *pitcher* is Susan.)

The NEW command You learned in Session 32 that the NEW command also assigns values. NEW gives every numeric variable a value of 0, and it gives every string variable a value of " ". This is called the **empty** string, since there are no characters between the two quotation marks.

Properties of variables Every variable has three main properties: its type, its name, and its value. When you read a LET statement in any program, you can find all three properties of one of the variables in the program.

How Variables Work

Session 32 gave you a lot of first-hand experience with variables. You found out that you could use a LET statement to tell the computer the value of a variable. After that, you could recall the value simply by using the name of the variable. Somehow, the computer remembered the value. When you entered the NEW command, the computer forgot the old value. Now is the time to understand how the computer remembers and forgets values.

Sample program The following program contains two LET statements and two PRINT statements:

```
10 LET YE = 1984
20 PRINT YE
30 LET YE = 2001
40 PRINT YE
```

You know from your own experience that this program will cause the computer to print the numbers 1984 and 2001 on the screen.

The model computer To help you understand how the computer handles variables, we will use the model computer again. Let's suppose you have entered the above program, cleared the screen, and entered the RUN command. The picture below shows the output scroll and the memory chalkboard after you enter those commands.

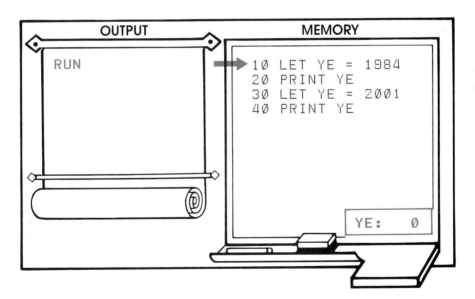

Note the box at the bottom of the chalkboard. It is named YE, and it contains 0 at the start. This box is a new feature of the memory in the model computer.

Perform first line The RUN program tells the computer to perform the line pointed at by the line pointer. It is now pointing to a LET statement. Here are the rules for performing a LET statement:

> **The computer's rules for performing the LET statement:**
>
> 1. Find the *value* of whatever is on the *right* side of the equal sign.
> 2. Write the value in the box whose *name* is on the *left* side of the equal sign.

Perform LET and move pointer The number on the right side of the equal sign in line 10 is 1984. The name on the left side is YE. Here is the model of the computer after it performs the LET statement and moves the pointer down:

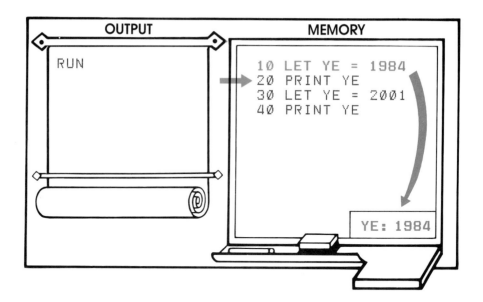

Note that the memory box named YE *now contains the value* 1984. The old value, 0, is forgotten.

Perform PRINT and move pointer The line pointer now points to a
PRINT YE statement, so the computer must perform it. What does that
mean? The answer is simple: It means that the computer should read
whatever is in the memory box named YE and print it on the output
scroll. Here is the model after the computer performs those tasks:

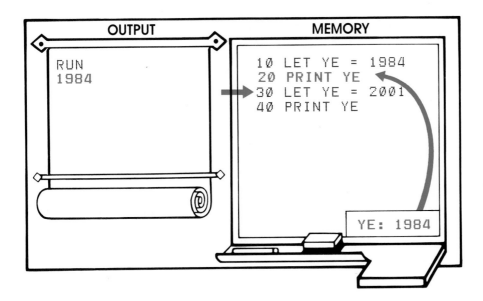

Note that the computer has written 1984 on the scroll and moved the
pointer down. The YE box still contains 1984.

Perform LET and move pointer You already know the computer's rules for performing the LET statement. This time, the right side of the equal sign has the value 2001. Here is the new model after the computer performs line 30:

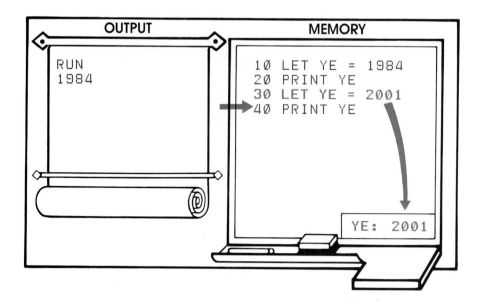

Note the change in the YE box in the memory. The LET statement told the computer to erase the old value (1984) and write a new value (2001) in the box. The old value is forgotten.

Perform PRINT and move pointer The line pointer now points to another PRINT YE statement, so the computer must perform it. As before, the computer reads whatever is *currently* in the YE box in memory and prints it on the output scroll. Here is the model after the computer performs those commands:

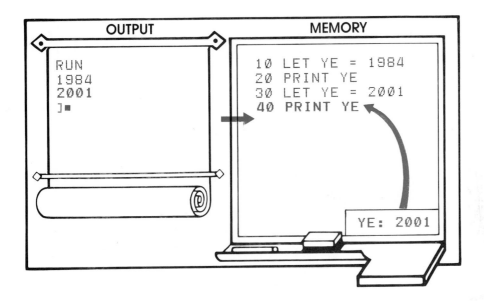

The computer wrote the current value in the YE box (2001) on the output scroll. Then it moved the arrow down. Since the pointer no longer points to a line, the RUN program ends, and the computer turns the cursor back on.

How to Think about Variables

The best way to think about a variable is to imagine that it is a *place in the memory* of the computer. Different places in the memory have different names. A place can hold one item of data at a time. A place that holds a number cannot hold a string, and vice versa.

Initial values of variables When the RUN program begins, it tells the computer to put 0 in all the places that can hold numbers and " " (the empty string) in all places that can hold strings. You saw in Session 32 that the NEW program tells the computer to do the same thing.

Variables in PRINT statements A variable name can appear in a PRINT statement. If so, the computer looks in memory for a place with the same name. Then it reads the data value stored there. Finally, it prints that value on the screen.

In LET statements, on the left A variable name is the *only* thing that can go on the left side of the equal sign (=) in a LET statement. The computer first finds the value of whatever is on the *right* side of the equal sign. Then the computer writes the value in the place in the memory that has the same name as the variable. The new value erases the data already there.

In LET statements, on the right It is also legal to have a variable name on the right side of the equal sign. Here is an example.

```
60 LET B$ = A$
```

At first glance, you may think this means to take the data out of location A$ and put it into location B$. That is almost correct, but not quite. According to the LET statement rules, the computer must first "find the value of whatever is on the the right side." This means it must go to the place named A$ and read the data stored there. Then the computer must put a *copy* of the data in the place named B$. *Note that the data in location A$ is not moved. Only a copy is moved.*

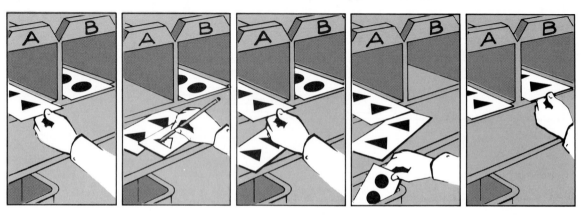

QUESTIONS

1. What two types of data have you learned about?

2. What is the name, type, and value of each variable below?

   a. LET X = 5
   b. LET A$ = "DOG"
   c. LET Z$ = "2"
   d. LET P = -3

3. Which variable names below are legal? If a name is illegal, explain why.

   a. FRED
   b. A3
   c. 3A
   d. GREAT
   e. $C
   f. 27

4. Can you think of two LET statements that will cause a ?TYPE MISMATCH ERROR message? Write them.

5. What happens to the values of variables after the computer carries out the NEW command?

6. Look at the last picture of the computer model. What would happen if you now entered the statement PRINT YE into the computer?

7. What would the computer print on the screen if you entered these four lines? Use the computer model to help you explain.

```
NEW
10 PRINT YE
20 LET YE = 2000
RUN
```

8. What would the computer print on the screen after it performed this program? Use the model to help you explain.

```
10 LET X$ = "HORSE"
20 LET X$ = "COW"
30 PRINT X$
```

9. What would the computer print on the screen after it performed this program? Use the model to help you explain.

```
10 LET X$ = "HORSE"
20 LET Y$ = X$
30 PRINT Y$
```

10. Suppose the first statement in a program says PRINT N. Explain why the computer prints a 0.

11. What number is in the P and Q memory boxes right after each statement in the program below is performed?

```
10 LET P = 7
20 LET Q = 11
30 LET P = Q
40 LET Q = P
```

34 Input and Processing Data

IN THIS SESSION YOU WILL:
- Use commas and semicolons in the PRINT statement.
- Use arithmetic operations in the LET statement.
- Use the INPUT statement with numbers.

PRINT with Commas and Semicolons

Until now, you have never used more than one piece of data in a PRINT statement. In this session, you will be using more than one. Now is a good time to learn more about the PRINT statement.

Start the computer with your diskette as usual. Then do the following things in immediate mode:

`PRINT 123`	No surprises here.
`PRINT , 456` `PRINT , , 789`	Notice where the numbers appear.
`PRINT 123, 456, 789`	See where the numbers are printed.
`PRINT 123; 456; 789`	This is quite different.
`PRINT 1; ; ; ; 2`	Extra semicolons do nothing.
`PRINT 2; " PLUS "; 2; " IS "; 4`	You can mix numbers and strings.

1. What does a comma in the PRINT statement tell the computer to do?
2. What does a semicolon in the PRINT statement tell the computer to do?

Doing Arithmetic

Computers solve many arithmetic problems. Perhaps you are wondering when you will have the computer do arithmetic. Now is the time.

`NEW` `HOME`	Erase memory and clear screen.
`50 PRINT P, Q` `RUN`	The Øs and their positions should not surprise you.

`20 LET P = 7`
`30 LET Q = 3`
`LIST`
`RUN`
	Line 5Ø says to print the value of the variables named P and Q.

```
40 LET R = P + Q
50 PRINT P; " PLUS "; Q; " IS "; R
LIST

RUN
```

Check this carefully. Try to guess what the computer will do with this program. Think about how R got its value.

Change the program so that it adds 12345 to 54321. Run the new version. Think about why you saw different numbers this time.

3. What part of your program tells the computer the values of P and Q?
4. What does the symbol + mean in line 40?
5. What does line 40 tell the computer to do? Explain in your own words.

Using the INPUT Statement

Your program now in the memory should look like this:

```
20 LET P = 12345
30 LET Q = 54321
40 LET R = P + Q
50 PRINT P; " PLUS "; Q; " IS "; R
```

The program falls nicely into two parts. One part tells the computer what the names P and Q stand for. The other part tells the computer what to do with P and Q, *no matter what P and Q stand for.* When you were writing lines 40 and 50, you did not have to worry about the actual values of P and Q. You just used their names. Lines 20 and 30 assign values, much as you do when you assign Susan to pitch and Larry to catch in a softball game. Lines 40 and 50 are like the rules of the game, no matter who is playing.

Your program is a big step forward because the processing part (line 40) and the output part (line 50) are *independent* of the numbers in the LET statements. Line 40 adds *any* two numbers, and line 50 prints the result. There is still one weakness in the program, though. To make it add different numbers, you have to rewrite lines 20 and 30. Let's see how to avoid that. **If the above program is not in memory, enter it now.**

```
20 INPUT P
LIST

RUN
```

Line 20 has a new statement.

Notice the ? and the flashing cursor.

The computer is waiting for you to type a number and press (RETURN). Do so, as follows:

```
?45678
```
...and RETURN. Notice what was printed.

```
RUN
?1
```
...and RETURN. Hmmm...

```
LIST
```
Think about how P got its value.

```
30 INPUT Q
LIST
```
Now both LETs are gone.

```
RUN
?21
```
...and RETURN.

```
?37
```
...and RETURN.

```
RUN
?12345
?67890
```
Be sure not to use commas in the numbers.

```
20
30 INPUT P, Q
LIST
```
Now there is only one INPUT statement.

```
RUN
?21, 37
```
Think how P and Q got values.

```
RUN
?444, 555
```
That worked too. Now let's make the program more "user friendly."

```
20 PRINT "ENTER TWO NUMBERS"
LIST
RUN
```
...and do what it says.

6. What does the INPUT statement tell the computer to do? Explain in your own words.

7. Your program now contains no data values. Why does that make it better than the old version with LET statements?

8. How does line 20 make the program "friendlier"—easier to use?

INPUT Errors

Users sometimes make errors when replying to a request for input. Use your last program to find out what happens when you make such an error.

```
RUN
?3
```
Enter only one number and press RETURN. Notice the ?? output.

```
??7
```
Enter the other number and press RETURN. That worked.

```
RUN
?3, 4, 5, 6
```
Note what happens.

```
RUN
?TWO, FOUR
```
——————————————————— Note what happens.

`15, 72`

——————————————————— Now it works OK.

9. What does the computer do if the input reply does not have as many numbers as there are variables in the INPUT statement?

10. What does the computer do if there are too many numbers in the input reply?

If you have extra lab time: EXPLORE

- Change the + in line 40 of the last program to a *. You may also want to change PLUS in line 50 to TIMES. Run the new version. Try out some large numbers.

- Change the arithmetic symbol in line 40 of the last program to the symbol /. Run the new version. See what happens when you try to divide by zero.

- Enter this new version of the program:

```
20 PRINT "ENTER TWO WORDS"
30 INPUT P$, Q$
40 LET R$ = P$ + Q$
50 PRINT P$; " + "; Q$;" = "; R$
```

Run the program and experiment with different string inputs. See whether quotation marks are needed in the input reply.

How Input and Processing Work

IN
THIS SESSION
YOU WILL:
- Learn how to use arithmetic and catenation operators.
- Learn what an expression is.
- Learn how to use the INPUT statement.
- Use the model computer to explain how input and arithmetic work.

Review

In Session 34, you found that BASIC gives you ways to input and process data. You used the INPUT statement to tell the computer to accept numbers and strings from the user. You used the LET statement and some new operations to process this data.

Commas and semicolons At the start of Session 34, you used commas and semicolons in PRINT statements. These punctuation marks do two things. They *separate* one item from another in the statement, and they say *where* the output is to appear on the screen. A comma tells the computer to print the next output at the start of the next **standard print column**: The standard columns are ten characters apart on the Apple II screen. A semicolon tells the computer that the next output should start wherever the last output ended.

Arithmetic operators The symbols +, -, *, and / tell the computer to add, subtract, multiply, and divide numbers. The symbols are called **arithmetic operators**. They usually appear in LET statements, such as these:

```
40 LET R = P + Q
60 LET A = B / C
```

These operators tell the computer to perform an arithmetic operation with the two pieces of numeric data, one on the left and one on the right of the operator.

Catenation operator There is only one operator that can be used with strings. It is called **catenation** and it is written as + in Applesoft BASIC. The word comes from the Latin word for "chain," and it means to link two strings together into a single string. For example, "NOW" + "HERE" is catenated as "NOWHERE".

Expressions In every programming language, there is a special word for combinations such as P + Q, B / C, and "NOW" + "HERE". They are called **expressions**. The main point about an expression is that it has a definite value. *In fact, anything that has a value is an* *expression.* For example, a single variable has a value, so a variable is also an expression. So is a constant. When people talk about expressions, however, they usually mean combinations of variables, constants, and operators.

Examples of expressions   Every one of the items shown below is an expression:

```
25
"HELLO"
6 + 2
"FAT" + "HER"
X - 4
2 * P + 3 * Q
```

Use of expressions   You saw in Session 34 that you can use an expression on the *right* side of the equal sign in a LET statement. In BASIC there is a simple rule that tells where you may use expressions: *You may write an expression anywhere that it is legal to write a constant.* You have used numeric constants in LET, PRINT, PLOT, HLIN, VLIN, COLOR=, and SPEED= statements. So you could also write a numeric expression in any of those statements. (Example: PLOT X + 2 , Y + 5.)

Use of variables   Variables are also expressions, so you can use their names anywhere you can use an expression. But there are a few places where you may not use anything but a variable name. You have seen the two main ones: Variable names must appear in (1) INPUT statements and (2) on the *left* side of the equal sign in LET statements. You must use variables there because you want to assign values, and you cannot assign a value to something unless you name it. For example, the computer will not accept these statements:

```
LET 5 = X
INPUT 932
```

How Input and Arithmetic Work

In Session 34, you experimented with a program that asked you to enter two numbers and then printed their sum on the screen. Let's take a close look at the steps the computer went through during that program.

The complete model Our computer model needs one more part to explain how your program worked. The part is called the **arithmetic and logic scratchpad**.

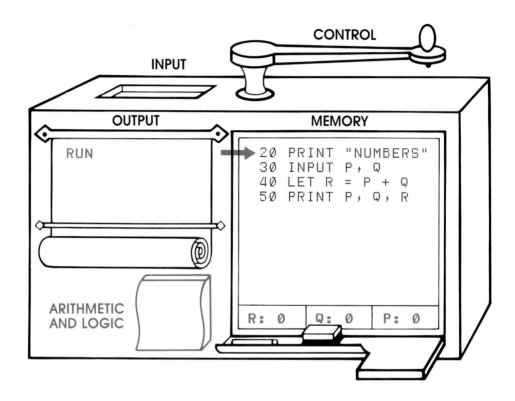

The model is now complete. *Using a model with only these five parts, you can understand how the computer performs any program.* The picture shows the computer just after the program has been entered, the screen cleared, and the RUN command entered. *Note the* P, Q, *and* R *variable boxes, initially with* 0s *inside.*

Perform PRINT and move pointer The RUN program tells the computer to perform the PRINT statement in the first line and then move the pointer down. Here is the new state:

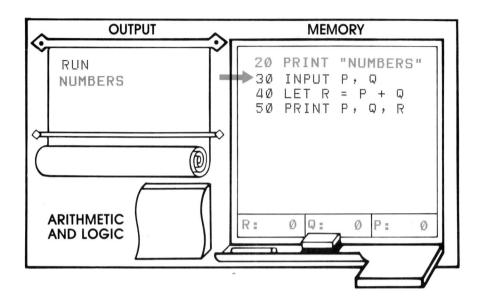

Perform INPUT statement Now the RUN program tells the computer to perform the INPUT statement. Here are the rules:

> **The computer's rules for performing the INPUT P, Q statement**
>
> **1.** Print a question mark on the output screen, turn on the cursor, and stop.
> **2.** Wait for two numbers, separated by commas, to be typed on the keyboard, and for the (RETURN) key to be pressed.
> **3.** Assign the first number to P and the second to Q.

Here is the computer while the INPUT statement is being performed. The question mark is on the screen, and the cursor is on. The numbers 234 and 765 are about to be dropped into the input slot.

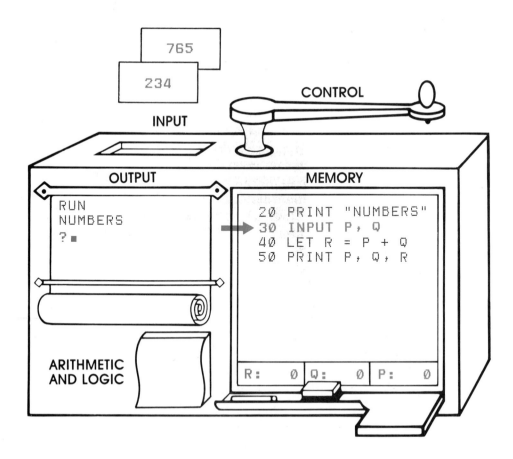

Finish INPUT and move pointer After the two numbers drop into the input slot of the model, the computer writes them on the output scroll and also in the P and Q memory boxes. After the computer moves the line pointer to the next line, the computer model looks like this:

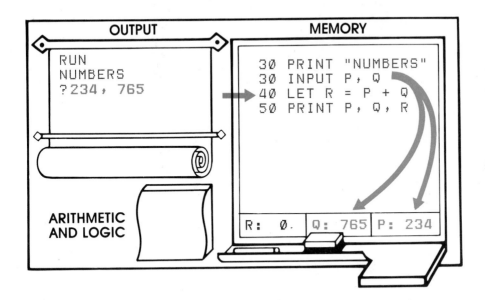

Perform the LET statement Now the computer must follow the rules for the LET statement. Rule 1 on page 180 says to "find the value of whatever is on the right side of the equal sign." Here is how the computer does that.

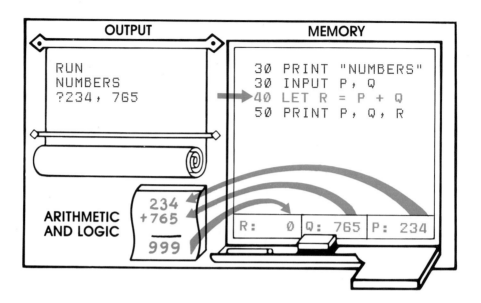

To find the value of P + Q, the computer used the arithmetic and logic scratchpad. First, it made copies of the data in the P and Q boxes in memory. Then it added them together to get 999, which is at the bottom of the scratchpad.

Finish LET and move pointer Rule 2 for performing the LET statement says to "write the value (999) in the box whose name appears on the left side of the equal sign." Here is how the model looks after the computer performs the LET statement.

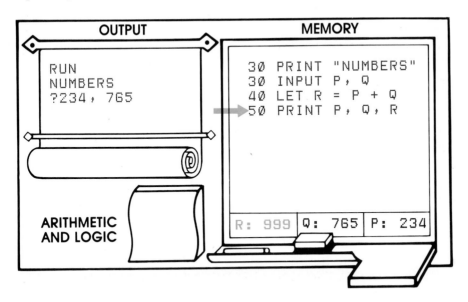

Notice that the R box in memory now contains the value that used to be on the scratchpad. Notice also that the computer threw away the scratch sheet it used for the calculation. Those numbers are gone and the scratchpad is clean. Finally, the computer moved the line pointer down one line.

Perform PRINT and stop Finally, the RUN program tells the computer to perform the last statement and then stop. Here is the final state of the computer:

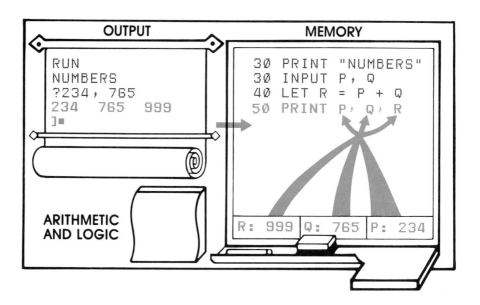

```
      OUTPUT                          MEMORY

   RUN                        30  PRINT  "NUMBERS"
   NUMBERS                    30  INPUT  P , Q
   ?234, 765                  40  LET R  =  P  +  Q
   234    765    999          50  PRINT P , Q , R
   ]■

                              R:  999  Q:  765  P:  234
  ARITHMETIC
  AND LOGIC
```

Other jobs for the scratchpad So far, you have seen the computer use the arithmetic and logic unit (ALU) in only one way—to do arithmetic. The computer also uses the ALU to catenate strings and to compare one piece of data with another. In other words, the computer processes data in the ALU.

Processing and LET statements The program line that told the computer how to process the data was the LET statement, line 40. Line 40 is an example of an assignment statement—a statement that tells the computer what value to assign to a variable. The assignment statement is nearly always the one that tells the computer how to process the data whether in BASIC or any other computer language.

QUESTIONS

1. What are the purposes of commas and semicolons in a PRINT statement?

2. What symbols are used in BASIC for the addition, subtraction, multiplication, and division operators?

3. What does a plus sign between two strings in an Applesoft BASIC program tell the computer to do?

4. What does the term *expression* mean?

5. Where do the rules of BASIC allow you to write an expression?

6. In what two places in a program must a variable name appear?

7. What is the computer's arithmetic and logic unit used for?

8. Is it true that the INPUT statement causes something to be output? Explain your answer.

9. What happens to the number a user enters into the computer while the computer is performing the statement INPUT X?

10. Suppose you run the following program and enter the string CAT. What is in the computer's memory afterwards?

```
10    LET A$ = "DOG"
20    INPUT A$
30    END
```

Projects with Variables and Input

IN THIS SESSION YOU WILL:
- Rewrite the NAMES program with a variable for the TAB position of each big letter.
- Add an input subroutine to the NAMES program.
- Write a new program to draw variable boxes on the graphics screen.
- Read programs that use input and variables.

Adding a Variable TAB to Program NAMES.

In Session 24, you wrote and saved on your diskette a program called NAMES. It printed Ann's, Nan's, or Ana's name in big letters. Then in Session 30, you changed the BIG N subroutine by adding TAB (11) to the PRINT statements. This made the big *N* appear always in column 11 on the screen.

The big *N* was always in the same place because 11 is a constant. Your goal now is to replace the constant with the name of a variable. That way, the BIG N subroutine will put the *N* in a different column whenever the main routine gives the variable a new value.

Start the computer with your diskette as usual. Load program NAMES and run it a few times. Then list it.

The main routine for printing Ann's name should look like this:

```
100 REM--PROGRAM NAMES
110:: HOME
120:: GOSUB 600: REM--BIG A
130:: GOSUB 400: REM--BIG N
140:: GOSUB 400: REM--BIG N
150 END
```

Line 400 should be the start of your BIG N subroutine, and line 600 should be the start of your BIG A subroutine. (If you have lost your NAMES program, enter the main routine now, but *not* the PRINT statements of the subroutines. You will be changing them now.)

Change the PRINT statements in your BIG N subroutine. The first item after the word PRINT should be TAB (C), followed by a semicolon. Here is a sample line:

```
420:: PRINT TAB (C); "***    ***"
```

Make exactly the same changes in your BIG A subroutine. Add the following line to the main routine:

```
115 LET C = 15
```

List the program and run it. If all goes well, you should see the three letters of Ann's name appear in a column down the middle of the screen. If not, list the program, find out what is wrong, and fix it.

Now add LET statements in lines 125 and 135. They should be like the one in line 115, but with different constants to the right of the equal sign. List the main routine and think about what it tells the computer to do. Run the program and find out.

Change the constants in lines 115, 125, and 135 and run NAMES again. Try to make Ann's name appear on a diagonal line from upper left to lower right. Then make the name appear on the other diagonal, from upper right to lower left.

Save this new version of the program on your diskette in the file NAMES, as before. If you locked NAMES, you will have to unlock it before you can save the new version.

1. What constants did you need in your three LET statements to get Ann's name to appear diagonally from upper left to lower right?
2. What do the LET statements in the main routine do? Explain in your own words.
3. What does TAB (C) tell the computer to do? Explain in your own words.
4. Why did changing the constants in the main routine cause the big letters to appear in different columns?
5. In Session 30, you needed to write two BIG N subroutines to get one N in column 11 and another in column 21. How many BIG N subroutines do you need now? Why?

Adding an Input Subroutine to NAMES

You probably got tired of retyping the three LET statements whenever you wanted the big letters to appear in different columns. The program would be more "user friendly" if it printed WHAT THREE COLUMNS DO YOU WANT LETTERS IN? and then waited for you to enter three numbers.

Write a new subroutine that asks the user to enter three numbers for the TAB positions of each letter in Ann's name. Here is an outline in a mixture of BASIC and English.

```
190:
200 REM--SUB INPUT
210::  prompt the user for 3 numbers
220::  input the numbers
230::  clear the screen
240 RETURN
```

You will have to convert this outline to all BASIC. You will need three new variable names for line 220. You might use C1, C2, and C3.

Next, add a GOSUB 200 statement to the main routine. Put it right after the HOME statement. Run the program and debug the new subroutine if necessary.

Next, change the LET statements to replace the three constants now in the program with the three variable names you used in line 220. For example, LET C = 11 might then become LET C = C1.

List the main routine and the new subroutine. Think carefully how they work together. For example, think about what would happen if the GOSUB 200 statement were missing.

Run the program and experiment with different numbers for the three inputs.

Again, save this version of the program in the file NAMES on your diskette. It is a good idea to lock it now.

6. How does the new input subroutine tell the computer where to print the big letters?

7. Why was it necessary to put a new GOSUB in the main routine after you added the new input subroutine?

8. Why was it necessary to change the LET statements after you added the new input subroutine?

Drawing Variable Boxes

Now let's write a completely new program. (If you forgot to save NAMES on your diskette, do so now.) The purpose of the program is to draw rectangular boxes on the screen. The program should ask the user to enter the left, right, top, and bottom of the box as well as the color to use.

Here is what the user should see when the program is run. The user's responses are printed in color:

```
ENTER THE LEFT AND RIGHT EDGES (0 - 39)
?5, 30
ENTER THE TOP AND BOTTOM (0 - 39)
?10, 25
WHAT COLOR DO YOU WANT? (0 - 16)
?4
```

Then the computer should draw the box on the graphics screen. Here are the steps of the top-down method for solving this problem.

Step 1. Begin by writing the main routine only. Write an outline first, on paper, and use only English for the statements in the body of the main routine. The body statements should tell the computer to do five things: (1) set the text mode, (2) clear the screen, (3) handle user input, (4) set the graphics mode, (5) draw the box.

Step 2. Convert each line of the body to BASIC. If no single BASIC statement can make the computer do what you want, use a GOSUB statement followed by a REM statement to explain the purpose of the GOSUB.

Step 3. Write on paper the outline and body of each subroutine, using only English for the body.

Step 4. Convert English to BASIC, as you did with the main routine.

You are now ready to go to the computer. Type NEW and then enter your program into the computer. Run it. Debug it if necessary. Save your program in the file MY BOX on your diskette. Lock it for safety.

9. Why do you need only one subroutine to draw the boxes, even though it can draw many different boxes?

10. Suppose your main routine outline had the phrase "handle input." Some people would convert directly to an INPUT statement. Others would use a GOSUB to an input subroutine. Which would you use? Why?

If you have extra lab time:

- Load program BOXES from the diskette and list it. See whether you can begin to see how it works, even though it contains some things you have not seen yet.

- Load program LITTLE TROT from the diskette. List lines 800 through 900. See whether you can figure out what this subroutine does and how it works.

37 The Information Machine

IN THIS SESSION YOU WILL:
- Learn that data can be stored and retrieved from on-line data bases.
- Recognize some applications of private data bases.
- Learn what a computer network is.
- Learn some applications of shared data bases.
- Find out some dangers of using shared data bases.

Data Storage and Retrieval

Almost every computer program tells the computer to do something with data. The computer moves data from place to place and makes changes in the data. For this reason, the computer is sometimes called an "information machine." In the last seven sessions, you have used the main BASIC statements—INPUT, LET, and PRINT—that tell the computer what to do with data.

Keyboard input, screen output You used the INPUT statement to tell the computer to accept data typed on the keyboard by the user. You used LET to tell the computer how to process data. You used PRINT to tell it what data to print and where on the screen to print the data. But data can come from places other than the keyboard, and it can go to places other than the screen.

File input and output You already know that programs are stored in files on your diskette. There can also be **data files**. BASIC and most other languages have a way to tell the computer to send its output to a data file on a diskette, a magnetic tape, or some other **storage unit** connected to the computer. (We will not show you how to use storage units here. For more information, read the Applesoft manuals.)

On-line data bases A large collection of information on one subject is called a **data base**. For example, your dictionary is a data base of English words and their definitions. If a data base is in a storage unit connected to a computer, we call that data base an **on-line** data base. The computer can take input from the data base or send output to the data base. On-line data bases have many important applications.

Spelling checker If you use a computer system to write letters or papers, you can use a program that checks for misspelled words. This is a common data-base application. The program tells the computer to compare each one of your words with all the words in an on-line "dictionary." The dictionary is usually stored in a data file on a diskette. The computer takes input from that file as it checks each of your words.

Some programs also allow you to add new words to the dictionary file. If so, the computer sends the new words as output to the data base.

Names and addresses Some people use a computer to keep their address books on line. The data base contains names, addresses, telephone numbers, and other useful information—birthdays, for example. Programs allow you to look up someone's phone number (input from the data base), add a person to the on-line address book (output to the data base), or change an address (input and output). Other programs can make the computer search the data base for all people with birthdays in January, for example.

Collections People who own many books, records, or other large collections can use a computer to manage the collection. They put together an on-line data base with information about every item in the collection. Computer programs allow them to search for a particular item by name, date, or some other category. Other programs have the computer print lists of everything in the collection, sorted into categories, for example, records listed by performer, type of music, or composer.

Travel agents use computers to reserve airplane seats and hotel rooms for their customers.

Computer Networks

The above are examples of **private data bases**. They are used by one person at a time, usually on a single computer that is not connected to any other computer. But there are also **shared data bases**: one collection of data that several people can get information from or add information to. Shared data bases are usually the largest, and they allow the most complex applications of computers to date.

Local networks One way to share a data base is to connect a group of computers to a single storage unit containing the data base. Usually the computers are located in the same room or building. This arrangement is called a **local network**, and it is often used in schools and offices. In fact, you may be using a local network along with this book. If so, programs such as ROCKET and TURTLE TROT are probably saved only once on the storage unit, and each person can load a copy into his or her computer.

Long-distance networks Sometimes one data base is shared by users a mile or so apart or even in different parts of the country. Stringing wires between the users can be very expensive. It is cheaper to use wires already there: the telephone system. A device called a **modem** changes data to a series of beeps that can be sent by telephone. Another modem changes the beeps back to data at the other end. In the near future, the cable TV system may link home computers to data bases in other cities.

Airline reservations A good example of a long-distance network is the airline reservation system. Here is how it works: A person goes to the ticket counter, for instance, at O'Hare Airport in Chicago and asks for a ticket on a flight from Denver to Dallas. The ticket clerk punches a few keys, and within 10 seconds the clerk's computer displays information about that flight. The clerk reserves a seat for the traveler just by punching a few more keys. At the same time, several hundred other clerks around the country are using the same data base to reserve seats. The data base they all use is in Ohio.

Electronic mail A different sort of data base is the set of messages that all the people in a network send to one another. The sender's computer adds a message to the data base. The receiver's computer searches the data base for "mail." If the receiver has a message, the receiver's computer gets a copy and displays it on the screen.

Above: Postal workers move tons of paper every day. Letters spend time just sitting in bags. Right: Computers can send and receive weightless electronic mail quickly over telephone lines.

Electronic banking Another kind of shared data base is the set of bank accounts of all the customers of a bank. For example, instead of billing customers by mail, the water company has its computer send the bank's computer a list of the amounts owed by the bank's customers. When the bill is due, the customer uses a home computer to call the bank's computer and find out how much the bill is. The customer tells the home computer how much to pay. The bank's computer then subtracts that amount from the customer's bank account and adds it to the amount the water company receives.

Other applications As home computers become cheaper, the number of computer network applications will grow. In the near future, people will do their shopping from electronic catalogs, read electronic classified ads from their home computer screens, get in touch with people who share their interests or hobbies via computer—even use the computer as an electronic newspaper.

Network Problems

Although the future for shared data bases looks bright, not everything about it is rosy. One person or family owns and uses a private data base, all one's own, but a whole community of people use and depend on a shared data base. The failure of a computer network affects many people. A few people who do not care about the good of the community may sabotage an application.

Down time Computer hardware may fail. A telephone line may fail. More likely, the computer software may have bugs that make the network stop working. How does the airline clerk sell tickets when "the computer is down"? How do you get your electronic mail, pay bills, get news, and so forth, if you become dependent on computer networks that sometimes fail? It is important to answer these questions before deciding to rely on a computer-network service. Usually, people do not rely on just one system. They have in reserve another way to get the job done.

Security of data If you put data in a shared data base, you want to be sure that it will not disappear or be tampered with. If you can use a home computer to get into your bank account, could someone else who owns a home computer raid your account and take all your money? A company that puts all of its vital data on line runs the risk of going out of business if the data is lost or incorrect.

Privacy of data Who will be able to look at data you put into a shared data base? How could those people harm you? What advantage might knowing things you thought were secret give those people? Will a government agency be able to see your data? If others are collecting data about you, what rights do you have to see that data and challenge them when it is wrong? None of these problems is new or caused by computers. But computer networks make it easier to collect data and analyze it. Therefore, citizens need to know of the dangers and consider whether new laws are needed.

Ownership of data Who owns the data in a shared data base? Does it belong to the person who collected it? Do you own data about yourself that someone else has collected? Suppose data about you is incorrect and someone bases a decision unfavorable to you on that data. Can you sue for damages, and if so, whom do you sue? Again, these are old problems, but they may occur more often as we depend more on computer networks and shared data bases.

Passwords An important way of controlling who may see or change data in a shared data base is to give a **password** to certain people but not to others. Before opening the data base, the computer asks the user to enter a password. Password protection is not perfect, though: If someone finds out your password and uses it, the computer will not be able to know that person is using your password illegally. Also, there must be a list of legal passwords somewhere in the computer system; otherwise, the computer could not check whether a password is correct. A clever programmer might be able to find the list and figure out which password goes with which user.

Coding A better way to assure privacy is by **encryption**. Instead of storing the data in a form that anyone can read easily, the computer rewrites the data in a code. To read the data, a person must not only gain entry into the data base but also know how to decode the data stored there. Since the only person who knows the code is the one who created the data base, that person can also control who is able to decode the data.

1. Why is the computer called an "information machine"?
2. What is an on-line data base?
3. What are two applications of private data bases?
4. What is a shared data base?
5. What is the difference between a local network and a long-distance network of computers?
6. What are two applications of shared data bases?

7. How can a computer hardware failure hurt an airline reservation system?
8. Why is security of data important for an electronic banking system?
9. Why is privacy of data important for an electronic mail system?

The stock market relies on a huge computerized data base. Investors use data to help them decide what to buy or sell.

Part 5

Vocabulary Table

Words printed in color were introduced in this part.

BASIC Vocabulary (Shaded Areas Show Standard BASIC Words)

Commands		Statements			Functions
Program	Diskette	Action	Action	Control	
RUN	LOAD	INPUT	SPEED=	GOSUB	——
LIST	SAVE	LET	FLASH	RETURN	——
NEW	DELETE	PRINT	INVERSE	END	——
DEL	CATALOG	REM	NORMAL	——	——
——	LOCK	PLOT	COLOR=	—	
——	UNLOCK	HLIN	TEXT	—	
——		VLIN	GR	——	
——		HOME			

New BASIC Words

LET   A statement that tells the computer to find or compute the value of whatever appears on the right side of the equal sign (=) and then assign that value to the variable named on the left side.

INPUT   A statement that tells the computer to ask the user to input data. The computer assigns those data values to variables.

TAB   An optional part of the PRINT statement. The number in parentheses after TAB tells the computer to begin the next output in the print column that has the same number.

New Ideas

arithmetic   Combining numbers by addition, subtraction, etc.

arithmetic operators   The symbols +, -, *, /, and ∧.

arithmetic and logic scratchpad   The arithmetic and logic unit in the model computer.

assignment statement   See LET.

catenation   Combining two strings of characters by joining the end of the first to the start of the second. Also called "concatenation."

catenation operator   In Applesoft BASIC, the plus sign.

constant   A piece of data that does not change its value.

data Pieces of information; information given as a pattern of symbols a computer can read.

data base A collection of information on one subject.

data file A set of data stored on a diskette, magnetic tape, or the like.

data-type error Use of numeric data when the computer expects string data, or vice versa.

expression A constant, variable, or combination of constants, variables, and operators in a statement.

network A group of computers connected to a central storage unit.

numeric data Data whose value is a number.

on-line Connected to a computer so that data can flow to and fro.

operator A symbol that tells the computer to perform an operation on two pieces of data. See *arithmetic operator* and *catenation*.

print line The characters sent to the screen by a PRINT statement. The longest print line for the Apple II is 255 characters.

string data Data whose value is a series of characters.

type of data The kind of information the data stands for. See *numeric data* and *string data*.

variable A place in the memory of the computer. Data values are stored there. In a program, the place is always referred to by its name.

variable properties The name, type, and value of a variable.

Part

Control Statements, Numbers, and Functions

In every program you have written, the computer has performed the INPUT, LET, PRINT, and graphics statements in *straight-line order,* starting with the first statement, then doing the second, and so on. You might think the GOSUB statement makes the computer interrupt this order, but it does not. GOSUB is a side trip to a subroutine, but the RETURN sends the computer back to the main route. GOSUB is not much different from PRINT: Both tell the computer to perform certain actions and then come back to straight-line order.

New statements In Part 6, you will learn two new statements: the GOTO and IF statements. They are not action statements. Unlike INPUT, LET, and PRINT, they do not affect data. They control the order in which the computer performs the statements that do affect it.

Repetition Without control statements, it would be hard to tell the computer to do something a thousand times. You would have to write the same statements a thousand times. The GOTO statement can tell the computer to go back to an earlier statement and start over.

Choice Without control statements, it would be impossible to tell the computer to do one of two different things. You could not tell it to ask for a number, decide whether it was even or odd, and then print *either* EVEN *or* ODD. The IF statement can tell the computer to make that kind of decision.

Computer languages give control All computer languages give you a way to tell the computer to repeat steps again and again. They all give you a way to tell the computer to make a choice between one set of steps and another set of steps. In Part 6, you will learn the BASIC statements for doing these things.

Numbers and functions These new statements will make it easy for you to explore numbers and arithmetic on the computer. You will also learn what functions are and how to use them.

213

Changing Statement Order

IN
THIS SESSION
YOU WILL:
- Use a GOTO statement to tell the computer to skip some of the statements in a program.
- Use a GOTO statement to create an infinite loop.
- Learn how to stop and restart the computer while running a program.
- Change programs on the diskette into infinite loops.

Skipping Statements

Start the computer with your diskette as usual. Then go on to the activities below.

```
LOAD ROCKET
RUN
```
Get the ROCKET program.
```
LIST
```
Look at the listing.

Like all the programs you have seen so far, ROCKET tells the computer to perform the first statement, then the second, and so on. The computer must perform all the statements. Now let's see how to skip some.

```
195 GOTO 250
LIST
```
What do you think the computer will do?
```
RUN
```
The rocket shrank!
```
LIST
```
Study the listing.
```
195 GOTO 270
LIST
```
What will this version do?
```
RUN
```
Now it is very short.
```
195
125 GOTO 290
LIST
```
What will happen now?
```
RUN
```
You probably knew this would happen.
```
125 GOTO 500
LIST
```
What do you think will happen now?
```
RUN
```
Now you know.

1. What does a GOTO statement tell the computer to do?
2. What happens if the computer performs the statement GOTO 380 when there is no line 380 in the program?

Repeating Statements

You have used the GOTO statement to jump forward over statements. Let's find out what happens when you tell the computer to jump backward.

```
LOAD ROCKET
LIST
```
Get a fresh copy of ROCKET.

```
300 GOTO 100
LIST
```
Try to figure out what the computer will do.

```
RUN
```
You have a flashing rocket now.

The GOTO statement at the end of the program told the computer to go back to the beginning. It started again at line 100, then went to 110, and so on. Finally it got to line 300, which told it to go back to 100. This program will never stop. You have created an **infinite loop**: It will run forever—or at least until your computer breaks or you stop it.

In Session 12, you learned two ways to force programs to stop. Let's review them.

[CONTROL] [S]
That command made the output pause.

[CONTROL] [S]
That started output again.

[CONTROL] [C]
That stopped the program.

Note that the cursor is now back on the screen. The computer is ready for your next command.

```
300 GOTO 120
LIST
```
The HOME statement is not in the loop now. What will happen?

```
RUN
```
Notice the difference.

Use [CONTROL] [S] to pause and [CONTROL] [C] to stop the program.

```
300 GOTO 200
```
What does this statement tell the computer to do?

```
RUN
```
Use [CONTROL] [C] to stop.

By changing only the GOTO statement, you have created very different effects. Now let's look at one more change.

```
300 GOTO 300
LIST
```
What will happen?

```
RUN
```
Is the computer broken?

This is another infinite loop. The computer is busy doing something, since the cursor is missing. Use ⌶CONTROL C⌶ to stop the program.

3. How can you tell the computer to repeat all the statements in a program again and again?
4. What is the difference between the ⌶CONTROL S⌶ and ⌶CONTROL C⌶ commands?

Making a Loop That Counts

In this section, you will write a new program that does arithmetic inside an infinite loop. Enter the following lines:

```
NEW
100 LET N = 1
110 PRINT N
120 LET N = N + 1
130 GOTO 110
LIST
```
Enter and check the program.

This program contains an infinite loop. The GOTO statement in line 130 tells the computer to perform line 110 next. Then the computer performs line 120 and comes back to line 130, which directs it back to line 110 again. The program will stay in the loop until you stop it. Let's see what the program does.

```
RUN
```
Watch the output on the screen.

The numbers keep scrolling up the screen until you tell the computer to pause. You know how to do that.

```
CONTROL S
```
Stop the output temporarily.

You can understand what is happening. Line 100 says that the variable N has the value 1. Line 110 tells the computer to print the value of N. Line 120 tells it to find the value of what is on the right side of the equal sign. Since N is 1, N + 1 is 2. So the computer must assign 2 as the new value of N. Then line 130 says to perform line 110 again; so the computer prints 2 this time. Then line 120 says to find the value of N + 1 again. This time N is 2, so N + 1 is now 3. Finally, line 120 says to assign the new value to N. Then line 130 says to start over at line 110.

```
CONTROL S
```
Restart the output.
```
CONTROL C
```
That stops the program.

Notice that the computer has told you the number of the line at which the program stopped. Let's see what we can learn. The PRINT statement in immediate mode is a good tool for snooping.

PRINT N _____ This is the value of N when the computer stopped.

CONT _____ This is a new command.

CONT tells the computer to *continue* running the program where it left off. CONT is like RUN, with two exceptions: The computer does not set variables to zero and empty strings, and the computer does not put the line pointer back at the first statement. Let's see what else we can do:

CONTROL C
PRINT N _____ Stop the program and print the value of N.

LET N = 10000 _____ Set the value of N to 10000.

CONT _____ Continue.

CONTROL C _____ Stop the program.

PRINT, LET, and CONT in the immediate mode are very useful for debugging programs.

5. How do you stop a running program and get the cursor back on the screen?
6. How do you restart a program at the place it was stopped?
7. After you stop a running program, how can you find out the value of a variable used in the program?

If you have extra lab time:

- Load program BLAST OFF from your diskette. Make the *main routine* into an infinite loop so that the rockets blast off again and again. Find out what happens to the print speed after you stop the program. Explain why the speed did not return to normal.
- Load program SYMMETRY from the diskette. Run it once and then delete line 135. Is the main routine an infinite loop now? Run the program. Explain why the computer remains in graphics mode after you stop the program. Use CONT to restart.
- Write a program in the form of an infinite loop. Put an END statement *inside* the loop. Run the program. See whether you can restart it by using the CONT command.

39 How the GOTO Statement Works

IN
THIS SESSION
YOU WILL:
• Learn how an infinite counting loop works.
• Learn the form of the infinite loop block.
• Understand the need to document programs and write clearly.

Review

In Session 38, you used the GOTO statement to skip statements in the ROCKET program. You also used the GOTO statement to tell the computer to repeat statements again and again.

The GOTO statement You found that the number after the GOTO tells the computer which line of the program to perform next. For example, the statement

    215 GOTO 270

tells the computer to perform line 215 and then continue with line 270 next.

Skipping lines In this example, the computer skips all lines in the program between lines 215 and 270. Skipping lines is one of the two uses of the GOTO statement. In sessions to come, you will see the need to skip lines.

Repeating lines The other purpose of the GOTO statement is to tell the computer to repeat some lines of a program again and again. In Session 38, you saw many examples of repetition. A group of statements performed again and again is called a *loop*. Every programming language gives you a way to make loops.

Infinite loops In Session 38, you created loops that never ended. The computer performed the statements in the loops again and again, forever. Such loops are called infinite. Common objects run by computers usually use infinite loops. For example, you would not want the computer in a car or a digital watch to stop running. The only way to keep the computer going is to loop back over the steps of the program again and again.

Breaking out of loops You learned how certain control keys affect infinite loops. The (CONTROL S) key makes the computer stop printing characters on the screen. Another tap of (CONTROL S) (or any other key) starts the printing again. The (CONTROL C) key stops the program and makes the cursor reappear on the screen.

Restarting a program   You learned that the `CONT` command tells the computer to restart a stopped program. The computer remembers the value of variables and also remembers the last statement it performed. You also found that while the program was stopped, you could use `PRINT` statements in immediate mode to find what values variables had. You could also use `LET` statements to change the value of variables before restarting. These are useful things to do when debugging long, complex programs.

GOTO errors   You found in Session 38 that the number after `GOTO` has to be an actual line number in your program. If not, the computer said `?UNDEF'D STATEMENT ERROR`. You found that it was legal to make the line number after `GOTO` the same as the line number of the `GOTO` statement itself, but the result was simply an infinite loop that did nothing.

A Loop That Counts

In Session 38, you wrote a four-line program that "counted." In other words, it printed integers (whole numbers), starting at 1 and going on forever. Counting is important in many programs. The computer in a digital watch counts the vibrations of a crystal. Video games count up your score. Program `TURTLE TROT` counts the moves of two turtles to see whether either one has crossed the finish line.

The program   You entered this program into the computer in Session 38:

```
100 LET N = 1
110 PRINT N
120 LET N = N + 1
130 GOTO 110
```

Line `130` tells the computer to "loop back to line `110`." There is no statement that tells the computer to stop looping, so this loop is infinite.

A contradiction?   Line `120` often confuses people. How can any number be the same as 1 plus that same number? If the value of `N` is `372`, for example, line `120` seems to be saying "Let `372` equal `373`." That is impossible, of course. In fact, line `120` does not say that `N` and `N + 1` are the same. It says something totally different, as you shall see.

The model computer Statements such as the one in line 120 occur often in programs, almost always inside loops. The model computer can help you understand how these statements work. Here is a picture of the computer with the program in memory. The HOME and RUN commands have just been entered.

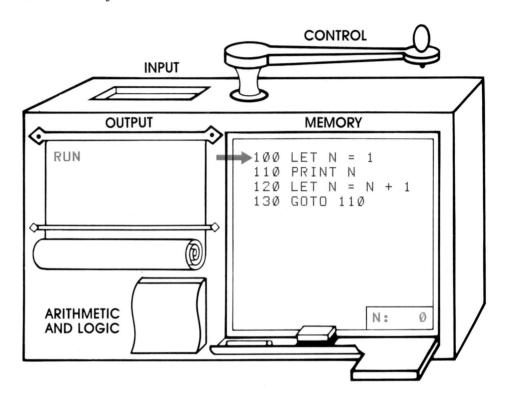

This is the complete model, with all its parts. The arithmetic and logic unit does the addition in line 120. Note the N variable box in the memory. The RUN program began by putting a 0 there.

Perform LET and move pointer The RUN program tells the computer to perform the LET statement in the first line and then move the pointer down. Here is the new state:

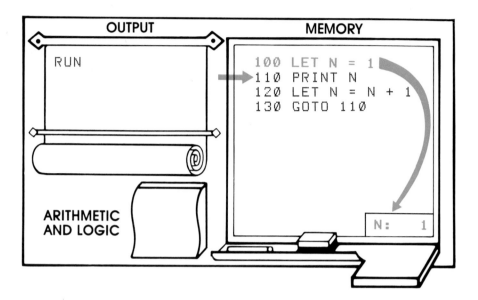

Now there is a 1 in the N box. The LET statement told the computer to write 1 there.

Perform PRINT and move pointer The computer must now perform the PRINT statement. Line 110 tells the computer to read the number in the N box and write that number on the output scroll. The RUN program then moves the pointer to the next line. Here is the new picture:

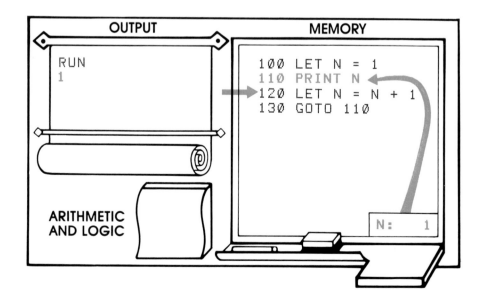

Start performing LET Now the computer performs line 120. Remember that the computer performs the LET statement in two steps. The first step is to "find the value of whatever is on the right side of the equal sign." The value of N is whatever is in the N box. The computer must add 1 to that value, so it uses the arithmetic scratchpad, as shown:

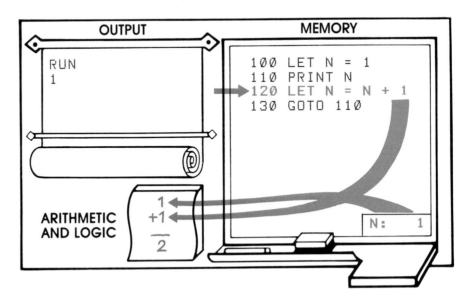

Finish LET and move pointer Now the computer must perform step 2 of the rules for the LET statement. The computer reads the number on the bottom of the arithmetic scratchpad, 2, and writes it in the N memory box—the box with the same letter that appears on the *left* side of the equal sign. So the computer erases the 1 in the N box and writes a new number in the box: 2. Here is the new picture:

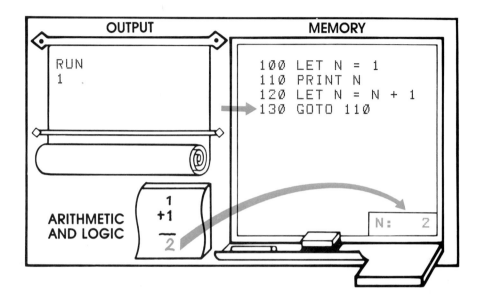

Perform GOTO Following the rules of the RUN program, the computer now places the pointer at line 130. The computer must perform the GOTO statement. The rule is very simple.

The computer's rule for performing a GOTO statement

Move the line pointer to the line with the same number as the one after the word GOTO.

Here is the picture after the computer performs the GOTO statement in your program:

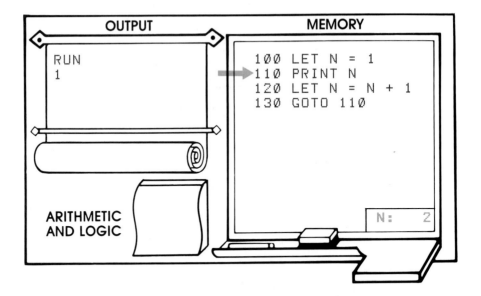

Perform PRINT and move pointer Now the line pointer is back at line 110, the PRINT statement. The computer performs it. Line 110 tells the computer to read the number in the N box and write that number on the output scroll. *This time the number in the box is 2.* Then the computer moves the pointer down. Here is the picture after that step:

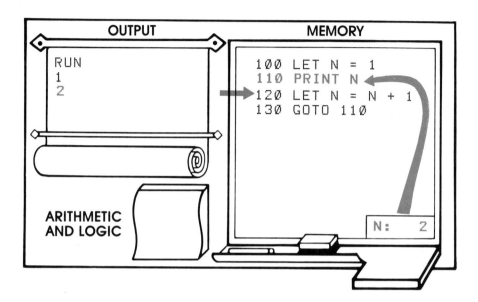

Repeat steps Now the computer must perform the LET statement in line 120 again. The LET statement tells the computer to find the value of the *right* side. Since there is a 2 in the N box now, the value of N + 1 is 3. Then the computer must write the new value, 3, in the N box. After that, the computer performs the GOTO, which tells the computer to put the pointer back at line 110.

Infinite loop You can see that the loop goes on forever. Each time around the loop, the computer prints the current value of N. Then the computer adds 1 to the current value, erases the current value, and writes the new value in the N box.

Standard Form of Infinite Loop

The infinite loop occurs so often in programs that it is important to write it clearly.

Hard to read You created infinite loop programs in Session 38 by putting a GOTO statement at the end of the program. That final position of the GOTO statement makes your programs hard to read. Readers will not know that you created a loop until they read the GOTO statement at the end. If the program is long, they will have a lot of reading.

Documenting a loop   To make programs easy to read, begin your infinite loops with a REM statement. The statement tells the reader that the block of statements after REM form an infinite loop. The block ends with a GOTO statement back to the REM. It is a good idea to put another REM after the GOTO, telling the reader that the loop ends there. These REM statements are examples of **documentation**: the written material that helps explain what the program is supposed to do.

Indent the body   You indented the body of a subroutine to make it easy to read. A loop also has a body of statements. You can make your loops stand out by indenting the body statements. (In Applesoft BASIC, you must use colons when you indent.)

The loop outline   Let's summarize all these good writing ideas in an outline you can use when you write any infinite loop:

```
___   REM--LOOP FOREVER  ◄─────────┐
___       first body statement     │
___       second body statement    │
___                                ▲
___       etc.                     │
___                                │
___   GOTO ___  ───────────────────┘
___   REM--END LOOP
```

The blanks stand for the actual line numbers you will use. The first line tells the reader that a loop block is beginning. The body statements are all indented. The final REM statement lets the reader know where the loop ends.

Jump arrow   The outline contains a new feature: the arrow from the GOTO back to the first REM. This is called a **jump arrow**. It reminds you that the number after the word GOTO *must* be the same as the line number of the REM statement at the beginning. You will use jump arrows often in the future.

Labeling the target   The line that the jump arrow points to is called the **target** of the GOTO. In this book, the targets will always be REM statements. The words after REM explain the reason for the jump. In the infinite-loop outline, the reason for the jump is to show that the loop runs forever. *Always use* REM *labels to explain the jumps in your programs.*

Readable programs   You should always try to make your programs easy to read so that other people will know what your programs are supposed to do. If others can read your program, they will be able to make helpful suggestions. Also, readable programs are easier to change. When you read one of your old programs after a few weeks or months, you will be able to understand it quickly.

Cost of bad writing Bad writing habits are expensive. People have to write the programs, change them, keep them up to date, and rewrite them for new hardware. Badly written programs make all these jobs very much more difficult and expensive. Over a long time, it is probably more expensive to correct badly written software than to buy computer hardware.

QUESTIONS

1. What are the two uses of the GOTO statement?
2. How can you create a program that has an infinite loop?
3. How can you tell the computer to pause and restart the screen output of a program?
4. How can you tell the computer to stop performing the statements in a program and then to restart?
5. What two steps does the computer follow when it performs a LET statement?
6. Suppose the Q box in memory contains the number 873. What is in the Q box after the computer performs the statement below?

   ```
   200 LET Q = Q + 3
   ```

7. Suppose the R box and the S box in memory each contain a 7. What numbers will be in each box after the computer performs this statement?

   ```
   300 LET R = R * S
   ```

8. What does documentation mean? What is its purpose?
9. What does the jump arrow in a program outline remind you to do?
10. What does the first REM statement in the infinite-loop outline tell the reader?
11. Why is it important to make programs readable?

Exploring Numbers

- See how the computer prints very large and very small numbers.
- Learn that there is a largest and a smallest number that the computer can store.
- Explore arithmetic and learn how to use parentheses in arithmetic problems.

Large Numbers

The infinite loop is a useful tool for exploring numbers on the computer. In the last two sessions, you saw how to make a counting loop. Let's get started with a multiplication loop this time. **Start the computer in the usual way, and then enter the program below.**

```
100 REM--PROGRAM NUMBERS
110:
120 LET P = 1
130 REM--LOOP FOREVER
140:: PRINT P
150:: LET P = P * 10
160: GOTO 130
170 REM--END LOOP
LIST
```

Check the program.

You will be running and changing this program throughout the session. Think about what it tells the computer to do.

1. What is the first value assigned to the variable P in program NUMBERS?
2. What two actions happen inside the loop in program NUMBERS?
3. What happens to the value of P each time around the loop in program NUMBERS?

Now let's see what the program does. **Run NUMBERS and type** CONTROL S **as soon as the screen is half full.** At the top of the output, the numbers are 1, 10, 100, and so on. Something strange appears after 100000000, though. The next line is 1E+09.

4. How many zeros are in each of the numbers before 1E+09?
5. What do you think 1E+09 means?

Type CONTROL S **to restart output. Watch the output until the computer stops.** There is a largest number the computer can store in its memory. This program shows roughly what that number is.

6. What was the last number the computer printed?

7. What do you think ?OVERFLOW ERROR IN 150 means?

Let's do this once more, but this time with numbers that are not multiples of ten.

```
150:: LET P = P * 3
LIST
```
Check the program.

```
RUN
```
Look at the output.

8. The largest number printed by the computer this time was 4.92696099E+37. What does E+37 mean?

9. How would you write the number 1,300,000,000 in E-notation?

10. About how big is the biggest number the computer can store?

Small Numbers

You have seen how the computer prints very large numbers. You have also seen the error message for a number that is too big to put into memory. Now, let's change the program and explore very small numbers.

```
150:: LET P = P / 10
LIST
```
Check the program.

The / symbol means "divided by." P is divided by 10 each time around the loop. P will get smaller and smaller. **Run NUMBERS again, but use** CONTROL S **right away to stop the output.** Notice the first three numbers: They are one, one-tenth, and one-hundredth, written with decimal points. The next number is 1E-03, which is the computer's way of writing one thousandth.

Type CONTROL S **again. This time, the output does not stop. After a while, there are nothing but zeros on the screen. Use** CONTROL C **to stop the program.** The computer uses E-notation again, but this time there are minus signs after the E's.

11. What do you think the number 1E-04 means?

12. What was the *smallest* number printed before the zeros began?

Making a Times Table

It is easy to change NUMBERS into a program that prints a multiplication table. If you want a times table for the number seven, just make these changes:

```
LIST
115 LET N = 7
140:: PRINT N; " TIMES "; P; " IS "; N * P
150:: LET P = P + 1
LIST
```
What will RUN tell the computer to do now?

```
RUN
```
Use (CONTROL S) to pause and (CONTROL C) to stop.

Make a times table for your age: Change line 115 so that N is your age. Then run the program.

Make a division table. An interesting value for N is 720720. Change N * P into N / P in line 140.

Immediate Mode Arithmetic

As you have seen, the computer can do addition, subtraction, multiplication, and division. You also know that you can enter the PRINT statement in the immediate mode, which gives you an easy way to use the computer as a calculator. Here are some examples:

```
NEW
PRINT 1001 / 13
```
The computer prints the answer immediately.

```
PRINT 3 * 4
PRINT 1 + 2 + 3 + 4 + 5
PRINT 1 * 2 * 3 * 4 * 5
PRINT 9999 - 3456
```
Here are more answers.

Pocket calculators are easier to use than the computer for this kind of problem, but once in a while it is handy to use the computer in this way. Typing PRINT each time is slow, so Applesoft BASIC gives you a substitute:

```
?100 / 4
?8 * 7
```
The question mark means the same as PRINT.

Order of Arithmetic

If you want the sum 8 + 4 + 2, it does not matter which numbers the computer adds first: Starting at the left, the computer adds 8 + 4, which is 12; it then adds 2, which is 14. But the computer would get the same answer if it started at the right: 4 + 2 is 6, and 8 + 6 is 14.

Sometimes the order matters. For example, what do you think PRINT 8 - 4 - 2 tells the computer to do? Starting at the left, the computer would do the subtraction 8 - 4, which is 4; then it would subtract 2 from 4 to get 2 for the answer. But if it started at the right, the computer would do the subtraction 4 - 2, to get 2; then it would subtract 2 from 8 to get 6. Which answer does the computer actually give? Let's see:

```
PRINT 8 - 4 - 2          Now you know.
PRINT 8 - 4 + 2          Did the computer start at the left?
PRINT 8 / 4 / 2          What order did the computer use?
PRINT 8 / 4 * 2          What was the order?
```

13. In what order did the computer perform the arithmetic operations in the last four examples?

When the computer is doing only addition and subtraction, the rule is simple. The computer uses the same rule when it is doing only multiplication and division. But suppose the computer must add or subtract *and* multiply or divide, all in the same problem. What happens then? Let's see:

```
PRINT 8 * 4 + 2
PRINT 8 * 4 - 2
PRINT 8 / 4 + 2          There are no surprises yet.

PRINT 8 + 4 * 2          This one is different.

PRINT 8 + 4 / 2
PRINT 8 - 4 * 2          These are also different.
```

14. When the computer adds and multiplies in the same program line, which operation is done first?

15. When the computer adds and divides in the same program line, which operation is done first?

You now know the rules the computer follows to decide which arithmetic operation to do first when there is more than one to do. Now you will see how you can change the rules and make the computer do things in the order *you* want:

```
PRINT 8 + 4 * 2
```
The multiplication was done first.
```
PRINT (8 + 4) * 2
```
Notice the different answer.
```
PRINT 8 + (4 * 2)
```
That gave the first answer.

Operations inside parentheses are done before operations outside. The last example shows that no harm is done when you put parentheses where they are not needed.

16. When there are several arithmetic operations in one line, how can you tell the computer to do one operation before all the others?

If you have extra lab time:

- Can the computer divide a number by zero? Find out.
- There is one more arithmetic operation in BASIC. The symbol is ∧, which is (SHIFT 6) (or (SHIFT N)) on your keyboard. Experiment with it. See what 3 ∧ 2, 4 ∧ 2, and 5 ∧ 2 are, for example. Then try 10 ∧ 1, 10 ∧ 2, 10 ∧ 3, and so on.

How Numbers Work

IN **THIS SESSION** **YOU WILL:**	• Review the form in which the computer prints numbers. • Learn the range of numbers allowed in Applesoft BASIC. • Learn the maximum length of a string in Applesoft BASIC. • Learn that the computer does not always give perfectly accurate numerical answers. • Learn the order in which the computer does arithmetic operations.

Review

In Session 40, you saw that the computer prints very big and very small numbers in an unusual way. You found that there is a largest and a smallest number that the computer can store in its memory. Finally, you discovered that the computer has rules for the order in which it performs arithmetic operations.

Big Numbers

In Session 40, you used a loop program to explore the way the computer handles large numbers. The loop program told the computer to assign 1 to P, print the value of P on the screen, multiply P by 1Ø, assign the result to P, print the new value of P on the screen, and so on.

Different notation   When you ran this program, you saw this list of numbers scroll up your screen:

```
1
1Ø
1ØØ
1ØØØ
1ØØØØ
1ØØØØØ
1ØØØØØØ
1ØØØØØØØ
1ØØØØØØØØ
1E+Ø9
1E+1Ø
1E+11
etc.
```

Each value of P was 10 times as big as the one before. When P reached the value of one billion, the computer did not print a 1 followed by nine zeros. Instead, it printed 1E+Ø9. This way of writing numbers is called **E-notation**. 1E+Ø9 means "move the decimal point 9 places to the right of the 1." Some pocket calculators also use E-notation, which is sometimes called **scientific notation**.

Biggest number When the computer finished printing $1E+38$, it printed $?OVERFLOW$ $ERROR$ IN 150 and stopped. The computer stopped because the multiplication by 10 in line 150 gave a number that was too big to assign to P. The P box in memory has limits, and numbers that do not fall within those limits will not fit in the box. When the number exceeds those limits, we say there is an **overflow**.

Little Numbers

Later in Session 40, you changed the program and had the computer divide P by 10 each time around the loop. When you ran this version of the program, the computer printed these numbers:

```
1
.1
.01
1E-03
1E-04
1E-05
etc.
```

As before, the number after the E tells where to move the decimal point; but the minus sign means "move the decimal point to the *left*." For example, $1E-03$ and 0.001 are the same number.

Smallest number After the computer printed $1E-38$, the next number that appeared on the screen was zero. The next number—$1E-39$—has too many decimal places to fit in the P box in memory. This is called an **underflow**. The computer does *not* send an error message for an underflow. Instead, it substitutes zero for this very small number.

Allowed Ranges of Data

You have seen that the computer cannot store every number. Some are too large or too small. There are also limits on strings.

Range of numbers As you saw, the computer could store numbers between $1E-38$, or

$$0.00000000000000000000000000000000000001$$

and $1E+38$, or

$$100000000000000000000000000000000000000$$

Numbers smaller or bigger than these seldom appear in real problems. For example, the distance from the earth to the sun, in feet, is $4.9E+11$; and the size of an atom, also in feet, is $3.3E-10$.

Range of strings There are also limits on string data. After all, the computer has to fit the characters of a string into its memory. Applesoft BASIC limits you to strings no longer than 255 characters. If you try to catenate two strings into one string that is too long, the computer will print ?STRING TOO LONG ERROR. Can you guess what the shortest string is? It is the empty string. It contains no characters.

Different computers Different versions of BASIC on different computers have different limits on the size of numbers and the length of strings. You should find out about these limits when you are working with a new computer.

Accuracy of Numbers

Besides the limit on the size of numbers, there is also a limit on accuracy. The computer handles some numbers, such as 1, 263, and 879432, with perfect accuracy. But the computer cannot handle others, such as 1/3, with the same accuracy.

Decimal fractions If you tell the computer to print the result of dividing 3 into 1, the computer will print

.333333333

Round-off errors This answer is not exactly correct. The computer would need to print an infinite number of 3s after the decimal point to give the correct answer. The P box in memory, of course, cannot store all those digits. So the computer rounds off to nine decimal digits. Rounded-off numbers are usually accurate enough for most problems. Once in a while, however, these tiny round-off errors can surprise you. Numbers that you think will be the same turn out to be slightly different.

The Order of Arithmetic

In Session 40, you experimented with expressions that contained several different operators. You saw that the computer does arithmetic in a certain order, and you used parentheses to control the order.

Long expressions You found that the computer can do arithmetic when there are several operators in a single expression. For example, the statements

```
PRINT 2 + 3 + 5 + 7
PRINT 2 * 3 * 5 * 7
```

are easy to understand. The first statement tells the computer to add the four numbers and print the sum. The second one tells the computer to multiply the four numbers together and print the product.

Mixing addition and subtraction You also found that you could mix plus and minus signs in an expression, such as this one:

```
PRINT 7 - 5 + 3 - 2
```

The computer starts at the *left;* computes 7 - 5 to get 2; then adds 3 to get 5; finally, it subtracts 2 and gets 3, which it prints on the screen.

Mixing multiplication and division If you enter this statement,
```
PRINT 1000 / 100 * 2 / 5
```
the computer again starts at the left; computes 1000 / 100 to get 10; then it multiplies 10 by 2 to get 20; finally, it divides 20 by 5 and gets 4, which it prints.

Mixing addition and multiplication If you enter these statements
```
PRINT 3 * 5 + 2
PRINT 2 + 3 * 5
```
the computer gives exactly the same answer. This time the computer does *not* start at the left; it does not give 17 as the first answer and 25 as the second. Instead, it performs the multiplication *before* the addition in both statements.

Using parentheses To make the computer do the additions first, you used parentheses. Here are the changed versions of the last two print statements:
```
PRINT 3 * (5 + 2)
PRINT (2 + 3) * 5
```
Now the computer will do the arithmetic inside parentheses before anything else. The first result is 21, and the second one is 25.

Order of arithmetic The computer follows a few simple rules when it performs arithmetic in long expressions. There is one main rule, which has two exceptions. The main rule is that the computer starts at the left and works its way to the right, just as you read words in a sentence. Here are the exceptions:

1. The computer multiplies and divides before it adds or subtracts.
2. The computer does the arithmetic inside parentheses before anything else.

The first line below shows a complicated example of arithmetic. Each line shows one step in finding the result, using the two rules above:

Step 1: 10 - 4 * (3 - 1) / (2 + 2) + 3

Step 2: 10 - 4 * 2 / (2 + 2) + 3

Step 3: 10 - 4 * 2 / 4 + 3

Step 4: 10 - 8 / 4 + 3

Step 5: 10 - 2 + 3

Step 6: 8 + 3

Result: 11

Extra parentheses You found in Session 40 that it was perfectly OK to put parentheses where none were needed. The computer ignored them. So, if you do not know whether you need parentheses, it is better to put extra ones in than to leave necessary ones out.

1. Write each one of these numbers in E-notation:
   a. `1000000000`   c. `50000`
   b. `125`   d. `1`

2. Convert each number below from E-notation to ordinary numbers. Use decimal points in your answers.
   a. `1E+04`   c. `9.876E+03`
   b. `1.23456E+02`   d. `3.2E+10`

3. Write each one of these numbers in E-notation:
   a. `.000000001`   c. `.00000007`
   b. `.0235`   d. `.1`

4. Write each number below as ordinary decimal numbers.
   a. `1E-04`   c. `6E-03`
   b. `1.34E-03`   d. `1E-01`

5. Why are computers unable to store numbers larger than a certain limit?

6. What range of numbers can Applesoft BASIC store in memory?

7. What range of string lengths can Applesoft BASIC store?

8. Can the computer handle the number one-third with perfect accuracy? Why not?

9. Use the computer's rules for arithmetic to find answers to all the problems below.
   a. `3 + 4 * 2`
   b. `(2 + 4) * 2 - 6`
   c. `2 + (6 + 3) / 3 * 2`
   d. `10 - 4 * (3 - 1) / (2 + 2) +3`

10. Look at the problems below. Which part of each problem will the computer perform first? Why?
   a. `8 - 4 - 2`
   b. `8 - (4 - 2)`
   c. `8 - 4 * 2`
   d. `2 + 3 * (4 - 2 * 3) + 2`

Exploring Functions

IN
THIS SESSION
YOU WILL:
• Explore the LEN, MID$, INT, SQR, and RND functions.
• Use the INT and RND functions to make random integers.
• Read programs that use random integers.

The LEN Function

You used the infinite loop to study numbers. Now you will use the loop to explore something new: **functions.** Start the computer with your diskette in the usual way. Then enter the program below.

```
100 REM--PROGRAM FUNCTIONS
110:
130 REM--LOOP FOREVER
140:: INPUT P$
145:: LET N = LEN (P$)
150:: PRINT N
160: GOTO 130
170 REM--END LOOP
```

Line 140 of this program asks the user to input a string. In line 145, LEN (P$) is an example of a BASIC function. Let's find out what that function does.

Run the program and enter each of these strings: DOG, AARDVARK, MISSISSIPPI, 5280, and Z. After each input, press the (RETURN) key and see what the computer does. See what happens when you simply press (RETURN). When you finish, use (CONTROL C) and (RETURN) to stop the program.

1. What do you think LEN (P$) tells the computer to do? Explain in your own words.
2. If A$ is "TELEVISION", what is LEN (A$)?

The MID$ Function

Let's go on to another function. Change lines 145 and 150 of program FUNCTIONS to look like this:

```
100 REM--PROGRAM FUNCTIONS
110:
130 REM--LOOP FOREVER
140:: INPUT P$
145:: LET A$ = MID$ (P$, 3, 1)
150:: PRINT A$
160: GOTO 130
170 REM--END LOOP
```

Notice that P$ appears both in the INPUT statement and as part of the MID$ function. Line 145 tells the computer to assign the value of the MID$ function to A$. **Run the program and enter the following strings: ABCDEF, **C**, CHARLIE, SKYSCRAPER, and 1234567. Remember to press** (RETURN) **after entering each string. See what the computer prints in response. Use** (CONTROL C) **and** (RETURN) **to stop the program.**

<u>145:: LET A$ = MID$ (P$, 2, 4)</u>   Make a change in line 145.

Run the program again and enter the strings TWINKLE, BLIMP, **and** PRICES. **Watch what happens in each case.**

3. What does the MID$ function do? Explain in your own words.
4. If W$ is "HOWDY", what is MID$ (W$, 2, 2)?
5. If B$ is "PARTNER", what is MID$ (B$, 1, 4)?

The INT Function

Make changes in lines 140, 145, and 150 so that program FUNCTIONS **looks like this:**

```
100 REM--PROGRAM FUNCTIONS
110:
130 REM--LOOP FOREVER
140:: INPUT A
145:: LET N = INT (A)
150:: PRINT N
160: GOTO 130
170 REM--END LOOP
```

Line 140 tells the computer to accept a number from the user. Line 145 tells it to assign to N the INT of that number. Line 150 tells the computer to print the value of N. **Run the program for each of the following inputs: 1, 2, 3, 3.5, 3.999, 4, and 53.7. Press the** (RETURN) **key after each input and see what the computer does.**

6. What does the INT function do?

Your computer should still be running the program. If not, run it again. Input each of the following values: 0, -1, -2, -2.1, -2.9, -3, -3.1, and -45.1. Press (RETURN) **after each input and see what the computer does. Use** (CONTROL C) **and** (RETURN) **to stop the program.**

7. You may wish to change your answer to question 6. How would you answer question 6 now?
8. What is the value of INT (153.21)?
9. What is the value of INT (-153.21)?

The SQR Function

Now, let's look at a new function. Change line 145 of program FUNCTIONS to look like this:

```
100 REM--PROGRAM FUNCTIONS
110:
130 REM--LOOP FOREVER
140:: INPUT A
145:: LET N = SQR (A)
150:: PRINT N
160: GOTO 130
170 REM--END LOOP
```

Let's see what the SQR function does. Run the program and enter the numbers 4, 9, 25, 49, 100, 2, and -25. Press the (RETURN) key after entering each number and see what the computer prints.

10. What the does the SQR function do?

11. What is SQR (36)?

12. What happens if the computer tries to use SQR with a negative number?

The RND Function

We will look at a very important function next. Delete line 140 and change line 145 so that program FUNCTIONS looks like this:

```
100 REM--PROGRAM FUNCTIONS
110:
130 REM--LOOP FOREVER
145:: LET N = RND (1)
150:: PRINT N
160: GOTO 130
170 REM--END LOOP
```

Notice that there is no INPUT statement this time. RND (1) is an unusual function: It produces numbers that do not depend on the number in parentheses. Run the program. Stop and restart the output several times with (CONTROL S). Each time you look at the output on the screen, think about the questions below. When you have seen enough, stop the program with (CONTROL C).

13. What was the largest number you saw on the screen?

14. What was the smallest number you saw on the screen?

15. Was there any pattern to the numbers?

Using Functions

Now that you know how these functions work, let's see how to put them to use. The RND function makes random numbers. INT turns numbers into integers. There ought to be a way to combine RND and INT to get random integers. Here it is.

`145:: LET N = 40 * RND (1)`   Multiply the RND function by 40.

Run the program. Stop and restart the output several times with CONTROL S . Look carefully at the numbers on the screen each time you stop the output. When you have seen enough, use CONTROL C to stop the program.

`145:: LET N = INT (40 * RND (1))`   Now use the INT function.

Think about what line 145 tells the computer to do. Run the program. Stop and restart the output as before. Examine the numbers produced by the program. Use CONTROL C to stop.

16. What was the largest number you saw?
17. What was the smallest number you saw?
18. What does this version of the program do? Explain in your own words.

If you have extra lab time:

- In the final version of program FUNCTIONS, you used the expression

  `INT (40 * RND (1))`

  Find similar expressions in program BOXES. Then explain how the expressions are used in BOXES.

- The RUN RACE subroutine in program LITTLE TROT uses the RND function. List the subroutine and try to understand the purpose the RND function serves in that program.

How Functions Work

IN THIS SESSION YOU WILL:
- Review the functions used in Session 42.
- Learn that a function has a name, a value, and a type.
- Understand that a function is a process.
- Learn that a function usually takes in a value and always returns a value.

The Form of Functions

Nearly all programming languages come with built-in words called *functions*. In Session 42, you explored five Applesoft BASIC functions.

Why have functions? Functions are important because they give you new ways to tell the computer to process data. You already know how to tell the computer to add, subtract, multiply, and divide numbers and to catenate strings. But without functions, it would be hard to tell the computer to take the square root of a number, to print the first character of a string, or to print the length of a string. You learned how to use functions for those jobs.

Form of a function In BASIC, all functions have the same form. When you type a function on the keyboard, you begin with its name. Then you type a left parenthesis. Then comes an expression, such as the name of a variable or a constant or combinations of variables and constants. Some functions, such as MID$, need more than one expression. Each expression is separated from the next by a comma. Finally, you type a right parenthesis. Here are examples of correctly written functions:

```
LEN ("AARDVARK")
INT (100 / 3)
SQR (49)
MID$ (W$, 1, J)
```

Parameters There is a special word for the expressions between parentheses in functions. They are called **parameters**. In the previous examples, "AARDVARK" is the parameter of the LEN function, and 49 is the parameter of the SQR function. Sometimes people use *argument* as a synonym for *parameter*.

Number of parameters In Applesoft BASIC, all functions have at least one parameter. The MID$ function has three parameters. In some versions of BASIC, there are functions with no parameters. For example, the statement

```
LET D$ = DATE$
```

would tell some computers to read today's date from its electronic calendar and assign the value as a string, such as "10/22/83", to D$.

DATE$, without any parentheses after the name, is an example of a function with no parameter. Again, there are no functions without parameters in Applesoft BASIC.

Result There is one more special term used to describe functions: **result**. The result is the value to which the function is equal. The result of SQR (49) is 7. The result of INT (100 / 3) is 33. People also say that a function "returns" its result: LEN ("AARDVARK") returns 8 as the result.

Type Like a variable or a constant, a function also has a *type:* either numeric or string. The type of a function is the same as the type of data it returns. For example, INT returns a number, so it is a *numeric* function. MID$ returns a string, so it is a *string* function. What type do you think LEN is? LEN has a string parameter, but it returns a number. The data returned is what matters, so LEN is a numeric function.

Expressions You learned in Part 5 that an expression is anything with a value. Variables, constants, and operators can be combined into expressions. Since a function also has a value, you can use a function in an expression. You may be glad to know that the list of things that can go into expressions is now complete. Here are examples of correct expressions that include functions:

```
40 * RND (1)
LEN ("SNAIL") / 2
MID$ ("RUNNER", 1, 4) + "ING"
INT (SQR (10))
```

Look over each expression above and think carefully about what it means. The last example is a function used as the parameter of another function. That expression is legal, since a parameter can be any expression, and a function is an expression. The computer first finds the square root of 10 (about 3.16) and then finds the integer part of that number (3).

Functions as Processes

Like variables, each function has a name, a type, and a value. For example, the name of the string-length function is LEN; its type is numeric; and its value is the number of characters in the string written in parentheses after LEN. But there is one big difference between functions and variables.

Variables are places Suppose you use the variable N in a program. It too has a name (N), a type (numeric), and a value (whatever is stored in the N box in the computer's memory). As you learned in Part 5, a variable is a *place* in memory. Variables get their values by assignment. For example, LET N = 10 tells the computer to put 10 in the place named N. INPUT P tells the computer to take the number entered by the user and put it in the place named P.

Functions are processes Functions are not places in memory. It would be incorrect to write LET INT (2.3) = 17. There is no place in memory named INT (2.3), so it makes no sense to try to assign 17 to it. Functions are *processes* that produce results. For example, the LEN function carries out this process: (a) count the characters in the string parameter; (b) return the number as the result.

Functions and subroutines A function behaves more like a subroutine than a variable. Each one tells the computer to carry out the steps of a process. The difference is that a function always returns a value, but a subroutine does not.

Where are the steps? You may be wondering how the computer knows the steps of the LEN function or the SQR function. Unlike the steps of a subroutine, which are just BASIC statements that *you* write, the steps of these *built-in* functions are machine-language instructions. They are stored on the same ROM chips that contain the LIST program, the RUN program, and all the other instructions that tell your computer how to perform a BASIC program.

Value-in Value-out Tables

Every function returns a value. Usually the value depends on the parameter (or parameters) that appear in parentheses after the function name. For example, SQR (9) returns the value 3 and SQR (16) returns the value 4. Think of the parameter as a value that goes in and the result as the value that comes out of the function. The function takes in one or more items of data, *processes* the data, and puts out one item of data. A very good way to find how a function works is to look carefully at what goes in and what comes out. The table on the next page should help you understand the functions you have been studying.

A function processes items in a computer's memory. An assembly line processes items in a factory.

Function	Value(s) In	Value Out
LEN	"AVERYLONGWORD"	13
	"ROCKET"	6
	"Z"	1
	" "	0
MID$	"COMPUTER", 4, 3	"PUT"
	"COMPUTER", 6, 1	"T"
	"COMPUTER", 2, 0	" "
INT	2.1	2
	2	2
	1.999	1
	1.1	1
	1	1
	0.1	0
	0	0
	-0.1	-1
	-1	-1
SQR	100	10
	64	8
	2	1.4142135
	0	0

The RND function The random-number function is not included in the value-in value-out table because the value out has little relation to the value in. This function returns numbers between 0 and .999999999 no matter what the parameter is. For all parameters greater than zero, RND returns numbers that seem to be scattered as if by chance. (Zero or negative parameters have other effects. For details, see the Applesoft manuals.)

Other functions Applesoft BASIC contains about 20 functions altogether. As you become more expert at using the computer, you will need some of them. The Applesoft manuals will tell you more about them when that time comes.

Making Random Integers

We close this session with two simulations that use functions. The RND and INT functions are used very often in programs to generate random integers. For example, you might like the integers 1 and 2 to stand for the two sides of a coin. If you want to "flip the coin" in a fair way, the computer must return these two integers at random. The random integers from the set 1, 2, 3, 4, 5, and 6 can stand for the roll of a die. In Session 42, you saw examples of random integers. Let's return for a closer look.

Heads or tails Suppose you want a computer to simulate a tossed coin by returning integers at random from the set 1 and 2. The following expression will do that.

```
INT (2 * RND (1)) + 1
```

Here is how the expression works. RND (1) returns a random number between 0 and 0.999999999. Next the computer multiplies that number by 2. The result, a number between 0 and 1.99999999, is the value in of INT. So INT returns 0 if the number is between 0 and 0.999999999 and 1 if the number is between 1 and 1.99999999. The last step is to add 1 and get either 1 or 2 as the value of the whole expression.

Dealing cards Suppose you wanted to simulate dealing cards from a deck. There are 52 cards in a deck, so you need a set of random integers from 1 to 52. This expression is just what we need:

```
INT (52 * RND (1)) + 1
```

You should be able to figure out how this works. For example, see what value comes out when RND returns 0.1; try again with 0.5. You should get 6 and 27 as the two results.

QUESTIONS

1. How is a function like a variable?
2. How is a function different from a variable?
3. Why does this statement make no sense?

```
LET LEN ("SNAILS") = 3
```

4. What is the parameter of INT (23.76)?
5. What is the result of INT (23.76)?
6. Can you use the terms *value in* and *value out* to explain how the LEN function works?
7. If A$ is "MISSISSIPPI", what is the result of MID$ (A$, 6, 2)?
8. What is the result of SQR (25)?
9. What happens if the parameter of SQR is negative?
10. What does RND (1) tell the computer to do? Explain in your own words.
11. What are the largest and smallest numbers that can come out of this expression?

```
INT (13 * RND (1)) + 1
```

A New Kind of Jump  44

IN THIS SESSION YOU WILL:
- Use an IF statement to tell the computer when to jump to another statement.
- Use the symbols =, < >, >, < =, <, and > = in IF statements.
- Use AND and OR in IF statements.

Fixed Statement Order

In Sessions 38 and 39, you learned how to use the GOTO statement to change the order in which the computer performs statements. For example, GOTO 215 tells the computer to put the line pointer at line 215 and start performing statements from there. In this session, you will learn about the IF statement. IF is similar to GOTO, except for this: GOTO always tells the computer to move the line pointer, but IF sometimes tells the computer to move the pointer and sometimes tells the computer to leave the pointer where it is.

Let's start with a very simple program. It will become part of an infinite loop soon; so let's type the colons that indent the body now. **Start the computer as usual and then enter these lines:**

```
40:: PRINT "NO ";
50:: PRINT "JUMP"
RUN
```
You should see NO JUMP printed under the RUN command.

```
30:: GOTO 50
RUN
```
Now you should see only JUMP.

```
LIST
```
Look at the program.

1. Why did the first version print NO and JUMP on one line?
2. Why did the second version print only JUMP?

Without the GOTO statement, the program did one thing. With the GOTO statement, it did another. Now let's make a change so that the program can do *both* things.

```
20:: INPUT A$
30:: IF A$ = "YES" THEN 50
LIST
```
Look this over carefully. Think about what line 30 tells the computer to do.

```
RUN
?NO
RUN
?YES
```

You should have `NO JUMP` first and `JUMP` second.

3. What do you think line `30` tells the computer to do when you enter `YES` as input to the program?
4. What do you think line `30` tells the computer to do when you enter `NO` as input to the program?

Exploring the IF Statement

You have just seen that the `IF` statement sometimes acts like a `GOTO` statement and sometimes does nothing. The explanation is in the phrase written between `IF` and `THEN`. The phrase is `A$ = "YES"`. Let's explore that phrase and some other ones. This will be much easier to do if the program is written as an infinite loop. **Change the program to look like this:**

```
10 REM--LOOP FOREVER
20::  INPUT A$
30::  IF A$ = "YES" THEN 50
40::  PRINT "NO ";
50::  PRINT "JUMP"
60: GOTO 10
70 REM--END LOOP
```

Run the program and reply to the input prompt with the following six strings, pressing (RETURN) **after each:**

```
X   Y   YE   YES   YESSIR   Z
```

When you finish, type (CONTROL C) and press (RETURN) to stop the program.

Now list the program. Retype line 30, changing the = symbol to < >. Then run the program again and enter the same input strings as before.

5. When you used the symbol =, which string or strings caused a jump?
6. When you used the symbol < >, which string or strings caused a jump?
7. What do you think the < > symbol means?

If you have not stopped the program, do so now. List it and change the < > symbol in line 30 to a > symbol. Run the program again and enter the same input strings as before.

Stop the program, list it, and change the > symbol in line 30 to a < = symbol. Run the program and enter the same input strings.

8. When you used the symbol >, which string or strings caused a jump?

9. When you used the symbol <=, which string or strings caused a jump?

10. What do you think the > symbol means when it is used with strings?

11. What do you think the <= symbol means when it is used with strings?

If you have not stopped the program, do so now. List it and change the <= symbol in line 30 to a < symbol. Run the program again and enter the same input strings as before.

Stop the program, list it, and change the < symbol in line 30 to a >= symbol. Run the program and enter the same input strings.

12. When you used the symbol <, which string or strings caused a jump?

13. When you used the symbol >=, which string or strings caused a jump?

14. What do you think the < symbol means when it is used with strings?

15. What do you think the >= symbol means when it is used with strings?

The IF Statement with Numbers

You have seen how the IF statement works with strings and the symbols =, < >, >, < =, <, and >=. Now let's see how these symbols work with numbers. Stop the program if it is still running. Then change lines 20 and 30 so the program looks like this:

```
10 REM--LOOP FOREVER
20:: INPUT N
30:: IF N = 7 THEN 50
40:: PRINT "NO ";
50:: PRINT "JUMP"
60: GOTO 10
70 REM--END LOOP
```

Run the program and reply to the input prompt with the following numbers, one at a time:

```
5  6  7  8  9
```

When you finish, type (CONTROL C) and press (RETURN) to stop the program.

Now list the program. Repeat the experiments you did before with strings, each time changing the symbol from = to < >, then to >, and so on. Enter the same five numbers each time.

16. For each of the six phrases below, which numbers that you entered caused jumps?

```
Phrase        Number Entered
N = 7         5   6   7   8   9
N <> 7        5   6   7   8   9
N > 7         5   6   7   8   9
N <= 7        5   6   7   8   9
N < 7         5   6   7   8   9
N >= 7        5   6   7   8   9
```

17. What do each of these six symbols mean when used with numbers?

More Than One Phrase

You should now have a very good idea of how the IF statement works and what those six special symbols mean. So far, the phrase in the IF statement has had only one symbol in it. Now let's look at a more complex phrase. **Stop the program if it is still running. Then change lines 20 and 30 so the program looks like this:**

```
10 REM--LOOP FOREVER
20:: INPUT N, A$
30:: IF N = 7 AND A$ = "YES" THEN 50
40:: PRINT "NO ";
50:: PRINT "JUMP"
60: GOTO 10
70 REM--END LOOP
```

Run the program and reply to the input prompt with the following number and string pairs. Press RETURN after each pair:

  7,YES   7,NO   5,YES   5,NO

When you finish all four pairs, type CONTROL C and press RETURN to stop the program.

18. Which pair or pairs caused a jump to happen?
19. What do you think AND means in line 30?

Now list the program. Change AND to OR in line 30, but leave everything else the same. Run the program and reply to the input prompt with the same four pairs as before, one pair at a time. Type CONTROL C and RETURN when you finish.

20. Which pair or pairs caused a jump to happen?
21. What do you think OR means in line 30?

If you have extra lab time:

EXPLORE

- Write a program that asks the user to enter a number and then prints the square root of the number. The program should be in the form of an infinite loop. Now use an IF statement to tell the computer to stop looping if the number entered is negative.

- Program SYMMETRY uses an IF statement to decide when to stop looping. Find this statement and explain how it works.

- Program LITTLE TROT uses an IF statement with more than one condition to make the computer decide when the race is over. Find this statement and see if you can figure out how it works. The statement you are looking for is in the RUN RACE subroutine.

Left: Old cash registers worked mechanically. *Right:* The new digital cash registers are much faster and can do many more things.

# How the IF Statement Works

- Learn how to write correct IF statements.
- Learn how the computer performs an IF statement.
- Learn how comparison operators work.
- Learn how compound conditions work.

The Power of the IF Statement

In Session 44, you explored a new feature of the computer. Until then, the computer always performed the statements in your programs in a fixed order. If they were all action statements, the computer performed them in straight-line order, starting at the top. Control statements allow you to change the order.

Jump every time If there is a GOTO statement in a program, the computer jumps to another statement. This is called an **unconditional jump**. There is no condition under which the computer will not make the jump. It always happens. So a program that contains only action and GOTO statements is very rigid: The computer always performs the statements in a fixed order.

Jump sometimes The IF statement tells the computer to make a jump, but not always. Certain **conditions** have to be met first. You explored conditions, such as A$ = "YES" and N > 7. If the condition was true, the computer made the jump. If not, the computer simply went on to the next statement after the IF statement. The IF statement in BASIC is an example of such a **conditional jump**.

Why conditional jumps? You used the GOTO statement to tell the computer to loop back to an earlier statement. You quickly found that such loops went on forever: They were infinite loops. The IF statement gives you a way to tell the computer to jump out of the loop if some condition becomes true. You also used the GOTO statement to tell the computer to skip forward over one or more statements. The IF statement gives you a way to tell the computer to skip only if some condition is true. Most of the remaining sessions in this book will show how to use the IF statement for these two purposes.

How Does the IF Statement Work?

Before you learn how to use the IF statement to solve problems, you need to know how to write IF statements correctly and to understand how they work. Most `IF` statements have this form:

    `IF condition THEN number`

The condition is composed of **comparisons**, such as `P >= 6` or `G$ = "QUIT"`. A **simple condition** contains one comparison. A **compound condition** has more than one comparison, such as `D = 5 AND P > 0`. The number after `THEN` must be the same as the line number of some statement in the program. All the `IF` statements you will see in this book tell the computer to jump forward. In other words, the line number after `THEN` is always greater than the line number of the `IF` statement itself. As you will soon see, programs written this way are easy to read and change.

The computer's rules for performing the IF statement

1. Decide whether the condition (the phrase between `IF` and `THEN`) is true.

2. If the condition is true, move the line pointer to the line with the number that appears after `THEN`. (If the condition is false, the `RUN` program moves the line pointer to the line after `IF`.)

Computer decisions   To carry out step 1, the computer uses its arithmetic and logic unit (ALU). This may come as a surprise, since making a decision does not seem very much like doing arithmetic, which is the only thing you have seen the ALU do before now. In fact, deciding whether $A > B$ is true is a kind of arithmetic. It is called **logical arithmetic**, and it is very similar to the arithmetic you already know.

A logical result   When you see the expression $A + B$, you know that the result is going to be a number. The expression $A > B$ also has a result, but it is not a number. Instead, the result can be one of only two things: either true or false. The rules of addition are wired into the circuits of the ALU; so it can calculate $53 + 32$ and get the result 85. The rules for comparing two numbers are also wired into the ALU; so it can calculate $53 > 32$ and get the result *true*. It is the true or false result that tells the computer whether or not to carry out the `IF`-statement jump.

New operators   You know that the symbols `+`, `-`, `*`, and `/` are operators. They tell the computer to perform the rules of arithmetic on the numbers to the left and right of the operator. The six symbols `=`, `<>`, `>`, `<=`, `<`, and `>=` are called **comparison operators**. They tell the computer to perform the rules of logical arithmetic on the numbers or strings to the left and right of the operator.

Comparison Operators

The condition in the IF statement is made up of one or more comparisons. A comparison is always formed by two pieces of data separated by a comparison operator. In Session 44, you used all of the six comparison operators possible in BASIC. You used them with both numbers and strings, and you found that the meanings were different in the two cases. Let's look closely at a numeric comparison.

Comparing numbers How does the computer make a comparison? Here is a typical numeric comparison:

```
X + 3 < 3 * Y
```

That expression is a mixture of arithmetic operators and a comparison operator. Which do you suppose gets done first? *The answer is that all arithmetic is done before the comparison begins.* The computer must first convert the numeric expressions on either side of the comparison operator ($<$) into numbers. In the case above, if X has the value 2 and Y has the value 4, the computer would translate the comparison to

```
5 < 12
```

The arithmetic and logic unit would judge this comparison as true. No matter how complicated the expressions in the comparison, the computer must be able to convert them into two numbers before making the comparison.

Numeric comparisons This table contains all six possible comparison operators and gives their meaning when used to compare numbers:

Comparison Operators

Operator	Meaning When Applied to Numbers
=	equal to
< >	not equal to
>	greater than
< =	less than or equal to
<	less than
> =	greater than or equal to

The terms *greater than* and *less than* refer to a number's position on the number line.

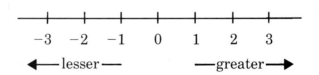

For example, 2 is greater than 1, and 2 is also greater than −3. This is true because, on the number line, 2 is to the right of 1 and also to the right of −3. Notice also that −1 is greater than −2 because −1 is "more positive" and to the right of −2.

Comparing strings A comparison using strings might look like this:

```
A$ >= W1$ + W2$
```

The computer does the catenation before it compares the strings, just as it does the arithmetic before it compares numbers. Suppose that the strings had these values: A$ = "HAMBURGER", W1$ = "HAM", and W2$ = "BONE". After catenation, the comparison would look like this:

```
"HAMBURGER" > "HAMBONE"
```

What do you suppose the symbol > means this time? As you may have guessed from your explorations in Session 44, the computer uses **dictionary order** to decide about strings. The arithmetic and logic unit judges this comparison true because HAMBURGER comes later in the dictionary than HAMBONE.

String comparisons This table contains all six possible comparison operators and gives their meaning when used to compare strings:

Comparison Operators

Operator	Meaning When Applied to Strings
=	at the same place in the dictionary
< >	not at the same place in the dictionary
>	later in the dictionary
< =	earlier or at the same place in the dictionary
<	earlier in the dictionary
> =	later or at the same place in the dictionary

Dictionary order Of course, not all strings are words in the dictionary; but the rules of dictionary order apply to nonwords. The comparison "AARRGH" > "AARDVARK" is true because AARRGH, if it were a word, would appear later in the dictionary than AARDVARK.

Other characters Strings can also contain punctuation marks, spaces, and numeric digits. You can think of all these as letters in one big alphabet: The space comes first, then most of the punctuation marks, then the digits, and finally the letters. It is legal to compare "ABC" to "123", but you cannot compare "ABC" to 123. If you compare a string to a number, the computer gives you a ?TYPE MISMATCH message. For more details, see your Applesoft manuals or do some experimenting on the computer.

Compound Conditions

In Session 44, you used the following compound condition:

```
IF N = 7 OR A$ = "YES" THEN 50
```

The condition in the `IF` statement is compound because there are two comparisons between `IF` and `THEN`. They are separated by the word `OR`. The compound condition is:

```
N = 7 OR A$ = "YES"
```

Compound with OR The whole condition above is true if either part is true. That is, if `N` is 7, or if `A$` is `YES`, or both, the condition is true. The whole condition is false only if `N` is not 7 *and* `A$` is not `YES`. In this example, there are only two comparisons in the condition, but there can be more than two. When the word `OR` is used between the parts, the whole condition is true if any one of the parts is true.

Compound with AND You also used the word `AND` between comparisons in Session 44. Here is another example:

```
A$ > B$ AND X = Y
```

The compound condition is true if *both* conditions are true. It is false if either comparison is false. A condition can have several comparisons separated by `AND`. Here is an example:

comparison 1 `AND` comparison 2 `AND` comparison 3

All the comparisons must be true for the whole condition to be true. If any one of the comparisons is false, then the condition is false.

Compound with both AND and OR Both `AND` and `OR` separate the comparisons in certain compound conditions. Here is an example:

```
A$ > B$ AND X = Y AND C > 0 OR W1$ = W2$
```

The logic of this compound condition is hard to follow, especially since there are no parentheses. There are four comparisons in the condition. Is the condition true if the first three comparisons are true *or* the last one is true? Is the condition true if the first two comparisons are true *and* either the third or fourth is true? Because of this confusion, it is best to steer clear of complicated compound conditions that use both `AND` and `OR`. If you need to use both `AND` and `OR`, be sure to use parentheses to make your meaning clear.

Condition determines outcome The important thing to keep in mind is that the `IF` statement uses a condition to determine what statement the computer performs next. It makes no difference whether the condition is simple or compound or whether numbers, strings, or both are used in the comparison. If the condition is false, the computer goes on to the next line after the `IF`. If the condition is true, the computer jumps somewhere else.

1. What is a compound condition?

2. If the condition in an `IF` statement is true, which statement will the computer do next?

3. If the condition in an `IF` statement is false, which statement will the computer do next?

4. Why is the `GOTO` statement sometimes called an *unconditional jump statement?*

5. Are the following comparisons true or false?

   ```
   a.  4 * 5 >= 16 + 2
   b.  "KIT" > "KITTYCAT"
   c.  350 >= 250
   d.  "ABACUS" < "COMPUTER"
   ```

6. Are the following conditions true or false?

   ```
   a.  4 > 2 OR "DOG" > "CAT"
   b.  3 > 4 OR 10 > 12 OR "A" > "B"
   c.  4 > 2 AND "DOG" > "CAT"
   d.  3 < 4 AND 10 < 12 AND "A" < "B"
   ```

Vocabulary Table

Words printed in color in the table were introduced in this part.

BASIC Vocabulary (Shaded Areas Show Standard BASIC Words)

Commands		Statements			Functions
Program	Diskette	Action	Action	Control	
RUN	LOAD	INPUT	SPEED=	GOSUB	INT
LIST	SAVE	LET	FLASH	RETURN	SQR
NEW	DELETE	PRINT	INVERSE	END	RND
DEL	CATALOG	REM	NORMAL	GOTO	LEN
CONT	LOCK	PLOT	COLOR=	IF	MID$
———	UNLOCK	HLIN	TEXT	———	
———		VLIN	GR	———	
———		HOME			

New BASIC Words

AND A logical operator that combines two conditions. The result is true if both conditions are true and false otherwise.

CONT A command that tells the computer to restart a program at the place it stopped.

GOTO A statement that tells the computer to move the line pointer to the line in memory with the same number as the number after the word GOTO.

IF A control statement that tells the computer to move the line pointer if the condition in the statement is true.

INT A function that returns the integer part of a number.

LEN A function that returns the number of characters in a string.

MID$ A function that returns a portion of a string.

OR A logical operator that combines two conditions. The result is true if either condition is true and false if both are false.

RND A function that returns a random number.

SQR A function that returns the square root of a number.

New Ideas

comparison operator The operators (<, >, <>, =, <=, >=) used to form a condition.

compound condition An expression with two or more conditions separated by either AND or OR. See AND and OR.

condition An expression that is either true or false. See IF.

documentation Written information used to clarify or explain a computer program.

E-notation A system of notation used to express very large and very small numbers; scientific notation.

function A process that generates a value.

jump arrow An arrow drawn to show the target of an IF or a GOTO statement.

straight-line program A program in which the computer performs the statements in line-number order.

target The line with a line number the same as the number following GOTO or after THEN in an IF statement. The target of a jump should always be a REM.

value in A value sent to a function.

value out The value returned by a function.

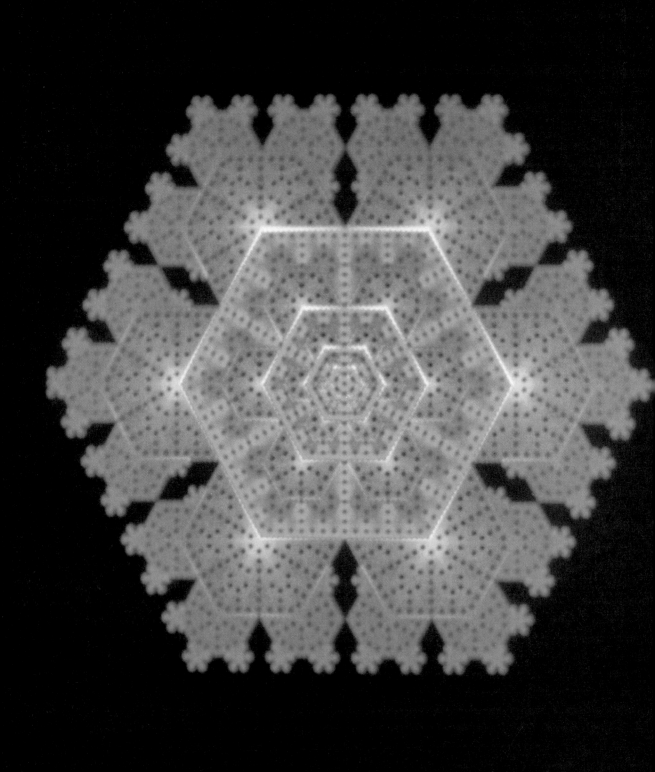

Part

Control Blocks: The Loop

You have reached a very important point in your work with the computer. *You now know all the BASIC statements needed to write any computer program.* You have seen that there are two main types: action statements and control statements.

Action statements The INPUT, LET, PRINT, and graphics statements are the main action statements in BASIC. Each one tells the computer to do something with data. Afterward, the computer *always* goes on to the next statement in the program listing.

Control statements In Part 6, you learned new statements that did nothing at all with data. Instead, the GOTO and IF statements told the computer the order in which to perform the action statements. These new statements, along with GOSUB, RETURN, and END, control the way the computer carries out the steps of a program.

Uses of control statements Control statements allow you to tell the computer to repeat a group of statements or to choose which of two groups to perform next. If there were no control statements in a programming language, it would be very hard to tell the computer to do the same thing again and again. It would be impossible to tell the computer to do either one thing or else another, depending on whether some condition were true.

Loops and branches In programming, a group of statements repeated over and over is called a *loop*. There is also a name for two groups of statements between which the computer must choose: a *branch. You can solve every programming problem by using only these two kinds of control blocks: loops and branches.*

The loop block In Part 7, you will learn a standard way to write any loop in BASIC. You will learn to use loops to solve many programming problems. You will find how to use the FOR and NEXT statements to repeat loops a certain number of times. In Part 8, you will learn about branches.

46 Programs with Loops

IN THIS SESSION YOU WILL:
- Read programs that contain loops.
- Change programs to form loops.
- Learn to indent and renumber programs.

Reading Program SYMMETRY

You can learn a lot about loops from examples. Two programs on your diskette are good examples to study.

Use the normal start-up procedure with your diskette.

```
LOAD SYMMETRY
RUN
RUN
RUN
```
Look at a few runs.
```
LIST 100, 190
```
List the main routine.

The main routine of program SYMMETRY contains a loop. This one is not an infinite loop, though. A statement in the program tells the computer when to stop looping. **Read the main routine carefully and then answer the questions below.**

1. Which statement marks the beginning of the loop?
2. Which statement marks the end of the loop?
3. Which statement tells the computer when to stop looping?
4. What does this loop tell the computer to do? Explain in your own words.

Reading Program LITTLE TROT

Program LITTLE TROT has a loop with a more complicated IF statement. Let's look at this loop next.

```
LOAD LITTLE TROT
RUN
```
Remind yourself how this program works.
```
LIST 1000, 1140
```
This is subroutine RUN RACE.

Subroutine RUN RACE contains a loop. Only one of the IF statements inside the loop tells the computer when to stop looping. **Study the list-**

ing of the subroutine carefully and then answer the questions below:

5. What is the first line of the loop?
6. What is the last line of the loop?
7. What statement tells the computer when to stop the loop?
8. When is the race over? (Hint: FL stands for the "finish line"; X1 and X2 tell where the two turtles are.)

Changing Program ROCKET

You have studied two examples of loops. Now make a loop of your own. Start with program ROCKET, which has no loop. You will add one to it.

```
HOME
LOAD ROCKET
RUN
```
That should be familiar.
```
LIST
```
Look at the program.

Here is the program you should have on your screen:

```
100 REM--PROGRAM ROCKET
110 HOME
120 PRINT "        ^"
130 PRINT "       # #"
140 PRINT "      #   #"
150 PRINT "      # M #"
160 PRINT "      # O #"
170 PRINT "      # O #"
180 PRINT "      # N #"
190 PRINT "      #   #"
200 PRINT "      # R #"
210 PRINT "      # A #"
220 PRINT "      # K #"
230 PRINT "      # E #"
240 PRINT "      # R #"
250 PRINT "     #       #"
260 PRINT "    #         #"
270 PRINT "   #  #####   #"
280 PRINT "#  #         # #"
290 PRINT "#  #           #"
```

When you ran this program, the computer drew a picture of the rocket on the screen. Let's make some changes.

```
105 REM--LOOP
300 GOTO 105
310 REM--END LOOP
LIST
```
Examine the new program.
```
RUN
```
Again and again, the computer erases the screen and draws the rocket.
```
CONTROL C
```
Stop the program.

The program contains an infinite loop. The only way to stop it is with CONTROL C . Let's give the computer another way out of the loop.

```
106 PRINT "WANT A ROCKET"
107 INPUT A$
108 IF A$ = "NO" THEN 310
LIST 100, 200
```
Look at the changes.

```
RUN
```
Answer the question.

```
?YES
?YES
?NO
```
That stopped the loop.

This version of program ROCKET kept drawing rockets until your answer was NO. The expression A$ = "NO" is the **exit condition** in this loop.

9. What statement in the new version of program ROCKET tells the computer when to stop the loop?
10. How does the new loop work?

Writing Tools

You know that indents help you write clear programs. The loops in SYMMETRY and LITTLE TROT are indented to make them easy to read. Program ROCKET works correctly with the loop added, but the loop is not indented. You could enter each statement again and give each line the correct indent, but that job would be very long and boring. Instead, learn to use a new tool on your diskette.

```
SAVE NEW ROCKET
```
Save the program for now under the name NEW ROCKET.

```
BRUN WRITING TOOLS
```
Don't forget the B before RUN.

WRITING TOOLS is on your diskette. It contains **machine-language programs** that tell the computer how to indent BASIC program lines and renumber them. To put these tools into the computer memory, you must use the BRUN command. (The B in BRUN comes from **binary**: These machine-language programs are stored in binary code on your diskette.)

```
LOAD NEW ROCKET
```
Bring your program back into the computer.

```
LIST
```
List it.

```
&INDENT
```
Be sure to type the &. It is the same as SHIFT 7 (or SHIFT 6 on older Apples).

```
LIST
```
Notice that all lines are indented two spaces.

```
&INDENT BY 4
LIST
```
Now they are indented four *more* spaces.

```
&UNDENT BY 6
```
&UNDENT undoes &INDENT.

All indents should be gone now. &INDENT and &UNDENT tell the computer to add or subtract *two* colons for indents. You can change the spacing by adding BY and the number of colons you want.

Like LIST and DEL, these new commands let you specify a range of lines. Here is how to indent only the lines inside the loop:

```
&INDENT 106,300
LIST
```
A block of lines have been moved right.

As a final improvement, let's "undent" the IF and GOTO statements by one space:

```
&UNDENT 108 BY 1
&UNDENT 300 BY 1
LIST
```
Lines 108 and 300 have been moved left.

The program is indented properly now. The loop in NEW ROCKET has the same form as the loops you saw in SYMMETRY and LITTLE TROT.

You can use your new writing tools to fix another problem. Suppose you wanted to insert a statement between the INPUT and the IF statements in your program. Right now, there is no way to do that; the INPUT statement is in line 107 and the IF statement is in line 108. You need a way to change the line numbers and "make room" for new statements. You can do this with a single command.

```
&RENUMBER
LIST
```
That did it.

Here is how your indented, renumbered program should look:

```
100 REM--PROGRAM ROCKET
110 REM--LOOP
120:: PRINT "WANT A ROCKET"
130:: INPUT A$
140: IF A$ = "NO" THEN 350
150:: HOME
160:: PRINT "        ^"
170:: PRINT "       # #"
180:: PRINT "      #   #"
190:: PRINT "      # M #"
200:: PRINT "      # O #"
210:: PRINT "      # O #"
220:: PRINT "      # N #"
230:: PRINT "      #   #"
240:: PRINT "      # R #"
250:: PRINT "      # A #"
260:: PRINT "      # K #"
270:: PRINT "      # E #"
280:: PRINT "      # R #"
290:: PRINT "     #     #"
300:: PRINT "    #       #"
310:: PRINT "  # ##### #"
320:: PRINT "# #       # #"
330:: PRINT "#           #"
340: GOTO 110
350 REM--END LOOP
```

The program was renumbered from top to bottom by 10s. Note that the line numbers after GOTO and THEN have also been renumbered properly. The targets of the GOTO and IF statements are still the correct REM statements.

You can also use &RENUMBER with a range of line numbers if you want to renumber only a part of a program. If you want the line numbers to increase by a number other than 10, you can add the word BY and the number you want.

11. What command did you use to put writing tools (indent and renumber) into the computer memory?

12. What will the command &INDENT 200, 300 BY 4 do?

If you have extra lab time:

EXPLORE

- Find out what happens to your new version of program ROCKET when you enter the following commands:

```
&RENUMBER BY 2
&RENUMBER AT 400
&RENUMBER AT 200 BY 5
&RENUMBER 200, 220 AT 100 BY 1
```

■ Find out what happens to your new version of program ROCKET when you enter the following commands:

```
&INDENT BY 10
&UNDENT BY 100
```

You may delete NEW ROCKET from your diskette now. You will not be needing it again.

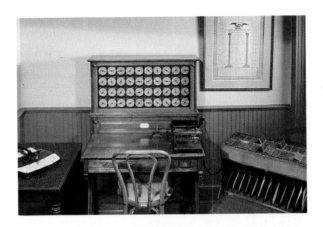

Computers have changed greatly over the years. *Left:* An early computer used by the government for the census. *Below:* A modern mainframe computer.

Structure of the Loop Block

IN THIS SESSION YOU WILL:
- Review indenting and renumbering program lines.
- Learn the structure of the loop block.
- Use loop-block structures to describe everyday events.
- See that the LIST program contains a loop block.
- Plan a programming project using loops.

Writing Tools

In Session 46, you saw that the command BRUN WRITING TOOLS put some new machine-language programs into the computer memory. Like LIST and RUN, these new programs tell the computer to do something to the BASIC program in memory. After you load the new machine-language programs into memory, you can use the commands &INDENT, &UNDENT, and &RENUMBER to change the indentions and line numbers of a BASIC program.

System programs in RAM You may wonder where these new programs go inside the computer. They are stored in a part of the random-access memory (RAM). Your BASIC programs are also stored in RAM, but in a different part. The command BRUN WRITING TOOLS tells the computer to do two things: to load the new machine-language programs into memory and to keep BASIC statements out of that part of memory. These machine-language programs stay there until you turn off the power or type PR#6. Here are some examples of ways you can use the new commands.

&INDENT 500, 560 BY 6 This is the most general form of the indent command. It tells the computer to indent statements in lines 500 through 560 by six spaces. The computer puts colons in the indented spaces because Applesoft BASIC does not allow spaces for indentions. The computer adds the new indentions to any already there.

&INDENT 500, 560 If you leave out the BY phrase, the command tells the computer to indent two spaces.

&INDENT 350 BY 4 You can indent single lines. This command tells the computer to indent line 350 four spaces.

&INDENT BY 6 If you do not give a line-number range in the command, the computer indents the entire program. This command tells the computer to indent every line six spaces.

Removing indention You can remove indentions with the &UNDENT command. Everything works exactly the same as with &INDENT except that colons are removed.

&RENUMBER This command tells the computer to renumber all the lines in the program. The first line keeps its original line number. Each line number after that is 10 greater than the one before. All target line numbers in GOSUB, GOTO, and IF statements are also renumbered properly.

&RENUMBER BY 5 This command tells the computer to renumber all lines. The first line keeps its original number, and each line number after that is 5 greater than the one before, not 10.

&RENUMBER 300, 390 BY 5 You can put a line-number range in the command to renumber portions of a program. This command tells the computer to renumber by 5 only the lines in the range 300 to 390. The first line number in the range stays the same.

&RENUMBER 300, 390 AT 800 BY 5 This command also renumbers lines 300 through 390 by a difference of 5, but line 300 becomes line 800. You can use this command to move a block of statements from one part of a program to another.

The Loop-Block Outline

In Session 46, you explored the way loops are used in programs. You saw that in some programs loops are a key part of the program structure, and you added loops to other programs.

Program SYMMETRY You found that an IF statement in this program told the computer to stop looping when the X and Y coordinates of a point were equal.

Program LITTLE TROT You studied the loop in subroutine RUN RACE and saw how it worked. You found that an IF statement told the computer to stop looping when either turtle crossed the finish line.

Program ROCKET You converted program ROCKET into an infinite loop that flashed the rocket again and again. Then you added an IF statement that told the computer when to stop looping.

The infinite-loop outline In Session 39, you saw the outline of the infinite loop. It looked like this:

```
___   REM--LOOP FOREVER
___
___      do something
___
___   GOTO ___
___   REM--END LOOP
```

The blanks stand for line numbers, and the jump arrow shows how the line pointer moves in response to the GOTO jump. Notice that the block begins and ends with REM statements. The first REM is the target of the jump. The phrase *do something* stands for one or more BASIC statements, which the computer will perform again and again. They can be any statements except for `IF` and `GOTO` jumps outside the loop, which would stop the loop.

The conditional-loop outline A loop that tells the computer to repeat statements until some condition becomes true is called a **conditional loop**, or simply a **loop**. Here is the outline for such a loop.

```
___   REM--LOOP
___
___       do something
___
___     IF  exit condition  THEN ___
___
___       do something
___
___     GOTO ___
___   REM--END LOOP
```

The exit condition in the `IF` statement tells the computer when to stop looping and jump to the second `REM` statement. Here is how the loop works:

The computer's rules for performing a loop block

1. Perform the first "do something."
2. Test the exit condition to see whether it is true or false. If true, stop looping and move the line pointer to the `REM--END LOOP` statement.
3. If the exit condition is false, perform the second "do something."
4. Move the line pointer back to the first `REM--LOOP` statement, and start over with step 1.

The loop works this way only if it is correctly written. There is nothing magical about the phrases `LOOP` and `END LOOP` in the `REM` statements. They are there to help the reader, but the computer ignores them. Steps 2 and 4 work correctly only if the numbers after `THEN` and `GOTO` match the line numbers of the two `REM` statements in the outline. It is up to you to get the numbers right.

Two "do somethings" There is one important difference between the two "do something" blocks in a loop: The computer must perform the first one at least once, but it may never get to the second one at all. This happens if the exit condition is true at the start.

A missing "do something" In some loop blocks, one or the other "do something" block may be absent. In other words, the IF statement may be the first statement inside the loop, or it may be the last except for the GOTO. You will see examples later.

Why Loops?

You may be wondering why you are spending so much time on the loop block. After all, how many loop problems can there be? You will probably be surprised to find out how often loops occur. This is true in everyday situations as well as in programming problems.

The boiling-water loop Think of the following directions from a cookbook: "Bring the water to a boil." That may not sound like a loop, but it is. Here is how to write directions to tell a very dumb assistant to boil a pot of water. The directions are written partly in English and partly in BASIC.

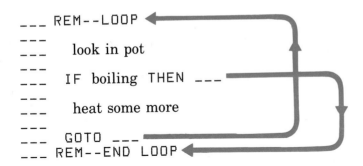

```
___  REM--LOOP
___
___      look in pot
___
___      IF boiling THEN ___
___
___      heat some more
___
___      GOTO ___
___  REM--END LOOP
```

The seasoning loop The same cookbook says to "add salt to taste" when you season a stew. That may not sound like a loop, but it is. Here is how to tell the helper to do the job.

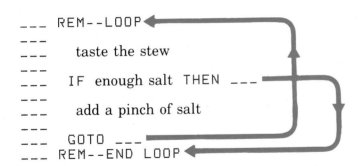

```
___  REM--LOOP
___
___      taste the stew
___
___      IF enough salt THEN ___
___
___      add a pinch of salt
___
___      GOTO ___
___  REM--END LOOP
```

The LIST Program Loop

In case you think these examples have nothing to do with computers, look at a programming example. Recall that the L I S T program looked like this in ordinary English:

The LIST Program

1. Move the line pointer to the first line of the BASIC program in the memory unit.

2. Repeat the following steps as long as the line pointer is pointing at a BASIC line:

   2a. Read the current line, and write it on the output screen.

   2b. Move the pointer to the next line of the program in the memory unit.

Structure of the LIST program The phrase "repeat the following steps" is a clue that the L I S T program in your computer contains a loop. Here is another way to outline the whole L I S T program.

```
___   move pointer to first BASIC line
___
___   REM--LOOP
___      IF not pointing at line THEN ___
___
___      read the current line
___      write it on the output screen
___      move pointer to next line
___
___      GOTO ___
___   REM--END LOOP
```

Step 1 of the L I S T program is a simple action. Step 2 is a loop. (The R U N program contains a similar loop.) These built-in programs (L I S T and R U N) are written in *machine language,* not BASIC, so you cannot list them on your screen and look at them. But if you could, you would find instructions for performing loops. *Every programming language allows you to write loops.*

Planning Programs That Use Loops

Try out what you have learned about loops. You will get the main routines for two programs, along with an explanation of what each of the subroutines is to do. Your job is to select one of the programs and write the subroutines to go with the main routine. **Be prepared to enter your program into the computer in Session 48.**

Problem 1: Reversing Words

If a friend gave you a list of words, one word at a time, you would know how to give the words back in the opposite order. (Putting lists of words or numbers in different orders is often a necessary part of solving problems on the computer.) Your job is to tell the computer how to reverse any list of words that your friend enters into the computer.

Some examples Let's suppose your friend enters the words CRACK and POTS. The computer should print POTS CRACK. Suppose the words are SHARKS, EAT, and PEOPLE. The computer should print PEOPLE EAT SHARKS.

The main routine The computer has three main jobs. The first is to get words from the user. The second is to reverse their order. The third is to print the reversed words. You will see that the first two jobs can be combined easily so that the computer adds words to the beginning of the string to be printed as each new word comes in. Here is the main routine:

```
100 REM--REVERSE WORDS
110:: GOSUB 200: REM--GET AND REVERSE
120:: GOSUB 400: REM--OUTPUT
130 END
```

Choosing variables The first subroutine will have to ask for input, one word at a time. Let's use W$ as the name of the variable that stands for each word the user gives. The second subroutine must print a string made up of the words in reversed order. Let's call that particular string R$.

Reversing order The idea here is to build up R$ one word at a time, putting each new word at the beginning. For example, suppose the word SHARKS has already been entered and that R$ is now equal to SHARKS. Next comes EAT, which is assigned to W$. This statement gives R$ the new value EAT SHARKS:

```
LET R$ = W$ + " " + R$
```

Repeating this statement with each new word will do the job. A loop is the answer. R$ must be set equal to the null string " " before the loop starts.

How many words? Of course, your friend has to have some way to tell the computer that there are no more words. One way to do this is to mark the end of the list with a **flag**, a word that will never be part of the data. For example, you could both agree that QUIT is the flag. The loop should stop as soon as W$ equals QUIT.

What to do Write the two subroutines needed to complete this program. Check them as carefully as you can and be prepared to enter the complete program into the computer in Session 48.

Problem 2: Finding an Average

What is the average age of the people in your family? To find out, you must add all the ages and then divide that sum by the number of people. Let's see how to tell the computer to do the work for you.

An example Suppose you enter the numbers 12, 16, 31, and 33. The computer must add the numbers, getting 92. The computer must also count the numbers as they are entered, getting 4. Then it must divide 92 by 4 and get the average, 23.

The main routine The computer has five main jobs. The first is to get the numbers from the user. The second is to find the sum. The third is to count the numbers. The fourth is to divide the sum by the count. The last is to print the result. You will see that the first three jobs can be combined easily, so that as each new number comes in, the computer adds it to the sum so far and adds 1 to a counter. The last two jobs can also be combined. Here is the main routine:

```
100 REM--PROGRAM AVERAGE
110:: GOSUB 200: REM--SUM AND COUNT
120:: GOSUB 400: REM--OUTPUT AVERAGE
140 END
```

Choosing variables The first subroutine must tell the computer to ask for input, one number at a time. Let's use N as the name of the variable that stands for each number the user gives. The program must also tell the computer to add the numbers and to count them. Let's call the sum S and the count C.

Summing and counting The idea here is to build up the sum S and the count C as each new number N is entered. These statements will build up the sum and keep track of the count:

```
LET S = S + N
LET C = C + 1
```

Repeating these statements with each new number N will do the job. A loop is the answer. Before the loop starts, S and C have to be set to 0.

How many numbers? Of course, you have to tell the computer that there are no more numbers. One way to do that is to mark the end of the list with a flag number that will never be part of the data. For example, you could use -999 as the flag. The loop should stop as soon as N is -999.

Output the average The average is the sum divided by the count, or S / C. The computer needs to calculate the average after the loop ends. Finally, it needs to print the result.

What to do Write the two subroutines needed to complete this program. Check them carefully and be prepared to enter the complete program into the computer in Session 48.

QUESTIONS

1. What must you do before you can use the tools for indention and renumbering?
2. What does &INDENT 200, 400 BY 4 mean?
3. What does &UNDENT 480 BY 1 mean?
4. What does &RENUMBER 600, 800 BY 20 mean?
5. What statement should be at the beginning and end of a loop block?
6. What statement in a loop block tells the computer when to stop looping?
7. What is the main difference between the two "do something" blocks in a loop?
8. A recipe says "beat the egg whites until they are stiff." How would you write these instructions in the form of a loop block?
9. Think of an everyday event and write a description of it in the form of a loop-block outline.
10. What is the exit condition from the LIST program loop?
11. What "do something" does the computer do if the exit condition in the LIST program loop is false?

Programming Project: Loops

**IN • Enter the program planned in Session 47.
THIS SESSION • Debug the program.
YOU WILL:**

Program REVERSE

If you planned program REVERSE in Session 47, enter it now. Test your program on the following set of data:

    SHARKS   EAT   PEOPLE   QUIT

Enter each word and press (RETURN). If your program is correct, you should see PEOPLE EAT SHARKS printed on your screen. If the computer does not print that, debug your program. A good debugging rule is to use simple test data for which you know the answer. Try these data:

(1) QUIT

(2) BUG   QUIT

Except for the flag QUIT, you enter no words the first time, so nothing should be printed. You enter only one word the second time, so you should see that word printed on the screen.

Program AVERAGE

If you planned program AVERAGE in Session 47, enter it now. Test your program on the following set of data:

    12   16   31   33

The correct average for this set is 23. If you don't get that number, debug your program. A good debugging rule is to use simple test data for which you know the answer. Try these data:

(1) 1   -999

(2) 5   5   5   -999

Remember, the average of one number is itself. Also the average of three 5s is 5.

If you have extra lab time:

■ Session 47 gave two programming projects, and you chose one. If you have time, work on the other project now.

In industry, computers are used to monitor factory operations. This man is looking at a panel of indicators showing what is happening in a paper mill.

 # Flowgraphs and Counting Loops

IN	• Learn the flowgraph description of a loop block.
THIS SESSION	• Learn how to write a counting loop.
YOU WILL:	• Plan a graphics program using a counting loop.

The Loop Block

You have learned that the loop block gives you a way to tell the computer to perform some action again and again. It tells the computer to do something over and over until the exit condition from the loop becomes true.

BASIC loop outline In Session 47, you learned the BASIC loop outline. This outline uses a mixture of English and BASIC to describe the structure of the loop block. Here it is again:

```
___   REM--LOOP
___
___       do something
___
___     IF  exit condition  THEN ___
___
___       do something
___
___     GOTO ___
___   REM--END LOOP
```

Control statements The BASIC loop block contains two control statements: The `IF` statement tells the computer when to exit from the loop. The `GOTO` statement tells the computer to keep looping.

Jump arrows As you have seen, the jump arrows in the loop block show the targets of the `IF` and `GOTO` statements. In the loop-block outline, the targets are `REM` statements that explain the purpose of the jumps.

The Loop Flowgraph

Another way to show the structure of the loop block, as well as other blocks you will study, is a **flowgraph**, built out of boxes and arrows. On the next page is the flowgraph for the loop block.

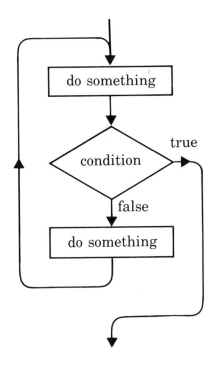

Reading a flowgraph You read a flowgraph by following the arrows, beginning at the top. The flow arrow comes first to the top "do something" and then the condition. (Remember, "do something" stands for one or more BASIC statements, and "condition" stands for an expression such as W$ = QUIT or N = -999.) If the condition is false, the arrow goes to the second "do something" and then back to the top of the loop. When the condition is true, the arrow goes out the side and to the bottom of the diagram.

Flowgraph arrows There are three different symbols in the flowgraph: arrows, rectangular boxes, and a diamond-shaped box. The arrows show the order in which the computer performs the boxes.

Flowgraph rectangles Rectangular boxes enclose "do somethings." "Do something" usually stands for one or more action statements, such as INPUT, LET, and PRINT. But it can also stand for a whole program block, such as another loop block. Or the box can stand for no statements at all.

Flowgraph diamonds A diamond-shaped box always stands for an IF statement. The computer tests the condition in the diamond to see whether it is true or false. This is sometimes called a **decision box**.

Identical ideas The loop flowgraph shows exactly the same structure as the loop outline. Both the flowgraph and the outline have advantages. The flowgraph gives a better picture of the order in which the parts get done. The outline, however, is more like the actual lines of a BASIC program.

The Abbreviated Loop Block

Sometimes one of the "do somethings" in the loop block is missing. Such a loop block is called an **abbreviated loop block**. Here is a loop block with the first "do something" missing:

```
___   REM--LOOP
___      IF exit condition THEN ___
___
___      do something
___
___      GOTO ___
___   REM--END LOOP
```

A counting loop   A counting loop is an example of an abbreviated loop block. Usually, the purpose of a counting loop is to perform some action (to "do something") a fixed number of times. The counting loop needs one statement before the loop block. That statement sets a counting variable to its first value. Here is the counting-loop outline:

```
___   LET C = first value
___   REM--LOOP
___      IF C > last value THEN ___
___
___      do something
___
___      LET C = C + 1
___      GOTO ___
___   REM--END LOOP
```

A counting-loop example   Let's see how to use the counting loop to tell the computer to print the numbers from 50 to 100. In the outline, "first value" stands for 50, "last value" stands for 100, and "do something" stands for PRINT C. Here is the outline for this example:

```
___   LET C = 50
___   REM--LOOP
___      IF C > 100 THEN ___
___      PRINT C
___      LET C = C + 1
___      GOTO ___
___   REM--END LOOP
```

How the counting loop works   The first line in the outline says to assign 50 to C. Inside the loop, the IF statement tests C to see if it is already greater than 1ØØ. It is not, so the computer performs the PRINT statement, and 5Ø appears on the screen. Then the LET statement adds 1 to C and assigns the sum, 51, to C. Finally, the GOTO statement sends the line pointer back to the beginning of the loop. Each time around the loop, the computer tests the condition in the IF statement to see if C has become greater than 1ØØ. Sooner or later, the condition becomes true and the loop stops. Until that happens, the PRINT statement prints each successive number through 1ØØ.

Flowgraph of a Counting Loop

You have seen how to draw the flowgraph of a loop. Let's use a flowgraph to describe a slightly different counting loop:

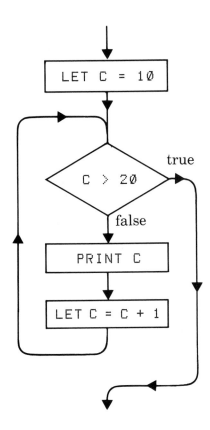

Action plus loop Notice that this flowgraph starts with the simple action of assigning 1Ø to C. In other words, 1Ø is the first value of the loop variable C. The rest of the flowgraph is a loop. The loop tells the computer to test C to see whether it is bigger than 2Ø, the last value, and if so, to stop looping. If not, the loop tells the computer to print the value of C on the screen, then add 1 to C, and then loop back to the test.

A Counting-Loop Project

Program BOXES on your diskette draws the borders of randomly located rectangles. Your next programming assignment is closely related to BOXES. **Be ready to enter your complete program in Session 50.**

Draw solid rectangles   Your problem is to write a program to draw solid rectangles on the screen. The computer should ask the user to enter the left, right, top, and bottom coordinates of the rectangle. (Recall that the left edge of the graphics screen is 0, the right edge is 39, the top is 0 and the bottom is 39.) Then the computer should pick a color at random and draw a solid rectangle in that color.

Outline of main routine   Here is an outline of the main routine, partly in BASIC and partly in English:

```
100 REM--PROGRAM SOLIDS
110:: set graphics mode
120:: REM--LOOP
130:::: ask if user wants a rectangle
140::: IF answer is "NO" THEN 180
150:::: ask for borders of rectangle
160:::: draw solid rectangle in random color
170::: GOTO 120
180:: REM--END LOOP
190:: set text mode and clear screen
200 END
```

Finish main routine   Notice that the body of the main routine contains a loop block in lines 120 through 180. Your first job is to convert the outline into BASIC. Most of the English descriptions of actions should be replaced with GOSUBs.

Counting loop   The next big job is to plan the subroutine to draw the solid rectangle. Picking one of 16 colors at random requires using the INT and RND functions. If your memory needs refreshing, read Session 43 again. One way to draw a solid rectangle is to use HLIN (or VLIN) again and again, inside a counting loop. Recall that the statement

```
HLIN L, R AT Y
```

tells the computer to draw a horizontal line from L (the left coordinate) to R (the right coordinate) at Y (the vertical coordinate). Your loop should use Y as the counter variable and should count from the top of the rectangle to the bottom. The "do something" in the loop should be the HLIN statement. For each new value of Y, the computer will draw another horizontal line from L to R.

Plan subroutines   Now start work on the subroutines you will need. You may want to look at program BOXES on your diskette for ideas.

1. What does the diamond-shaped box stand for in a flowgraph?
2. What does the rectangular box stand for in a flowgraph?
3. What do the flow arrows stand for in a flowgraph?
4. Why is a counting loop an abbreviated loop?
5. Suppose the first value of the variable C in a counting loop is 1, the last value is 10, and the "do something" is the statement PRINT C. What does this program tell the computer to do?
6. What line of the counting loop outline would you change if you wanted it to count by 2s instead of 1s?
7. What does a counting loop tell the computer to do if the first value is greater than the last value?
8. Suppose a computer runs the program shown in the flowgraph on page 281. What numbers will the computer print on the screen?
9. What is the value of C after the exit from the counting loop shown in the flowgraph on page 281?

50 Programming Project: Graphics

IN • Enter the program planned in Session 49.
THIS SESSION • Debug the program.
YOU WILL:

Computer Work

Enter the program you started planning in Session 49. Debug the program and make sure it is working properly.

Here are some bugs to watch out for in this program:

1. Did you set graphics mode in the main routine?
2. Does the counting loop start from the top and go to the bottom of the rectangle? (Or, if you are using VLIN, does it go from left to right?)
3. Did you remember to add 1 to the counting variable inside the counting loop?
4. Are you using the counting variable after AT in the HLIN (or VLIN) statement?
5. Does the user know that the number for the top of the rectangle has to be smaller than the number for the bottom?

If you have extra lab time:

- Change the subroutine that asks the user for the edges of the rectangle into a subroutine that picks the edges at random, as in program BOXES.
- Next, change the main routine into an infinite loop.

284   Control Blocks: The Loop / 50 • Programming Project: Graphics

What Computers Do Well

- • Recognize that computers are good at repetition, arithmetic, logic, data handling, and speed.
- • Recognize that computers are poor at seeing patterns, using judgment, handling incomplete information, and adapting to new situations.
- • Learn ways that computers can be misused and overused.
- • Learn what artificial intelligence is.

Easy Things to Do

The computer is a tool. Like any tool, it is good for some jobs and bad for others. It is important to recognize both the strengths and the weaknesses of the computer. Here are the main things the computer can do well.

Repetition In the past several sessions, you have learned that it is extremely easy to tell the computer to repeat a group of statements again and again. In fact, once you have written the group of statements, you only have to add a `GOTO` statement at the bottom to create an infinite loop. Loops are easy to create in all computer languages. Any task that needs to be done again and again is usually easy to do on a computer.

Arithmetic As you have seen, the computer is good at doing accurate arithmetic. It can add, subtract, multiply, and divide. It does not make mistakes (unless the numbers are too big or too small).

Logical decisions Your work with the `IF` statement showed you that the computer can tell whether certain conditions are true or not. You will see a lot more of this in Part 8. No matter how complex these conditions are, the computer will discover whether the condition is true or false.

Storing quantities of data A computer can output vast amounts of data to an on-line data base. It can later input data from the data base. The computer almost never loses or destroys data.

Speed Computers do all the above tasks at amazing speeds. Small computers can do thousands of arithmetic operations in a second. Large machines may be a thousand times faster than that.

Hard Things to Do

You have learned the main things that computers are good at doing. Fortunately, there are vast numbers of problems that call for these abilities. But there are many other problems that computers cannot easily solve. Here are some examples.

Seeing patterns People are very good at finding patterns in things. For example, you can probably figure what the next thing in each series below should be:

1, 2, 4, 8, 16,...
M, T, W, T, F,...
31, 28, 31, 30, 31,...

Think how hard it would be to write a program to tell the computer how to find a pattern in a series of five numbers or letters.

Exercising judgment When you walk up to an intersection with a stop light, there is usually a light that says WALK or DON'T WALK. You pay attention to the signal, but you also judge for yourself whether it makes sense to obey it. If there is a car about to cross your path, you do not walk into the street, no matter what the signal says. Nor do you stop walking if you happen to be in the middle of the street when the signal switches to DON'T WALK. You use your own judgment to decide what to do. The computer, on the other hand, does *exactly* what it is told. If there are special conditions, the programmer has to know what they all are and tell the computer exactly how to handle each one. The computer will not make judgments of its own.

Although computers can help, this air traffic controller must make the vital decisions that only a person can make.

Handling incomplete information People are very good at accepting incomplete directions. They fill in the details in some reasonable way. If someone asks you to "go to the store and get some bread," you will usually know what to do. There are many missing details in those directions, though: Which store? What kind of bread? How much bread? You work out reasonable answers to these questions and act accordingly. But a computer needs to be given complete and clear instructions.

Adaptation No matter what rules you know, you can adapt them to new situations. If a recipe for a cake calls for two cups of milk and you have only one cup, you might substitute a cup of water, even though the recipe has no instructions about substitutions. But a computer does only what it is told. It cannot handle a new situation unless it is told how to recognize the situation and what to do if it happens.

Dangers in Computer Use

The computer is a new and powerful tool. People are discovering one new application after another. Naturally, excitement about computers is very high. At the same time, it is a good idea to guard against misuse and overuse of computers.

Deliberate misuse Some people believe any results that come out of a computer, as though the computer had knowledge of its own. Yet a horoscope printed by computer is no more accurate than the one in the newspaper. Computers only run programs. A bad program usually gives bad results. It is a misuse of the computer to claim that the results are true or better just because they come out of a computer.

Bad judgment Just because a job can be done on a computer does not mean that the computer is the best tool for the job. When people first learn to use a computer, they may be tempted to try to apply it to everything. Many people, for example, write a program to help them balance their checkbooks each month. This job is much easier to do with a simple pocket calculator.

Overuse We may become so busy exploring the things computers are good at that we simply ignore all problems which are not "computable." We cannot compute tastes, smells, or emotions; but if we ignore all such things, our lives will be very empty. Writing a program for a computer is a rewarding experience, but so is writing a letter to a friend, learning a piece of music, or walking through the woods.

Artificial Intelligence

If you look over the list of things that computers do poorly, you will see that they are all things that people do fairly well. It takes intelligence to see a pattern, use judgment, handle incomplete information, and adapt to new situations. If intelligence could be written into a computer program, perhaps a computer could do some of the things people do well.

Computers control the behavior of robots.

A new subject Many people have tried to create **artificial intelligence** in computer programs. Examples include programs that play chess as well as experts, programs that ask patients questions and diagnose their illnesses, programs that find error patterns in students' answers to arithmetic problems, programs that understand simple English sentences, and programs that recognize simple shapes in TV pictures.

Intelligence in the program   The computers in all these applications are just like the one you are using, although usually a lot bigger and faster. The computer itself has no built-in intelligence. All the knowledge about chess, medicine, arithmetic errors, and English must be written into the programs by people who understand the subjects. Because the computer lacks intelligence, these programs are always very long, complex, and hard to write.

The future   It is still too early to tell whether many practical applications of artificial intelligence will be created. Some people would like to "talk" to their computers in English sentences; they would like to give incomplete instructions and get reasonable results. On the other hand, there are advantages in working with computer languages that force you to say exactly what you mean and leave nothing to chance.

QUESTIONS

1. What are three things that computers do well?
2. What makes it easy, in BASIC, to tell the computer to repeat steps again and again?
3. What are three things that computers do poorly?
4. What information do you have to know to decide what comes after M, T, W, T, F?
5. If the computer had to make the decision in question 4, where would the computer get the information it needs?
6. What are two dangers in using computers?
7. What is an example of something important to you that is not "computable"?
8. What is artificial intelligence?

FOR/NEXT Loop Abbreviations  52

IN	• Use FOR and NEXT statements to rewrite a counting loop.
THIS SESSION	• Explore the FOR and NEXT statements.
YOU WILL:	• Explore the exit values of a loop variable.
	• Read programs containing FOR and NEXT statements.

Experiments with the Counting Loop

In Session 49, you learned how to use the BASIC loop outline to write a loop that would repeat until a counter got larger than a certain value. There is a program on your diskette that uses such a counting loop.

Start the computer with your diskette in the usual way. Then type the following commands:

`LOAD COUNT`	
`LIST`	Find the counting loop.
`RUN`	Answer the question.
`?5, 10`	Note the list of numbers.
`RUN`	
`?90, 100`	Note this list.
`RUN`	
`?-10, 10`	This list began at -10.
`RUN`	
`?5, 5`	There is only one number this time.
`RUN`	
`?5, 4`	There are no numbers this time.
`LIST`	Look at the program again.

1. Which variable in program COUNT stands for the first value of the counting loop?
2. Which statement sets the counter equal to the first value?
3. What is the exit condition in this loop?
4. Which statement adds 1 to the value of the counter?

The FOR/NEXT Abbreviation

You just experimented with a program that asked you to enter a first value and a last value and then printed a list of numbers starting with the first value and increasing by 1 each time. The program looked like this:

```
100 REM--PROGRAM COUNT
110:: PRINT "FIRST & LAST VALUES"
120:: INPUT F, L
130:: LET C = F
140:: REM--LOOP
150::: IF C > L THEN 190
160:::: PRINT C
170:::: LET C = C + 1
180::: GOTO 140
190:: REM--END LOOP
200 END
```

There is a simpler way to write this same program. Change the program so that it looks like this:

```
100 REM--PROGRAM COUNT
110:: PRINT "FIRST & LAST VALUES"
120:: INPUT F, L
140:: FOR C = F TO L
160:::: PRINT C
190:: NEXT C
200 END
```

The new FOR statement takes the place of three statements in the original version of COUNT. So does the new NEXT statement. Notice also that the variables F and L appear in the FOR statement. Suppose F equals 5 and L equals 10. What do you think the program says to do? Let's find out.

Turn back to the first page of this session and enter each pair of numbers you used with the original version of program COUNT.

As you see, the old program and the new, shorter program usually work alike: The same series of numbers usually appears on the screen. The experiment with the pair 5, 4 shows up a bug in Applesoft BASIC. You'll come back to that bug in Session 53.

5. Which three statements in the original version of program COUNT does the FOR statement replace?
6. Which three statements in the original version of program COUNT does the NEXT statement replace?

Exit Values

The loop variable C has some value after the loop stops. That value is its **exit value**. Let's explore exit values next. List your program. Add the following line right after the NEXT statement:

```
195:: PRINT "EXIT VALUE = "; C
```

Think about what line 195 tells the computer to do. What do you think will be printed if F is 5 and L is 10? **Turn to the first page of this session and enter the same pairs of numbers for F and L that you did before. Pay attention to the exit value each time.**

When answering the questions below, ignore the last experiment you just did. (It shows the same Applesoft bug you saw before.)

7. How is the exit value of the loop variable C related to the last value L?

8. Look at line 150 in the original version of program COUNT. Why is the exit value of C equal to 11 if L is 10?

Changing the STEP

So far all your counting loops have counted by 1s. Next you'll see how to make them count by 2s and other numbers. **Clear the screen and list the program. Change the FOR statement to this:**

    140:: FOR C = F TO L STEP 2

Note the STEP phrase. Now do these new experiments:

RUN
?0, 20 _____ Note the numbers *and* the exit value.

RUN
?0, 21 _____ Think about these results.

RUN
?0, 21.9999
RUN
?0, 22 _____ Think about these results too.

Next, let's try another STEP phrase in the FOR statement in line 140. **List the program and change the FOR statement to this:**

    140:: FOR C = F TO L STEP 10

List the program again and check it. Then do these new experiments:

RUN
?0, 100 _____ Note the numbers and the exit value this time.

RUN
?1, 100 _____ Think about these results.

9. What does the STEP phrase in a FOR statement tell the computer to do?

10. What one change would you have to make in the original version of program COUNT to make it count by 10s?

Counting Down

So far, all your experiments have resulted in lists in which the numbers got bigger. You can also tell the computer to count backward. List the program and change the 10 after STEP to -1. The FOR statement should look like this:

```
140:: FOR C = F TO L STEP -1
```

List the program and check it. Then do these new experiments:

```
RUN
?10, 5
```
————————————————————— Note the list; look at the exit value.
```
RUN
?20, 0
```
————————————————————— Think about these numbers.

11. What does a negative value in the STEP phrase of a FOR statement tell the computer to do?

12. How is the exit value of C related to L when there is a negative STEP value?

A Few Details

There are only a few more details to learn about the FOR/NEXT abbreviation for counting loops. Change the program to this:

```
100 REM--PROGRAM COUNT
140:: FOR C = 3 + 4 TO 3 * 4
160:::: PRINT C
190:: NEXT C
195:: PRINT "EXIT VALUE = "; C
200 END
```

Think what this changed program tells the computer to do. Then run the program and see if you are right.

You just saw that the computer calculates the first and last values of a FOR/NEXT loop before the computer starts the loop. Now let's see whether you can change the last value from inside the loop. Change the program to this:

```
100 REM--PROGRAM COUNT
120:: LET L = 10
140:: FOR C = 1 TO L
160:::: PRINT C
165:::: LET L = 5
190:: NEXT C
195:: PRINT "EXIT VALUE = "; C
200 END
```

Notice that L starts out as 10; but inside the loop, L is changed to 5. Will the program count to 10 or to 5? Run it and find out. Then, type PRINT L in immediate mode and find what L is equal to.

The last experiment shows something important: *The first and last values of a* FOR / NEXT *loop are computed only once, before the loop starts. They cannot be changed from inside the loop.* You can change L inside the loop, but that change will not affect the last value of the loop variable C.

13. When does the computer decide what numbers to use for the first and last values of the loop variable in a FOR / NEXT loop?

14. Can a LET statement inside the body of a FOR / NEXT loop change the last value of the loop variable?

If you have extra lab time:

- Write a FOR / NEXT loop that prints the integers from 0 to 20. Next to each integer, the program should print its square root. Use the function SQR.

- Load program BLAST OFF into your computer. One of the subroutines contains 23 identical statements. Rewrite that part of the subroutine as a FOR / NEXT loop that tells the computer to repeat the statement 23 times.

- Load program HI THERE into your computer and run it. What does the FOR / NEXT loop tell the computer to do? How many times does it tell the computer to print your name? Make it print the message 200 times.

- Load program SYMMETRY into your computer and run it. Change the loop in the main routine into a FOR / NEXT loop that repeats the two GOSUB statements 50 times.

- Load program QUILT into your computer and run it. The FOR / NEXT loop in the main routine is easy to understand, but the loops in the subroutine at line 400 are tricky. Can you figure out what those loops do?

How the FOR and NEXT Statements Work

IN THIS SESSION YOU WILL:
- Learn the details of the FOR and NEXT statements.
- Learn why the exit value is always outside the range of the loop variable.
- Plan a programming project using FOR and NEXT statements.

Experiments with the FOR/NEXT Loop

The FOR/NEXT loop is just a short way of writing the counting loop. You saw in Session 52 that you really do not need the FOR/NEXT loop. Anything you can do with a FOR/NEXT loop, you can do with a loop made with REM, IF, and GOTO statements. (The reverse is not true. You cannot solve every loop problem with a FOR/NEXT loop.)

Your FOR/NEXT loop This is the loop you studied in Session 52:

```
140 FOR C = F TO L
160:: PRINT C
190 NEXT C
```

Positive ranges The set of numbers from first (F) through last (L) is called the **range** of the loop variable (C). In Session 52, you found that when the first number was 90 and the last number was 100, the loop told the computer to print 90, 91, 92, and so on up through 100.

A negative first value You also tried a range from -10 through 10 and found that the loop variable started at -10 and then went to -9, -8, etc., all the way up through zero and on to 10.

A short range When you used 5 for both ends of the range, the FOR/NEXT block went through the loop exactly once. It used the value 5 for the loop variable.

Exit values You learned that the value of the loop variable after the computer finished performing each loop is called the *exit value*. The exit value is always the first value outside the range given in the FOR statement.

A different step Then you added the phrase STEP 2 to your FOR statement. You found that the variable started at the first value and increased by 2 each time around the loop.

A negative step You found that you could count down from a big number to a small one by adding the phrase STEP -1 to the FOR statement.

Outline Form of the FOR/NEXT Loop

Like all other BASIC blocks, the FOR/NEXT loop has a general outline form. Here it is:

```
___  FOR  variable = first TO  last  STEP  step
___
___      do something
___
___  NEXT  variable
```

The words *first, last,* and *step* each stand for a number or an expression that has a numeric value (examples: 23, 10, X + 5, LEN (A$)). If you omit the STEP phrase, the computer uses a step value of 1. The word *variable* stands for the name of a BASIC variable (examples: C, J). The phrase *do something* stands for the block of BASIC statements to be repeated.

Nothing new here The FOR/NEXT loop is not really a new kind of loop. It is just a much shorter way of writing a counting loop. If the step value is positive, the outline below means exactly the same thing as the FOR/NEXT outline above:

```
___  LET  variable = first
___  REM--LOOP
___      IF  variable > last  THEN ___
___
___          do something
___
___      LET  variable = variable + step
___      GOTO ___
___  REM--END LOOP
```

When the step value is negative, the symbol > in the third line must be changed to <.

How the FOR/NEXT Loop Works

The best way to see how any FOR/NEXT loop works is to rewrite it in the long form. That way you can see every detail of what is going on. Here is a program similar to one that you wrote in Session 52:

```
100 REM--PROGRAM COUNT
110:: PRINT "FIRST & LAST VALUES"
120:: INPUT F, L
140:: FOR C = F TO L STEP 3
160:::: PRINT C
190:: NEXT C
195:: PRINT "EXIT VALUE = "; C
200 END
```

Lines 110 through 120 ask the user to enter numbers for F and L. The FOR/NEXT loop is in lines 140 through 190. Line 195 prints the exit value of the loop variable C.

Convert to long form The FOR statement in line 140 is an abbreviation for three statements. So is the NEXT statement in line 190. Here is the long form of the same loop:

```
100 REM--PROGRAM COUNT
110:: PRINT "FIRST & LAST VALUES"
120:: INPUT F, L
130:: LET C = F
140:: REM--LOOP
150::: IF C > L THEN 190
160:::: PRINT C
170:::: LET C = C + 3
180::: GOTO 140
190:: REM--END LOOP
195:: PRINT "EXIT VALUE = "; C
200 END
```

Loop initialization Line 130 in the long form assigns the value of F to the loop variable C. This process, which happens before the loop begins, is called **initialization**. We say that line 130 "initializes C to equal the value of F." This value will be the initial, or first, value of C inside the loop.

Exit test The first statement inside the loop is the IF statement. Before performing the body of the loop, the computer tests whether C is already greater than L. If so, the loop stops with a jump to line 190. If not, the computer performs the body of the loop.

Perform body of loop The PRINT statement in line 160 tells the computer to print the current value of C on the screen. Then line 170 tells the computer to add 3 to C and assign the sum back to C.

Loop back Finally, line 180 tells the computer to jump back to the start of the loop block, line 140. As before, the first action the computer takes inside the loop is to test whether C is greater than L. The loop repeats until C is greater than L.

Exit value When the exit condition C > L finally becomes true, the computer exits the loop by jumping to line 190. After that, it must perform line 195, which says to print the value of C when the exit condition became true. For this reason, the exit value is always the first value *outside* the range in the FOR statement.

An Applesoft BASIC Bug

You saw strange results on your Apple computer when you ran a program similar to this:

```
100 FOR C = 5 TO 4
110:: PRINT C
120 NEXT C
```

The computer printed 5 and stopped. The exit value of C was 6. Now is the time for an explanation of this bug in Applesoft BASIC and a few other BASICs.

Standard FOR/NEXT loop Let's see how the FOR/NEXT loop is supposed to work. First, we convert the loop into the long form:

```
100 LET C = 5
102 REM--LOOP
104: IF C > 4 THEN 120
110:: PRINT C
116:: LET C = C + 1
118: GOTO 102
120 REM--END LOOP
```

This version tells how the Standard BASIC FOR/NEXT loop is performed. Line 100 sets C to the first value, 5. Inside the loop block, the IF statement tells the computer to see whether C is greater than 4. Of course, it is; so the computer exits the loop at once. The PRINT statement is never performed. The exit value of C is 5, the first value assigned to it.

The Applesoft FOR/NEXT loop In Applesoft BASIC, the computer performs the "do-something" part *before* testing whether to exit the loop. Here is how Applesoft BASIC performs the loop:

```
100 LET C = 5
102 REM--APPLESOFT LOOP
110:: PRINT C
116:: LET C = C + 1
117: IF C > 4 THEN 120
118: GOTO 102
120 REM--END LOOP
```

The computer goes through the body of the loop (lines 110 and 116) once, no matter what. That is why your computer printed 5 on the screen and why the exit value of C is 6, not 5, in Applesoft BASIC.

Loop bug appears rarely This bug in Applesoft BASIC does not show up often, since you usually write loops that are supposed to be performed at least once. But the Applesoft loop bug may appear in a program like this one:

```
400 PRINT "HOW MANY STARS DO YOU WANT?"
410 INPUT N
420 FOR S = 1 TO N
430:: PRINT "*";
440 NEXT S
```

If you enter a 0, a computer using Standard BASIC will print *no* stars, but a computer using Applesoft BASIC will print *one* star. You can avoid this problem, the few times it comes up, by using the long form of the counting loop instead of the FOR/NEXT shorthand.

More about Range Values

You know you can use constants, variables, or more complicated expressions to assign the range to a FOR loop.

Computing range values   You discovered that it was legal to write the following block.

```
140 FOR C = 3 + 4 TO 3 * 4
160:: PRINT C
190 NEXT C
```

The computer did the arithmetic in line 140 *before* it started the loop. It found the first value was 7 and the last value was 12. Then it performed the PRINT statement with C ranging from 7 to 12.

Variables as range values   You ran the following program, which has a variable as the last value of the range:

```
120 LET L = 10
140 FOR C = 1 TO L
160:: PRINT C
165:: LET L = 5
150 NEXT C
```

You probably were not sure at first whether the computer would go through the loop ten times or five times. L starts with a value of 10, but inside the loop the value of L is changed to 5. When you ran the program, though, you found that line 165 had no effect on the range of the loop. The computer did the loop ten times.

Rules on FOR/NEXT ranges   Your experiments can be summed up in the following rule: Before performing a FOR/NEXT loop, the computer first calculates the first and last values of the range. You cannot change the range by changing the values of any variables inside the body of the loop.

A FOR/NEXT Loop Project: Making Graph Paper

Take the rest of the time available to start planning a programming project. **Be prepared to enter the program into the computer in Session 54.** The project is to make the screen look like a sheet of graph paper. Ordinary graph paper is made by drawing a set of vertical and horizontal lines on a blank sheet. The spacing between the lines is usually constant.

What you will need   Here are some things you should think about. What color should the screen be? How far apart horizontally should the lines across the screen be? What should the vertical spacing be? What color should the lines be?

Main routine outline Here is a top-level outline of the project:

```
100 REM--PROGRAM GRAPH PAPER
110:: get colors and line spacing
120:: cover the screen with background color
130:: draw the set of horizontal lines
140:: draw the set of vertical lines
150 END
```

What you should do As usual, your first task is to substitute GOSUBs for the English statements in the main routine. Then start planning the subroutines you will need. You might want to refer to page 92 in Session 17, which has a table of all the Apple II colors. The same table gives the shades of gray available on a black-and-white screen.

Three FOR/NEXT loops You will need a FOR/NEXT loop to fill the entire screen with one color. This loop will be much like the one you wrote for your project in Session 50, except that you can use the FOR/NEXT abbreviation this time. You will also need a FOR/NEXT loop with a STEP phrase to draw the set of vertical lines, and another loop with a STEP phrase for the horizontal lines. Remember that screen positions are from 0 to 39 in both directions.

QUESTIONS

1. What is meant by the range of a FOR/NEXT loop?

2. If you open a loop with the statement

    ```
    250 FOR M = 21 TO 21
    ```

    how many times will the computer perform the body of the loop?

3. What will the exit value of M be after the computer finishes the loop in question 2?

4. Which three lines of the long loop outline on page 295 can be shortened to a single FOR statement?

5. Which three lines of the long loop outline on page 295 can be shortened to a single NEXT statement?

6. Suppose the program on page 296 is run and the user enters each one of the sets of values for F and L shown below. For each set, use the long form of the counting loop to say what the program tells the computer to print on the screen.

    a. F = 2, L = 8   c. F = 2, L = 2
    b. F = 2, L = 9   d. F = 2, L = 1

7. Why is the exit value of a loop variable always the first value outside the range given in the FOR statement?

8. When does the computer test the exit condition in the Applesoft BASIC FOR/NEXT loop?

9. When is the range of a FOR/NEXT loop computed?

10. Can you change the range of a FOR/NEXT loop from inside the body of the loop?

Sometimes your classmates can help you find the bugs in your program.

Programming Project: FOR/NEXT Loops

IN • Enter the program you planned in Session 53.
THIS SESSION • Debug the program.
YOU WILL:

Computer Work

If you have not finished writing program GRAPH PAPER, do so now. Then enter it into the computer and debug it.

If you have extra lab time:

- Add to your program a subroutine to draw a solid rectangle anywhere on the screen. It can be similar to the one you wrote in Sessions 49 and 50, except that you may want to use a FOR/NEXT loop this time. Then make your program draw a series of colored rectangles on the diagonal blocks of the graph paper your program now draws.

- Program LITTLE TROT contains a subroutine for drawing solid rectangles. Load the program and find the subroutine. See how it is used by other subroutines.

Words printed in color in the table were introduced in this part.

BASIC Vocabulary (Shaded Areas Show Standard BASIC Words)

Commands		Statements			Functions
Program	Diskette	Action	Action	Control	
RUN	LOAD	INPUT	SPEED=	GOSUB	INT
LIST	SAVE	LET	FLASH	RETURN	SQR
NEW	DELETE	PRINT	INVERSE	END	RND
DEL	CATALOG	REM	NORMAL	GOTO	LEN
CONT	LOCK	PLOT	COLOR=	IF	MID$
BRUN	UNLOCK	HLIN	TEXT	FOR	
&INDENT		VLIN	GR	NEXT	
&UNDENT		HOME			
&RENUMBER					

New BASIC Words

BRUN   A command used to load and run a binary code program stored on diskette.

FOR   A statement used to open a counting loop.

NEXT   A statement used to close a counting loop.

&INDENT   A command used to indent portions of a program.

&RENUMBER   A command used to renumber all or portions of a program.

&UNDENT   A command used to remove indents from portions of a program.

New Ideas

abbreviated loop block   A loop that does not have one of the two usual "do somethings."

artificial intelligence   The attempt to build into computer programs some of the following things: knowledge, pattern recognition, adaptation, judgment, and the ability to understand human languages.

counting loop   A loop used to perform some action a fixed number of times.

flag   A variable that is never part of data, used to signal the end of a set of data.

flowgraph   A diagram using boxes and arrows to show the structure of a program block.

infinite loop   A loop with no exit condition.

loop   A program structure that causes a group of statements to be repeated.

loop block A set of statements that defines a loop in a program.

loop body The statements inside a loop block.

loop exit condition The condition that when false allows a program loop to continue and when true stops the loop.

loop exit value The value of a loop variable after a loop ends.

loop range The set of numeric values a counting loop variable can have inside the loop.

loop variable The variable that is tested to exit from a counting loop.

Left: Early telephone systems needed people to make the connections. Right: Today, computerized switching centers route all calls automatically.

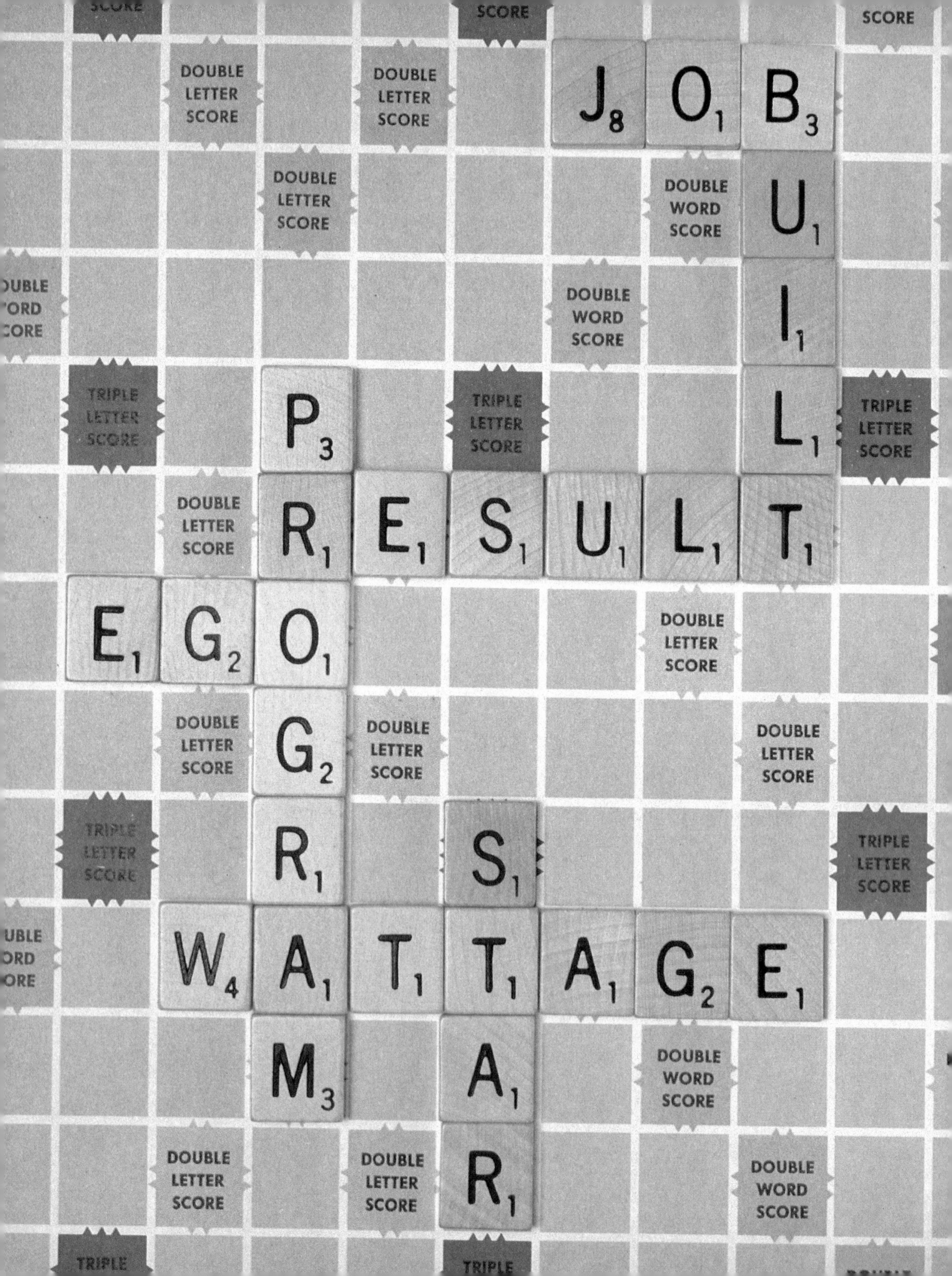
JOB
BUILT
RESULT
EGO
PROGRAM
WATTAGE
STAR
DOUBLE LETTER SCORE
DOUBLE WORD SCORE
TRIPLE LETTER SCORE

Part 8

Control Blocks: The Branch

In Part 7, you learned to use the loop block to solve many programming problems. In this part, you will learn about branches.

Branch blocks A branch can handle an either-or situation. Branches allow you to tell the computer to do either one or the other of two possible groups of statements, depending on whether a condition is true or false. Suppose, for example, that you use the RND function to stand for the toss of a coin. Then you can use a branch block to tell the computer to print either HEADS (if RND (1) is less than one-half) or TAILS (if RND (1) is greater than one-half). Without a branch block, the program could not tell the computer to print HEADS or TAILS.

Actions, loops, and branches Only the simplest program can be written as a straight-line list of action statements. You must put a loop in the program if you want the computer to perform the same block of statements again and again. You must put a branch in the program if you want the computer to choose between two blocks of statements and perform only one of them.

Nothing else No other control blocks are needed, though. *No matter how complex a programming problem seems when you first look at it, you can solve it by using only three types of blocks: actions, loops, and branches.* Remember this fact if you are stumped when writing a program. To decide what comes next, you need only figure out which of the three blocks is the right kind to use.

Filling in the outline After you choose the correct block, you then write its outline and fill in the details. Usually, you can handle the details with one or two BASIC statements. Sometimes, however, you may need to put a loop block or a branch block inside another loop block or branch block. You will see examples in this part. This way of planning and writing is often called **structured programming**. Careful studies show that people who use structured programming methods are far more successful than others at handling complex problems.

 # Structure of the Branch Block

IN	• Learn the structure of the branch-block outline.
THIS SESSION	• Learn the flowgraph form of the branch block.
YOU WILL:	• Use the branch-block outline to describe everyday events.
	• Find the branch block in the RUN program.

Branch-Block Outline

In Session 47, you learned how to write an outline of the loop block. You used a mixture of BASIC and English words. In this session, you will write an outline of the **branch block**.

Purpose of a branch A branch block is used for an either-or situation. The computer begins by testing a condition to see whether it is true or false. If true, the computer performs one group of statements. If false, it performs a different group of statements. In either case, the computer goes on to the next statement after the branch block.

Components of a branch The first part of a branch block is an IF statement that contains the condition to be tested. After that, there must be one group of statements the computer performs if the condition is true and another group the computer performs if the condition is false. There must be a GOTO statement between the two groups to tell the computer to skip the second group if it has performed the first. Here is the outline:

```
___   IF condition THEN ___
___      REM--FALSE
___
___         do something
___
___      GOTO ___
___   REM--TRUE
___
___         do something
___
___   REM--END IF
```

Parts of the outline As in the loop-block outline, the blanks show where line numbers will be used. The jump arrows remind you that the numbers after THEN and GOTO must match the line numbers of the targets. REM statements remind readers of the reason for the jumps. *Condition* stands for an expression such as A1 > 5 or A$ = "STOP". The indented phrase *do something* stands for one or more BASIC statements. Here is how the computer performs a branch:

The computer's rules for performing a branch block

1. Test the condition to see whether it is true or false.
2. If the condition is false, move the line pointer to the REM--FALSE statement and perform the first "do something" block. If the condition is true, move the line pointer to the REM--TRUE statement and perform the second "do something" block.
3. Move the line pointer to the REM--END IF statement.

Differences in jump arrows The outline shows that the branch block is very different from the loop block. In the loop block, there is a jump arrow from the GOTO statement at the end *all the way back to the beginning*. In the branch outline, both jump arrows go forward.

Different uses of the IF statement The IF statement appears in both types of blocks, but it has a completely different purpose in each one. In the loop block, the IF statement tells the computer when to exit from the loop. In the branch block, the IF statement tells the computer which "do something" to perform.

Different uses of GOTO statement The GOTO statement also appears in both types of blocks, but the uses are totally different. In the loop block, the GOTO statement at the end tells the computer to loop back to the beginning. In the branch block, the GOTO statement tells the computer to skip the true "do something" if it has performed the false "do something."

Flowgraph of the Branch Block

In Session 49, you learned how to draw a loop block as a flowgraph. You can use the same flowgraph symbols to diagram a branch block. Remember that in a flowgraph, the rectangular boxes stand for blocks of statements, the diamond-shaped boxes stand for IF statements, and the lines show the order in which the computer performs the boxes.

Branch-block flowgraph Since the branch block begins with an IF statement, the flowgraph must start with a diamond. On the next page is the complete flowgraph of the branch block.

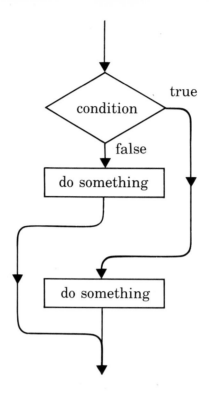

If the condition is false, the computer follows the vertical path, performs the upper "do something" block, and then skips the lower one. If the condition is true, the computer follows the path at the right and performs the lower "do something" block.

Branches in Everyday Life

Branches are not limited to computer programs. You probably use branches often when you tell another person how to do something. You also find branches in the instructions people write for doing everyday tasks. Let's look at some examples.

Adding "ly" Think about these sentences: "The right lane on a highway is the slow lane. People drive slowly in the right lane." *Slow* is an adjective in the first sentence. *Slowly* is an adverb in the second sentence. You can change the adjective to the adverb by adding *ly*. But, is that rule always true? *Speedy* is also an adjective. If you add *ly,* you get *speedyly*. The correct word is *speedily*.

Instructions for adding "ly" When you were younger, you learned the following spelling rule for changing adjectives to adverbs. "If the adjective ends in *y*, change the *y* to *i* and add *ly*. Otherwise, add *ly*."

Not an action or a loop If you think about this spelling rule as a program block, you'll see that it is not a loop. Nothing gets done again and again. It is a branch: Either one thing gets done or another thing gets done. Here is how you could write the spelling rule, using a mixture of BASIC and English.

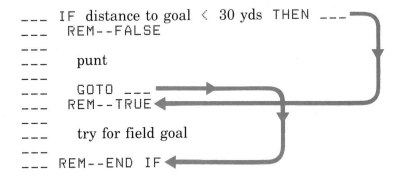

```
___   IF  last letter is y  THEN  ___
___      REM--FALSE
___
___         add ly
___
___         GOTO ___
___      REM--TRUE
___
___         change y to i
___         add ly
___
___   REM--END IF
```

Field goal or punt?   A second example of an everyday branch block is a problem every quarterback has faced in a football game. It is fourth down. Should you punt or try for a field goal?

The coach's instructions   The coach might give these instructions: "If the ball is inside the opponent's 30-yard line, try for a field goal. Otherwise, punt." Here are those instructions written as a BASIC branch block:

```
___   IF  distance to goal < 30 yds  THEN  ___
___      REM--FALSE
___
___         punt
___
___         GOTO ___
___      REM--TRUE
___
___         try for field goal
___
___   REM--END IF
```

Paul Revere's ride   Paul Revere faced a problem we can describe with a branch block. This example is interesting because it needs an action and a loop block as well as a branch block.

Paul's problem   Paul Revere's mission was to warn the Minutemen at Lexington whether the British forces were coming by land or by sea. His instructions to a fellow patriot might have been these: "Climb up in the tower of Old North Church, from where you can see what the British are doing. If they come by land, hoist one signal lantern. If they come by sea, hoist two. Once I see the signal, I'll ride and spread the alarm."

A block description There are three separate parts to Paul's instructions. First, climb the tower. Second, wait until you see the British. Third, give one alarm or the other. Here is a BASIC outline of the orders.

```
___   climb the church tower
___
___   REM--LOOP
___
___      look for movement
___
___      IF British are coming THEN ___
___
___      wait awhile
___
___      GOTO ___
___   REM--END LOOP
___
___   IF British coming by sea THEN ___
___      REM--FALSE
___
___      light one lantern
___
___      GOTO ___
___      REM--TRUE
___
___      light two lanterns
___
___   REM--END IF
```

Branch block is essential You cannot describe any of these instructions with the action and loop blocks alone. With the branch block as well, you can give any instructions, no matter how complex. This is true whether you are giving instructions to a person or to a computer.

QUESTIONS

1. Why must a jump arrow go backward in a loop block but not in a branch block?
2. What is the purpose of the IF statement in the branch block? In the loop block?
3. What is the purpose of the GOTO statement in the branch block? In the loop block?

4. What do the three REM statements in the branch outline on page 306 tell a reader of the program?

5. Why must the first statement in a branch block be an IF statement?

6. What is the meaning of a diamond-shaped box in a flowgraph?

7. What is the meaning of a rectangular box in a flowgraph?

8. Why does the branch-block flowgraph begin with a diamond?

9. Which line in the branch-block flowgraph corresponds to the jump arrow from the GOTO statement in the branch outline?

10. Which line in the branch-block flowgraph stands for the jump arrow from the IF statement in the branch outline?

11. Look at the revised version of the RUN program on page 132. Step 2b says: "If step 2a just moved the line pointer, leave the pointer there; if not, move the pointer to the next line of the program in the memory unit." Write step 2b in the form of a BASIC branch outline.

12. A friend telephones you and says: "Let's go on a picnic Saturday. If it rains, we'll go to a movie instead." Rewrite this suggestion in the form of a BASIC branch outline.

13. Make up your own either-or situation and write instructions for it in the form of a BASIC branch outline.

Exploring the Branch Block

IN THIS SESSION YOU WILL:
• Find branch blocks in programs `DECISION` and `LITTLE TROT`.
• Write a branch block that simulates the toss of a coin.

Reading Programs with Branches

In Session 55, you learned about the branch block. You saw several examples of everyday instructions that could be written as BASIC branch outlines. In this section, you will read programs, look for branch blocks, and make changes in the blocks.

The BASIC branch outline begins with an `IF` statement and ends with a `REM--END IF` statement. Here is the outline:

```
___   IF condition THEN ___
___      REM--FALSE
___
___         do something
___
___         GOTO ___
___      REM--TRUE
___
___         do something
___
___   REM--END IF
```

Notice that each of the two "do somethings" comes after a `REM` statement. `REM--FALSE` reminds the reader that the first "do something" block of statements is done if the condition is false. `REM--TRUE` is the target line of the `IF` statement; so the second "do something" block is done only if the condition is true. The `GOTO` statement after the false "do something" tells the computer to skip over the true "do something."

Start the computer with your diskette as usual. Then load and run program `DECISION`. Notice the pattern it produces. Think about how you would tell the computer what color to use on different parts of the screen.

Now, list program `DECISION`. Locate the branch block. Think about how it works.

1. What lines of program DECISION contain the branch block?
2. What is the condition in this branch block?
3. What are the two "do somethings" in this branch block?
4. What does this branch block tell the computer to do? Explain in your own words.

Changing the Branch Block

You have seen a branch block that tells the computer how to choose a color. Next, let's change the condition and see what happens.

Change X < 20 to Y < 20 in the branch block in program DECISION. Think about what the branch block now tells the computer to do. Run the program and find out if you were correct.

Now, change the expression to X + Y < 40. Think about what this new condition means. Mentally try some values of X and Y to see which values produce which colors. Run the program and test your ideas.

Now, let's make an error: Remove the GOTO statement from the branch block. List the program and think about what this incorrect branch tells the computer to do. Run the program and find out if you were right.

5. Suppose you use the condition Y < 20 in the branch block in program DECISION. What does that condition tell the computer to do?
6. Why did removing the GOTO statement from the branch block cause the trouble you saw?

The Branch in LITTLE TROT

Program LITTLE TROT tells the computer to race a black turtle against a green one. As the turtles race, the program must tell the computer either to move the black turtle or else to move the green turtle. Since the race is really an either-or situation, there must be a branch in the program.

Load LITTLE TROT and run it a few times. Now list the main routine only. Try to decide which one of the subroutines is going to contain the branch block. List that subroutine and find the branch block. Think about what it tells the computer to do.

7. How does this branch block tell the computer which turtle to move? (Hint: Remember that RND (1) results in random numbers between 0 and 1.)
8. What are the two "do somethings" in this branch block?

9. If you wanted to give one turtle a better chance of winning than the other, what part of the branch block would you have to change?

Writing a Coin-Tossing Branch Block

Now that you have seen a few branch blocks, you can write one. Your job is to write a program that simulates the tossing of a coin. The program should print HEADS or TAILS after each "toss." Use the RND function to get random numbers, much as the LITTLE TROT branch block does.

Here is a top-level description of the main routine of your program:

```
100 REM--PROGRAM COINS
110::  ask user how many coins to toss.
120::  toss coins; print HEADS or TAILS for each.
130 END
```

You should convert line 110 to a GOSUB to an input subroutine. Line 120 should become a GOSUB to the subroutine that does most of the work. Write that subroutine in the form of a FOR/NEXT loop. Inside the loop, there should be a branch that decides which word to print on the screen.

Complete the writing and debugging of program COINS. Run it several times and make sure that it behaves as randomly as a tossed coin.

If you have extra lab time:

EXPLORE

- Suppose you want program COINS not only to "toss coins" but also to count the number of heads and the number of tails. Then, when the tossing loop is over, you want the computer to print the two counts. Change the program so that the computer keeps track of how many heads and how many tails and also prints the count.

- Change your program so that the "coin" comes up heads 60 percent of the time and tails 40 percent of the time, on average.

- Program SPAGHETTI behaves exactly like LITTLE TROT, but it is written very differently. Try to find the part of SPAGHETTI that tells the computer which turtle to move. Which program is easier to read?

Nesting Program Blocks

IN THIS SESSION YOU WILL:
- Learn what a computer simulation is.
- Learn that computer simulations may not be accurate.
- Review the coin-tossing simulation.
- Learn how to nest one program block inside another.
- Plan a programming project using nested blocks.

What Is a Computer Simulation?

In Session 56, you wrote program COINS, which gives results as random as the results of tossing a coin over and over. Program COINS is an example of a **computer simulation**. "To simulate" means "to pretend" or "to behave similarly." The computer does not really toss coins, of course. But your program made the computer behave randomly, much as we think tossed coins behave. People use computer simulations to study many real things, such as a rocket journey to the moon, economic changes in a town, and even the decisions that can lead nations to war. Most electronic games are also computer simulations.

Accuracy of a simulation A computer simulation is only as accurate as the ideas of the programmer who wrote the program. To simulate a rocket trip to the moon, the programmer has to know the laws of physics and use them correctly. The laws of physics have been tested for centuries and are quite accurate. The laws of economics are not as well understood, so economic simulations are likely to be less accurate than rocket simulations. *Remember this: Results are not correct just because they come out of a computer.*

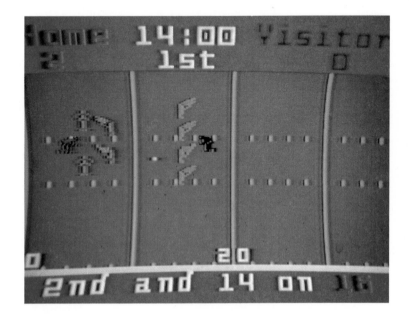

Many computer programs are simulations

Review of Program COINS

There is no single correct way to write an English composition or to write a computer program. For example, there are several correct ways to write program COINS. Here is how one person wrote program COINS:

```
100 PROGRAM COINS   (BRUCE'S VERSION)
110:: GOSUB 200: REM--INPUT NUMBER
120:: GOSUB 400: REM--TOSS COINS
130 END
140:
200 REM--SUB INPUT NUMBER
210:: PRINT "HOW MANY COINS DO YOU WANT?"
220:: INPUT N
230 RETURN
240:
400 REM--SUB TOSS COINS
410:: FOR J = 1 TO N
420:::: GOSUB 600: REM--ONE TOSS
430:: NEXT J
440 RETURN
450:
600 REM--SUB ONE TOSS
610:: IF RND (1) > .5 THEN 650
620::: REM--FALSE
630:::: PRINT "HEADS"
640:::: GOTO 670
650::: REM--TRUE
660:::: PRINT "TAILS"
670:: REM--END IF
680 RETURN
```

Main routine The main routine is divided into two main actions. GOSUB 200 tells the computer to ask the user how many coins to toss. GOSUB 400 tells the computer to toss that number of coins and print HEADS or TAILS.

Input subroutine The subroutine in line 200 simply does two things: It asks (prompts) the user for a number and then it waits for an answer (input) from the user. The INPUT statement assigns the number to a variable named N.

Toss loop The body of the subroutine at line 400 is a FOR/NEXT loop. It tells the computer to repeat the statement GOSUB 600. The number of repetitions is equal to the value of N.

One-toss branch The subroutine in line 600 simulates the toss of a coin. It uses the RND function to get a random number between 0 and 1. If the number is less than .5 (one-half), the computer prints HEADS. Otherwise, the computer prints TAILS. The structure of this subroutine is a branch block.

Another Version of COINS

Although correct, Bruce's version of COINS is not the only one. Here is how another person wrote program COINS:

```
100 PROGRAM COINS  (JENNIFER'S VERSION)
110:: GOSUB 200: REM--HOW MANY
120:: GOSUB 400: REM--FLIPPEM
130 END
140:
200 REM--SUB HOW MANY
210:: PRINT "HOW MANY FLIPS?"
220:: INPUT C
230 RETURN
240:
400 REM--SUB FLIPPEM
410:: FOR A = 1 TO C
420:::: IF RND (1) > .5 THEN 460
430::::: REM--FALSE
440:::::: PRINT "HEADS"
450:::::: GOTO 480
460::::: REM--TRUE
470:::::: PRINT "TAILS"
480:::: REM--END IF
490:: NEXT A
500 RETURN
```

Small differences The two writers did things differently, but both programs work correctly. Some differences are small. The names of the subroutines at lines 200 and 400 are different. Bruce used variables named N and J; Jennifer named them C and A.

Big difference There is one very big difference, though. Bruce used three subroutines, and Jennifer used only two. Bruce's FOR/NEXT loop contained a GOSUB 600 to the third subroutine, which tossed the coin and decided whether to print HEADS or TAILS. But Jennifer's FOR/NEXT loop is much longer and contains no GOSUB statement.

The loop body Let's take a close look at the body of the loop in Jennifer's version of the program. Here it is:

```
420:::: IF RND (1) > .5 THEN 460
430::::: REM--FALSE
440:::::: PRINT "HEADS"
450:::::: GOTO 480
460::::: REM--TRUE
470:::::: PRINT "TAILS"
480:::: REM--END IF
```

It is easy to see that the body of the loop is a branch block. It begins with an IF statement and ends with a REM--END IF statement. In fact, it is exactly the same branch block (except for line numbers) that appeared as the last subroutine in Bruce's version of the program.

A branch inside a loop The big difference between the two versions is the way the two writers thought about the branch. Bruce thought of it as a separate action and put it into a subroutine of its own. Jennifer thought of the branch as the body of the `FOR`/`NEXT` loop, and she wrote it there.

Nesting of Blocks

Jennifer's version of program `COINS` is an example of **nesting**—putting one program block inside another program block. In this section, you will learn how to read programs with nested blocks.

Complex looking The first time you see a lot of nesting, the program looks very complex. For example, here is Jennifer's coin-tossing subroutine:

```
400 REM--SUB FLIPPEM
410:: FOR A = 1 TO C
420:::: IF RND (1) > .5 THEN 460
430::::: REM--FALSE
440:::::: PRINT "HEADS"
450:::::: GOTO 480
460::::: REM--TRUE
470:::::: PRINT "TAILS"
480:::: REM--END IF
490:: NEXT A
500 RETURN
```

Start at outer level The trick is to start reading at the outer level. Try to get the big picture before looking at the details. The outer level is the subroutine itself. The first thing to do is find the body of the subroutine. Let's draw a box around the body:

```
400  REM--SUB FLIPPEM

410 │   FOR A = 1 TO C
420 │   :: IF RND (1) > .5 THEN 460
430 │   ::: REM--FALSE
440 │   :::: PRINT "HEADS"
450 │   :::: GOTO 480
460 │   ::: REM--TRUE
470 │   :::: PRINT "TAILS"
480 │   :: REM--END IF
490 │    NEXT A

500  RETURN
```

Look inside the box Now you can see that lines `410` to `490` make up the body of the subroutine. The next step is to see what is inside the box. The box contains an entire FOR/NEXT loop. Inside every loop is a "do something." Let's draw another box, this time around the "do something" part of the loop:

```
400  REM--SUB FLIPPEM

410 │ FOR A = 1 TO C
    │
420 │   IF RND (1) > .5 THEN 460
430 │   : REM--FALSE
440 │   :: PRINT "HEADS"
450 │   :: GOTO 480
460 │   : REM--TRUE
470 │   :: PRINT "TAILS"
480 │    REM--END IF
    │
490 │ NEXT A

500  RETURN
```

Look inside again The inner box contains the whole body of the loop. The next step is to look inside the inner box. This time, you find an entire branch block. A branch block has two "do somethings." Let's draw a box around the true "do something" and another box around the false "do something":

```
400  REM--SUB FLIPPEM

410 │ FOR A = 1 TO C
    │
420 │   IF RND (1) > .5 THEN 460
430 │     REM--FALSE
    │
440 │     PRINT "HEADS"
    │
450 │     GOTO 480
460 │     REM--TRUE
    │
470 │     PRINT "TAILS"
    │
480 │   REM--END IF
    │
490 │ NEXT A

500  RETURN
```

Look inside The two inner boxes contain the true and false "do somethings" of the branch block. When you look inside this time, you see only simple action statements. There is nothing left to box.

Conclusions This way of looking at lines 400 to 500 helps you understand the block. First, the whole block is a subroutine. Second, the body of the subroutine is a FOR/NEXT loop, so something will be repeated C times. Third, the thing to be repeated is a branch block. Fourth, the true and false "do somethings" of the branch are simple PRINT statements.

Boxing and indenting You will not want to draw boxes around the parts of every program you read. Fortunately, you do not have to. That is, you do not have to if the writer indents each block nested inside another block. By looking at the indents, you can see the nesting without drawing boxes.

Planning a Program with Nesting

Jennifer's program COINS is an example of a branch block nested inside a loop block. In this section, you will plan a program that nests one branch block inside another branch block. In Session 58, you will enter your program into the computer and debug it.

The problem Your problem is to write a program that begins by asking the user to enter two words. The program must tell the computer to decide first whether the words are the same or different. If the words are the same, the computer must print a message saying so. If they are different, the computer must tell which one comes first in the dictionary.

Three-way branch This program has a three-way branch: Word 1 is the same as word 2, or word 1 comes before word 2, or word 1 comes after word 2. The branch blocks you have seen are only two-way, either-or branches. But you have learned that you can nest one block inside another. You can create a three-way branch by putting one two-way branch inside another.

Outer branch You can start by writing the BASIC branch outline that you have learned. Choose a condition that tests whether the two words are the same.

Inner branch If the words are the same, the computer tests no further. If not, the computer must test the words again to see which comes first in the dictionary. This test is the first line of the inner branch, which must be nested inside the outer branch.

Planning the program You should be able to plan the whole program now. Write a top-level description first. Then fill in the details. In the next session, you will enter the program into the computer and debug it.

1. What is a computer simulation?

2. What determines how accurate a computer simulation is?

3. Program COINS uses the RND function to get random numbers. Suppose that RND does not give truly random numbers. How would that affect the accuracy of the simulation?

4. In Bruce's version of program COINS, what is the condition in the branch block?

5. In Bruce's version of program COINS, what are the two "do somethings" in the branch block?

6. In Bruce's version of program COINS, what is the "do something" in the loop block in the subroutine at line 400?

7. What is the main difference between Bruce's and Jennifer's versions of program COINS?

8. Which version of program COINS, Bruce's or Jennifer's, do you like better? Explain your answer.

9. What does it mean to say that one program block is "nested" inside another block?

10. Each box on page 319 is nested inside a program block. What type of block is each box inside?

11. How do indents help you read programs with nested blocks?

Programming Project: Nested Blocks

IN THIS SESSION YOU WILL:
• Enter the program planned in Session 57.
• Debug the program and save it on the diskette.

Three-Way Branch Problem

The program you designed should do two things. First, it should ask the user to enter two words. Second, it should do *only one* of these three things:

1. Print SAME if the two words are identical.
2. Print a message saying that the first word comes before the second in the dictionary, if that is true.
3. Print a message saying that the first word comes after the second in the dictionary, if that is true.

Start the computer as usual with your diskette. Enter your program. Run it several times and check it with words that cause all three messages to be printed.

Save your program with the name DICTIONARY before finishing this session.

Empty Branches 59

- Learn the outline of the branch block when one branch is empty.
- Learn the opposites of all the comparison operators.
- Write one-line branches.
- Plan a program with empty branches.

Examples of Empty Branches

You have seen that the branch block lets you write programs that do one thing or another. The branch outline contains both a false "do something" and a true "do something":

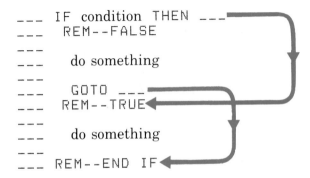

```
___  IF condition THEN ___
___     REM--FALSE
___
___        do something
___
___        GOTO ___
___     REM--TRUE
___
___        do something
___
___  REM--END IF
```

Doing nothing There are many times, however, when you want to tell the computer either to do something or else to do nothing. If you wanted to show these changes in the above outline, you would make one of the two "do somethings" **empty**. In other words, there would be no BASIC statements in one of the two branches. In this session, you will see examples of this special case, and you will learn how to shorten the outline when there is an empty branch.

Everyday examples Empty branches occur often in everyday life as well as in computer programs. Think about each one of these sentences:

1. If it is raining, take your umbrella.
2. If you have enough money, buy a bag of oranges.
3. If the room is too hot, turn down the thermostat.

Ask yourself what each sentence says to do if the condition is false. If it is not raining, what should you do? If you do not have enough money, what should you do? If the room is not too hot, what should you do?

Do nothing   The answer to all three questions is the same: "Do anything." The instructions say nothing at all about what to do if the condition is false. If these sentences were written as BASIC branch outlines, the false "do something" would be empty.

The branch outline   Let's see how to put sentence 1 into the form of a BASIC branch. Here is how it looks:

```
___   IF  it is raining  THEN  ___
___      REM--FALSE
___
___        do nothing
___
___        GOTO  ___
___      REM--TRUE
___
___        take umbrella
___
___   REM--END IF
```

A Shortened Branch Outline

You just saw that the standard BASIC branch outline can be used for empty branches. However, it is long and clumsy. There is a shortcut for empty branches.

Hard to read   The "do nothing" part of the "if it is raining" branch does not really tell you anything. You can simply leave this part of the branch out:

```
___   IF  it is raining  THEN  ___
___      REM--FALSE
___        GOTO  ___
___      REM--TRUE
___
___        take umbrella
___
___   REM--END IF
```

Although this version is correct, it is very hard to read. It seems silly to have a false branch with nothing in it, and then a GOTO to get around the true branch.

A better way   It would be better if the false branch had something to do and the true branch were empty. Then there would be no need for a GOTO statement. *You can switch the false and true "do somethings" in any branch block by changing the condition to its opposite.* On the next page is the sentence with the condition changed from "it is raining" to "it is not raining".

```
___   IF  it is not raining  THEN  ___
___      REM--FALSE
___
___         take umbrella
___
___         GOTO ___
___      REM--TRUE
___
___         do nothing
___
___   REM--END IF
```

This version says exactly the same thing as the original one.

Shortening the branch This version of the branch is no easier to read, but a small change will make it more readable. The "do nothing" part is really empty, so there is no need for the GOTO statement. Also, there is no need for the REM--TRUE statement, since the true branch is empty. Here is the shortened branch:

```
___   IF  it is not raining  THEN  ___
___      REM--FALSE
___
___         take umbrella
___
___   REM--END IF
```

More readable This version of the empty branch is the easiest one to read. The IF statement tells when to skip the "do something" instructions—"take umbrella."

Opposite Conditions

You just saw how to shorten the BASIC branch outline when one branch is empty. Here is the shortened form:

```
___   IF  skip condition  THEN  ___
___      REM--FALSE
___
___         do something
___
___   REM--END IF
```

The skip condition You found that you had to change the condition in the long branch outline into a **skip condition**, which tells the computer when to skip over the "do something" block. In this section, you will practice changing conditions into skip conditions.

Opposites In the last section, you changed the English phrase "it is raining" into the opposite phrase "it is not raining." In mathematics, these two phrases are called **complementary**. That word comes from the word *complete*. The two phrases together are complete: Either it is raining or it is not raining. There are no other possibilities.

BASIC comparisons All the conditions in your BASIC programs are based on comparisons between two pieces of data. Are they equal? Is one greater than the other? To change a BASIC condition into a skip condition, you will need practice in finding opposites of the BASIC comparisons.

Opposite of "equal" Let's suppose you start with the condition A$ = B$, and you want to find the opposite condition. Two pieces of data are either equal (=) or not equal (< >). So the conditions A$ = B$ and A$ < > B$ are opposite and also complementary, because there are no other possibilities.

Opposite of "greater than" Suppose you start with the condition P > Q, which is true if the value of P is greater than the value of Q. What is the opposite, or complement, of *greater than*? It is natural to say that *less than* is the complement of *greater than*, but that is wrong. The conditions P > Q and P < Q are not complete: The condition P = Q is not included in either one.

Less than or equal The complement of *greater than* (>) is *less than or equal* (< =). P is either greater than Q or else it is less than or equal to Q. The conditions P > Q and P < = Q are complete. There are no other possibilities.

Complementary operators The table below shows a complete list of all the comparisons possible in BASIC and their complements.

Comparisons		Complements	
equal to	A = B	A < > B	not equal to
less than	A < B	A > = B	greater or equal
greater than	A > B	A < = B	less or equal

Notice that you can read this table from right to left or left to right. For example, the complement of < > is =, the complement of > = is <, and the complement of < = is >.

Skip conditions You need to figure out the complement, or opposite, of a BASIC comparison when you want to use the short form of the branch block. Recall that you need to know how to tell the computer when to skip the "do something" block. It is natural for you to think about the condition for performing the "do something," not for skipping it. If you think about the "do something" condition first, you must then change it to the skip condition.

Another Short Branch

Applesoft BASIC allows you to write some special empty branches in a very short form. In this section, you will find out how to do that. You will also find out when *not* to use this form.

The IF statement You have learned that the `IF` statement has this form:

```
IF condition THEN number
```

Number stands for the line number of another statement in a program. Every version of BASIC has such an `IF` statement. A few versions, including Applesoft, allow you to use another kind of `IF` statement:

```
IF condition THEN statement
```

Statement stands for any BASIC statement at all. If the condition is true, the computer performs the statement. If the condition is false, the computer skips the statement.

Examples Here are a few examples of this kind of `IF` statement:

```
230 IF X > 39 THEN LET X = 39
350 IF A$ = "NO" THEN END
480 IF P = 1 THEN GOSUB 800
```

The first example might be used in a graphics program to make sure that an X coordinate does not get too big. The second example could be used to stop a program if the user had just typed `NO` in answer to an `INPUT A$` statement. The third example tells the computer to perform the entire subroutine at line `800` if `P = 1`.

Advantages This one-line branch block is very easy to think about and use. You do not have to figure out the complement of the comparison. The statement is also very easy to read.

Disadvantages If the "do something" part of a branch block is more than one statement, this form of the `IF` statement is a poor choice. There are tricky ways to put more than one statement after `THEN`; but the results are often hard to predict, and the `IF` statement becomes very hard to read. Finally, you may not find this kind of `IF` statement on another computer.

Advice Do not use the one-line branch if the "do something" has more than one statement or if you are likely to add statements in the future.

Planning a Programming Project

Spend the rest of your time in this session designing a program that uses a branch block with one empty branch.

The first problem Your problem is this: Write a program that asks the user to enter a sentence. The program should then print the number of words in the sentence on the screen.

Tools needed Words are always separated by blank spaces; so your program will have to loop through the characters of the user's input string and look for spaces. You will have to use the MID$ function to make the computer look at one character at a time. You will need the LEN function to tell the computer when to stop looping. If your memory needs refreshing about these functions, reread Session 43 or look at the Applesoft manuals.

The branch Your program has to count a word whenever it finds a space. That means you will need a branch inside your loop. The branch will tell the computer either to add 1 to a counter or else do nothing, depending on whether the computer has found a space.

Second problem When that program looks right, add this new feature to it: As the computer finds each new word, have the computer print just that word on a line by itself. The words of the sentence should appear in a vertical column when the program ends.

More tools You will need the MID$ function again to extract words from the input string. Your program must have a way to make the computer remember where the previous space was so that the computer can tell what characters to get from the string.

OBOB You will probably meet OBOB in this project: the **off-by-one bug**. Unless you are very careful, your count of words will be one less than is correct. OBOB is the most common bug in programming. This is a good time to think about how it happens.

QUESTIONS

1. What does the term *empty branch* mean?
2. Pick sentence 2 or 3 on page 323 and write it in the form of a complete BASIC branch with both a true part and a false part.
3. What had to be done to the condition "it is raining" to make "take umbrella" become the *false* branch?
4. Pick sentence 2 or 3 on page 323 and rewrite it in the form of the shortened branch outline.
5. Why is the condition in the shortened branch outline called a *skip condition*?
6. What does it mean to say that one comparison is the complement of another comparison?

7. What is the complement of each comparison below?

   a. `A$ <> B$`   d. `A > 5`
   b. `X <= 0`   e. `R = S`
   c. `P$ < Q$`   f. `M1 >= M2`

8. Pick sentence 1, 2, or 3 on page 323 and write it in the form of a one-line branch.

9. What are one advantage and one disadvantage of using the one-line branch?

Left: Once, we had only simple instruments to help us predict the weather. Right: Now, forecasters get help from computers that can simulate weather patterns.

 # Programming Project: Empty Branches

IN • Enter the program planned in Session 59.
THIS SESSION • Debug the program and save it on the diskette.
YOU WILL:

Empty-Branch Problem

The program you designed should do two things. First, it should ask the user to enter a sentence. Then it should print the number of words in the sentence.

Start the computer as usual with your diskette. Enter your program. Run it several times and check it with different sentences. What happens if the sentence has only one word? What happens if the sentence is an empty string? Watch out for OBOB!

When this first version of your program is working correctly, make the additions given at the end of Session 59: Have the computer print the words of the sentence in a vertical column at the left.

Enter the additions to your program and debug it. Save your program with the name WORDS before finishing this session.

There were no new BASIC words introduced in this part.

BASIC Vocabulary (Shaded Areas Show Standard BASIC Words)

Commands		Statements			Functions
Program	Diskette	Action	Action	Control	
RUN	LOAD	INPUT	SPEED=	GOSUB	INT
LIST	SAVE	LET	FLASH	RETURN	SQR
NEW	DELETE	PRINT	INVERSE	END	RND
DEL	CATALOG	REM	NORMAL	GOTO	LEN
CONT	LOCK	PLOT	COLOR=	IF	MID$
BRUN	UNLOCK	HLIN	TEXT	FOR	
&INDENT		VLIN	GR	NEXT	
&UNDENT		HOME			
&RENUMBER					

New Ideas

branch block A program block that has the computer perform either one group of statements or another.

complementary conditions Two conditions that together include all possibilities. Example: $X > Y$ and $X <= Y$ are complementary.

computer simulation A program that makes the computer behave like some real process.

nested block A program block inside another program block.

skip condition A condition in a branch block that, when true, tells the computer to skip the "do something" part of the block.

structured programming A program method that uses only action, loop, and branch blocks.

Part 9

Putting It All Together

In the first eight parts, you have seen the main features of the BASIC language. You have discovered what the computer can do. You have learned to use subroutines to organize a program. You have studied the action block, the loop block, and the branch block.

Other languages No matter what computer language you use, solving problems on the computer always means the same thing. You must begin with a clear, top-level description of the problem. As you fill in the details, you must decide whether an action, a loop, or a branch block is the right structure to use. Every programming language has the structures you need for the job. Grammar and spelling will be different in other computer languages, but the ideas you have learned will be the same.

A big project You have learned these ideas one at a time by exploring them in fairly small programs. It is time to pull together the main ideas of computer problem solving and put them to work on a large project. You have all the tools you need. Now you can apply what you know.

Plan first People who work with computers have a saying: "The sooner you start writing program statements, the longer it will take you to finish the job." Badly written programs, such as SPAGHETTI, happen when the writer dives into the problem and writes one statement after another. This trial-and-error approach often works with small problems, but it fails badly with big ones. There is no substitute for careful top-down planning before writing a single statement. The block structures you have learned—subroutines, actions, loops, and branches—will help you plan your program.

The payoff Though planning takes time away from programming, there are big rewards. Usually, your program will be working correctly sooner when you plan than when you just start writing statements without a plan. More important, a well-planned, well-organized, and well-documented program is much easier to add to and improve.

Playing a Game

IN • Play a word-guessing game.
THIS SESSION • Write a top-level description of the game.
YOU WILL:

Pulling Ideas Together

There will be no new tools or ideas introduced in Part 9. Instead, you will follow easy steps to write a complex program. You will use the tools and methods you have learned to solve the problem. In this session, you will define and become familiar with a game that you will program into the computer. In later sessions, you will write, debug, and change the program.

A Guessing Game

It takes two to play the game, so find a partner and decide who will be partner A and who will be partner B. You will play a word game.

Rules of the game   First, what is the game? Here are the rules:

1. Partner A thinks of a short secret word.
2. Partner B tries to guess the secret word.
3. Partner A says one of three things:
   a. "You got it. The game is over."
   b. "My word is earlier in the dictionary. Try again."
   c. "My word is later in the dictionary. Try again."

Play the game   Take a few minutes to play the game. Switch roles so that each person gets a chance to pick a secret word. While playing the game, try to find a method for guessing the secret word as quickly as possible.

Know the rules   The rules of the game should be clear to you by now. It is always important to know precisely what the problem is before you start to put a program into the computer. Often, programmers have trouble because they begin to write a program before they understand exactly what it is supposed to do.

Describe the Game in English

Your goal is to teach the computer to play the game. *The best way to start is to write a description of the game in English.* This description will bring you closer to knowing what the computer will have to be told. Here is how one person described the game:

"Susan and Bill are playing. The game starts when Susan thinks of a secret word. After that, Bill tries again and again to guess the word. Each time, Susan tells Bill whether the secret word is earlier or later in the dictionary than the one Bill guessed. As soon as Bill guesses correctly, Susan says 'You got it!' and the game is over."

Computer can't do it That description seems accurate and simple. Most people would understand it easily, but your computer cannot. Your goal, therefore, is to rewrite the English-language description in the programming language BASIC, which your computer understands. You will move from the English-language description to the final BASIC program in easy steps.

Converting to the Main Routine

The wrong thing to do at this point is to begin writing down BASIC statements. *The best way to reach your goal of a BASIC program is to think first about the structure of the game. Reread the English paragraph and look for the major topics. Create an outline, just as you do in English class.* Here is how one person outlined the game:

1. Susan thinks of a secret word.
2. Bill guesses again and again, and Susan gives hints until he gets it right.
3. Susan congratulates him.

Main routine outline Much as you did in earlier programming projects, the best thing to do now is to convert this description into the main routine of the program. Here is the first stage of the conversion, partly in BASIC and partly still in English:

```
100 REM--PROGRAM GUESSING GAME
110 ::  get secret word
120 ::  guess words
130 ::  wrap up game
140 END
```

Think at high level Note that the outline gives no details. How does the computer get the secret word? How does the user guess words? How does the computer wrap up the game? At this point, it makes no difference how the computer does these things. In fact, these details are exactly the wrong thing to think about now. You will take care of details later, when you write subroutines that tell the computer what these top-level instructions mean.

Convert to GOSUBs The next stage of planning is to convert the main routine completely into BASIC statements. There are no simple BASIC statements that you can substitute for the English phrases. That means you should use a GOSUB for each one:

```
100 REM--PROGRAM GUESSING GAME
110:: GOSUB 200: REM--SECRET WORD
120:: GOSUB 400: REM--GUESS WORDS
130:: GOSUB 600: REM--WRAP UP
140 END
```

Plan the Subroutines

Now that the main routine is finished, you can start thinking about the subroutines. Again, the trick is to avoid getting bogged down in details. Keep thinking at as high a level as possible. Think about what kinds of program *structures* you will need.

Secret word You do not know very much about the first subroutine, SECRET WORD. You do know where the subroutine begins and what it is supposed to do. With this information, you can write a skeleton of the subroutine.

```
200 REM--SUB SECRET WORD
210:: PRINT "SECRET WORD SUBROUTINE"
---
---     get secret word
---
380 RETURN
```

You will remove the PRINT statement in line 210 later. You put it there now to get the computer to print a message whenever it performs the subroutine. This is an example of a **debugging message**. It will help check the program when you first enter and run it in Session 62.

Guess words Here is a similar skeleton for the second subroutine, GUESS WORDS.

```
400 REM--SUB GUESS WORDS
410:: PRINT "GUESS WORDS SUBROUTINE"
---
---     keep guessing until right
---
---     give hints if guess is wrong
---
580 RETURN
```

The computer will print the debugging message in line 410 whenever it performs the GUESS WORDS subroutine. You will remove line 410 later. The English phrases tell what you must translate into BASIC later.

Wrap up Finally, here is the skeleton outline of the WRAP UP subroutine, which also has a debugging message:

```
600 REM--SUB WRAP UP
610:: PRINT "WRAP UP SUBROUTINE"
---
---     give congratulations
---
780 RETURN
```

Complete outline Now you can combine the main routine and the skeletons of the subroutines. Blank lines separate the main routine and subroutines.

```
100 REM--PROGRAM GUESSING GAME
110:: GOSUB 200: REM--SECRET WORD
120:: GOSUB 400: REM--GUESS WORDS
130:: GOSUB 600: REM--WRAP UP
140 END
190:
200 REM--SUB SECRET WORD
210:: PRINT "SECRET WORD SUBROUTINE"
---
---     get secret word
---
380 RETURN
390:
400 REM--SUB GUESS WORDS
410:: PRINT "GUESS WORDS SUBROUTINE"
---
---     keep guessing until right
---
---     give hints if guess is wrong
---
580 RETURN
590:
600 REM--SUB WRAP UP
610:: PRINT "WRAP UP SUBROUTINE"
---
---     give congratulations
---
780 RETURN
```

A giant leap Even though you have not been thinking about the details of the program, you have made valuable gains. You now have a strong framework that will allow you to concentrate on one block of the program without worrying about the others.

How to start *any* program

The first step in planning a program is to work out the *main block structure* without worrying about details inside the blocks.

---

1. According to the rules, what happens if Bill guesses Susan's secret word?

2. If Bill fails to guess the secret word, how does it help for Susan to tell him that the word is either earlier or later in the dictionary?

3. What does line 1 1 0 of the main program correspond to in the English language outline on page 335?

4. Which line of the main program corresponds to step 2 of the English-language outline on page 335?

5. What does it mean to plan a solution to a problem at a "high level"?

6. Why should you write the main routine before you write any other parts of a program?

7. Why is it a good idea to avoid thinking about details in the early stages of planning a program?

Entering the Program 62

IN • Enter the complete main routine.
THIS SESSION • Enter skeleton subroutines.
YOU WILL: • Verify that the computer performs the subroutines in the proper order.

Writing a Complex Program

In Session 61, you played a game to guess a secret word. You also constructed the framework of a program to tell the computer how to play the game. Most of the details in the program are still missing. However, you can now enter this framework into the computer and verify that the computer performs the steps in the proper order.

The Main Routine

Start the computer in the usual way with your diskette.

```
100 REM--PROGRAM GUESSING GAME
110:: GOSUB 200: REM--SECRET WORD
120:: GOSUB 400: REM--GUESS WORDS
130:: GOSUB 600: REM--WRAP UP
140 END
```
Enter the main routine.

```
LIST
```
Check for errors.

```
RUN
```
Surprise?

1. Why did you get the message you saw when you ran the main routine?
2. How is the main routine like a table of contents for the program?

Subroutine Skeletons

Next you need the skeletons of the three subroutines. Enter lines 190 through 780 of the framework shown here:

```
100 REM--PROGRAM GUESSING GAME
110:: GOSUB 200: REM--SECRET WORD
120:: GOSUB 400: REM--GUESS WORDS
130:: GOSUB 600: REM--WRAP UP
140 END
190:
200 REM--SUB SECRET WORD
210:: PRINT "SECRET WORD SUBROUTINE"
380 RETURN
390:
400 REM--SUB GUESS WORDS
410:: PRINT "GUESS WORDS SUBROUTINE"
580 RETURN
590:
600 REM--SUB WRAP UP
610:: PRINT "WRAP UP SUBROUTINE"
780 RETURN
```

List the program and read it carefully. Fix any errors.

3. Where in the program should you put the details that tell the computer to ask the user for guesses and to decide whether the user has guessed the correct word?

4. What is the purpose of the subroutine beginning in line 600?

Check the Program

Now, let's make sure that the program is working correctly. Run the program and make sure you get the following output:

```
SECRET WORD SUBROUTINE
GUESS WORDS SUBROUTINE
WRAP UP SUBROUTINE
```

This output confirms that the framework of your program is correct. Most of the details are still missing, but you will insert them in the next few sessions.

Save the program under the name GUESSING GAME.

5. What would the computer print if you removed line 130 and then ran the program?

6. What would the computer print if you left out line 380?

Designing the Subroutines

IN THIS SESSION YOU WILL:	• Write the subroutines in a mixture of English and BASIC.
	• Convert the subroutines to BASIC statements.

Status of Program GUESSING GAME

In Session 62, you entered the framework of program GUESSING GAME into the computer and saved it on your diskette. The main routine is complete and needs no more work. The subroutines, however, are skeletons and have no details. In this session, you will begin writing the body of each of the subroutines in a mixture of English and BASIC, just as you did for the main routine. Then you will convert the bodies of the subroutines into BASIC statements.

Subroutine SECRET WORD

Remember that when you played the game with a partner, one person had to think of a secret word. The purpose of subroutine SECRET WORD is to get the secret word from one of the players. Also, you want the screen to be clear before the players begin the game. Finally, you want the program to be friendly to the players; so you want the computer to display a message that tells the players what to input.

First try at subroutine With the information above, you can fill in the body of the subroutine with phrases that tell the computer what to do. Here is the revised subroutine.

```
200 REM--SUB SECRET WORD
210::  clear the screen
220::  ask for secret word
230::  input secret word
380 RETURN
```

Lines 200 and 380 are the same ones you entered in Session 62. English phrases show the details that you have not yet worked out.

Finish the subroutine The next step is to replace each English phrase with one or two BASIC statements to carry out the task described. (Remember that if the task is too complicated for one or two BASIC statements, you can insert a GOSUB statement to another subroutine that will handle the details.) On the next page is the subroutine with BASIC statements replacing the English phrases.

```
200 REM--SUB SECRET WORD
210:: HOME
220:: PRINT "WHAT'S THE SECRET WORD";
230:: INPUT S$
380 RETURN
```

Compare each new BASIC statement with the English phrase it replaced.

Subroutine GUESS WORDS

The next subroutine handles the details of guessing. Recall how you played the game. Once your partner thought of a secret word, you guessed again and again, getting hints along the way, until you guessed the right word. What kind of program structure tells the computer to do something again and again until some condition becomes true? If you are thinking of a loop block, you are right. The exit condition from the loop is that the guess matches the secret word.

Filling in the details Here is a loop framework that uses English phrases for the body and also for the exit condition:

```
400 REM--SUB GUESS WORDS
410:: REM--LOOP
___:::: print message to ask for guess
___:::: input guess
___::: IF guess is correct THEN 500
___:::: give a hint
490::: GOTO 410
500:: REM--END LOOP
580 RETURN
```

Complete the subroutine You can easily replace the first two phrases with BASIC statements. You need a condition in the IF statement to test whether the guess is correct. If the guess is incorrect, the computer must "give a hint." No single BASIC statement can give a hint, so you must use a GOSUB. Here is the refined version of the subroutine:

```
400 REM--SUB GUESS WORDS
410:: REM--LOOP
420:::: PRINT "WHAT IS YOUR GUESS";
430:::: INPUT G$
440::: IF G$ = S$ THEN 500
450:::: GOSUB 800: REM--HINT
490::: GOTO 410
500:: REM--END LOOP
580 RETURN
```

In the version of the program you entered in Session 62, there was no subroutine HINT. You discovered you needed the new subroutine when you were filling in the details in subroutine GUESS WORDS. (You may find you need even more subroutines when you fill in the details of subroutine HINT.) Forget about HINT now. Putting off complicated details by using GOSUBs is the right way to write long programs.

Subroutine WRAP UP

The last subroutine in the main program is easy to write. You need only two PRINT statements. Here is the finished subroutine:

```
600 REM--SUB WRAP UP
610:: PRINT "CONGRATULATIONS, YOU GOT IT"
620:: PRINT "THE SECRET WORD WAS "; S$
780 RETURN
```

Subroutine HINT

You have now completed the main routine and all the subroutines it uses. But the job is not over. Subroutine GUESS WORDS has a GOSUB 800 to a subroutine named HINT. HINT does not yet exist.

What structure is needed? The job of HINT is to tell the user that the secret word is either earlier or later in the dictionary. You need to use a branch block for such an either-or situation.

First try at subroutine HINT The body of the subroutine is in lines 810 through 870 below. The subroutine is in the form of the branch block that you learned about in Part 8.

```
800 REM--SUB HINT
810:: IF secret earlier than guess THEN 850
820::: REM--FALSE
830:::: give "later" hint
840:::: GOTO 870
850::: REM--TRUE
860:::: give "earlier" hint
870:: REM--END IF
980 RETURN
```

Finish the subroutine If the secret word (S$) is earlier in the dictionary than the guess (G$), then the computer should print the message EARLIER THAN. Otherwise the computer should print the message LATER THAN. Here is the complete subroutine:

```
800 REM--SUB HINT
810:: IF S$ < G$ THEN 850
820::: REM--FALSE
830:::: PRINT "LATER THAN "; G$
840:::: GOTO 870
850::: REM--TRUE
860:::: PRINT "EARLIER THAN "; G$
870:: REM--END IF
980 RETURN
```

Complete Program

All the necessary details are now in the subroutines. Here is the complete program:

```
100 REM--PROGRAM GUESSING GAME
110:: GOSUB 200:   REM--SECRET WORD
120:: GOSUB 400:   REM--GUESS WORDS
130:: GOSUB 600:   REM--WRAP UP
140 END
190:
200 REM--SUB SECRET WORD
210:: HOME
220:: PRINT "WHAT'S THE SECRET WORD";
230:: INPUT S$
380 RETURN
390:
400 REM--SUB GUESS WORDS
410:: REM--LOOP
420:::: PRINT "WHAT IS YOUR GUESS";
430:::: INPUT G$
440::: IF G$ = S$ THEN 500
450:::: GOSUB 800: REM--HINT
490::: GOTO 410
500:: REM--END LOOP
580 RETURN
590:
600 REM--SUB WRAP UP
610:: PRINT "CONGRATULATIONS, YOU GOT IT"
620:: PRINT "THE SECRET WORD WAS "; S$
780 RETURN
790:
800 REM--SUB HINT
810:: IF S$ < G$ THEN 850
820::: REM--FALSE
830:::: PRINT "LATER THAN "; G$
840:::: GOTO 870
850::: REM--TRUE
860:::: PRINT "EARLIER THAN "; G$
870:: REM--END IF
980 RETURN
```

QUESTIONS

1. What variable name stands for the secret word in the program GUESSING GAME?

2. Why is there no need for GOSUBs in the body of subroutine SECRET WORD?

3. Why is a loop needed in subroutine GUESS WORDS?

4. What variable name stands for the guess?

5. Why is there a GOSUB statement in line 450?

6. Why don't you have to worry about the condition S$ = G$ in subroutine HINT?

7. Why must the body of subroutine HINT be a branch block?

8. What steps should you take to go from a skeleton subroutine to a finished subroutine?

9. When you fill in details in a subroutine, what should you do if you run across a task you cannot describe in a few BASIC statements?

Right: Computerized scanning devices let us make color movies of the body's inner workings. Left: Traditional diagnostic tests will always have their place in modern medicine.

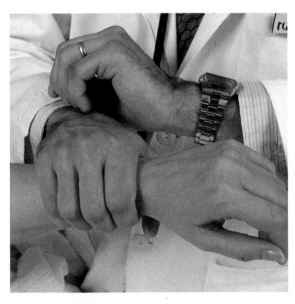

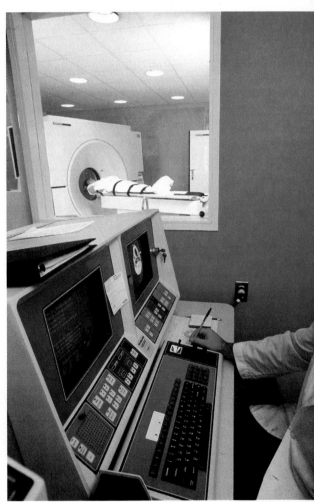

Entering the Subroutines

IN **THIS SESSION** **YOU WILL:**	• Enter the new subroutines. • Run and debug the program. • Find weaknesses in the program.

Filling in the Subroutines

Enter the bodies of the subroutines you worked out in Session 63. Start the computer with your diskette as usual.

```
LOAD GUESSING GAME
LIST
```
Check the program you saved in Session 62.

```
210:: HOME
220:: PRINT "WHAT'S THE SECRET WORD ";
230:: INPUT S$
```
Now enter the body of the subroutine SECRET WORD.

```
LIST 200, 380
```
List the subroutine.

Check your listing carefully and fix any errors. Here is what the complete subroutine should look like:

```
200 REM--SUB SECRET WORD
210:: HOME
220:: PRINT "WHAT'S THE SECRET WORD ";
230:: INPUT S$
380 RETURN
```

Debugging and refining are important stages in writing a computer program.

Enter and check the rest of the subroutines. Your new program should look like this:

```
100 REM--PROGRAM GUESSING GAME
110:: GOSUB 200:   REM--SECRET WORD
120:: GOSUB 400:   REM--GUESS WORDS
130:: GOSUB 600:   REM--WRAP UP
140 END
190:
200 REM--SUB SECRET WORD
210:: HOME
220:: PRINT "WHAT'S THE SECRET WORD";
230:: INPUT S$
380 RETURN
390:
400 REM--SUB GUESS WORDS
410:: REM--LOOP
420:::: PRINT "WHAT IS YOUR GUESS";
430:::: INPUT G$
440::: IF G$ = S$ THEN 500
450:::: GOSUB 800: REM--HINT
490::: GOTO 410
500:: REM--END LOOP
580 RETURN
590:
600 REM--SUB WRAP UP
610:: PRINT "CONGRATULATIONS, YOU GOT IT"
620:: PRINT "THE SECRET WORD WAS "; S$
780 RETURN
790:
800 REM--SUB HINT
810:: IF S$ < G$ THEN 850
820::: REM--FALSE
830:::: PRINT "LATER THAN "; G$
840:::: GOTO 870
850::: REM--TRUE
860:::: PRINT "EARLIER THAN "; G$
870:: REM--END IF
980 RETURN
```

Take a few moments to check all your entries. Notice the blank lines between the parts of the program.

1. Why are the PRINT statements that were in the original skeletons of the subroutines no longer useful?

2. Suppose you decided to change the whole program into an infinite loop so that a new game started as soon as the old one was over. What part of the program would you have to change?

3. Suppose you wanted to improve the hints given by the computer. What part of the program would you need to change?

Try out the Program

Let's try a secret word to see how the program works.

```
RUN
SAM
```
_____ This is the secret word.

```
BEE
TRY
HOW
SAM
```
_____ Did you get the right hints?

The program is working now! It gives good hints when the guess is not right, and it prints the congratulatory message when you guess the secret word. However, you can improve the program, as you will see in the next session.

Save the program under the name GUESSING GAME before leaving the computer.

4. If the secret word is COW and you guess CAT, what message would you see on the screen?
5. If the secret word is DOG and you guess DOG, what message would you see on the screen?

If you have extra lab time:

- Change the congratulatory message in subroutine WRAP UP to your own message.
- Change the prompt message in subroutine SECRET WORD to your own prompt.

Refining the Program

IN • Identify areas in the program that need improvement.
THIS SESSION • Revise the subroutines.
YOU WILL:

Program Improvements

At the end of Session 64, you had a chance to think about some problems with your game program. The program works, but it still needs some improvements. Here is a list of some remaining problems:

1. After you type the secret word, it stays on the screen. The game is not a challenge if the second player can look on the screen and see the answer.

2. If you typed ANTIDISESTABLISHMENTARIANISM as the secret word, it might take a while for the person playing against you to guess it. You should limit the length of the secret word.

3. To make the game more challenging, you should limit the number of guesses a player can have.

Removing the Secret Word

The first problem to solve is making the secret word disappear from the screen after you enter it.

Main routine is a directory When you are deciding what part of a program to change, you can use the main routine as a directory. Here it is:

```
100 REM--PROGRAM GUESSING GAME
110:: GOSUB 200:  REM--SECRET WORD
120:: GOSUB 400:  REM--GUESS WORDS
130:: GOSUB 600:  REM--WRAP UP
140 END
```

You can see that subroutines GUESS WORDS and WRAP UP have nothing to do with getting the secret word. But subroutine SECRET WORD does. Here is how it looks now:

```
200 REM--SUB SECRET WORD
210:: HOME
220:: PRINT "WHAT'S THE SECRET WORD";
230:: INPUT S$
380 RETURN
```

When the user responds to the INPUT statement, the secret word stays on the screen. Getting rid of it is easy: Just put this line after the INPUT statement:

```
240:: HOME
```

As soon as one player enters the secret word and presses [RETURN], the computer clears the screen. The other player must look away while the first player types in the word, but afterward, it is gone from the screen.

Limiting the Length of the Secret Word

The second problem you need to solve is limiting the length of the secret word. Once again, you need to change subroutine SECRET WORD. Here is how it now looks:

```
200 REM--SUB SECRET WORD
210:: HOME
220:: PRINT "WHAT'S THE SECRET WORD";
230:: INPUT S$
240:: HOME
380 RETURN
```

What is needed Let's change the subroutine so that if the first player enters a secret word longer than three characters, the computer will reject the word and ask the player to type a word of the right length. If the secret word is three or fewer characters, the game should go on.

Choosing a block Once again, the main question you need to ask is: "What kind of block do I need to use? Is it an action, a loop, or a branch?" The clue lies in the fact that if you keep entering words longer than three characters, the computer should keep asking for another word. As soon as you type one of the proper length, the computer should stop asking. You need a loop block.

Add loop to subroutine The loop should begin after the first HOME statement and end before the second. Here is a first try at the loop structure:

```
200 REM--SUB SECRET WORD
210:: HOME
215:: REM--LOOP
220::::  PRINT "WHAT'S THE SECRET WORD";
230::::  INPUT S$
234:::  GOTO 215
235:: REM--END LOOP
240:: HOME
380 RETURN
```

Note that the lines inside the loop are indented farther to the right.

Add exit condition The problem now is that there is no way out of the loop: It is an infinite loop. You need an IF statement that tests some exit condition and tells the computer to stop looping if the condition is true. The condition is met if the secret word has three or fewer characters. You learned about the LEN function in Session 42. LEN (S$) returns the length of the string S$. Here are the changes you need:

```
200 REM--SUB SECRET WORD
210:: HOME
215:: REM--LOOP
220:::: PRINT "WHAT'S THE SECRET WORD";
230:::: INPUT S$
231::: IF LEN (S$) <= 3 THEN 235
232:::: PRINT "TOO LONG"
234::: GOTO 215
235:: REM--END LOOP
240:: HOME
380 RETURN
```

Now, if the secret word has three characters or fewer, the computer leaves the loop. If not, the computer goes on to line 232, which says to tell the first player that the secret word is too long. Then the computer returns to the beginning of the loop.

A change of structure When you first planned subroutine SECRET WORD, it contained only an action block. With the improvement you just made, the subroutine is now a loop with action blocks inside. Programmers often make similar changes in block structure when they refine programs.

Limiting the Number of Guesses

Now you can start thinking about how to limit the number of guesses. First, which program block should you change? It certainly is not the SECRET WORD subroutine nor is it the WRAP UP subroutine. The GUESS WORDS subroutine needs changing. Here is that subroutine as it now stands:

```
400 REM--SUB GUESS WORDS
410:: REM--LOOP
420:::: PRINT "WHAT IS YOUR GUESS";
430:::: INPUT G$
440::: IF G$ = S$ THEN 500
450:::: GOSUB 800: REM--HINT
490::: GOTO 410
500:: REM--END LOOP
580 RETURN
```

Compound exit condition At present, the computer stops looping only when the guess is correct. You want the loop to stop when the guess is correct *or* when the player uses up the allowed number of guesses, so you need a *compound* condition in the IF statement. Let's use the variable C to count the number of guesses and limit the guesses to ten. Here is what the new IF statement should look like:

```
440::: IF G$ = S$ OR C = 10 THEN 500
```

Counting loop needed The subroutine says to end the loop if C equals 1Ø. But how does the computer know where to start counting? And how does it keep track of the number of guesses? You need two new statements. First, you must set the value of C to Ø *outside* the loop. Second, you must have the computer add 1 to C each time the player guesses. Here is the subroutine with the new IF statement and the statements that define and keep track of C.

```
400 REM--SUB GUESS WORDS
405:: LET C = 0
410:: REM--LOOP
420:::: PRINT "WHAT IS YOUR GUESS";
430:::: INPUT G$
435:::: LET C = C + 1
440::: IF G$ = S$ OR C = 10 THEN 500
450:::: GOSUB 800: REM--HINT
490::: GOTO 410
500:: REM--END LOOP
580 RETURN
```

A New Problem

You have made all the improvements suggested at the beginning of this session. However, you have a new problem. Suppose the user does not guess the secret word before using up all ten tries. The computer leaves the loop, returns to the main routine, and then goes to subroutine WRAP UP, which gives an encouraging message. The player who does not guess the word in ten tries is congratulated! You need to change subroutine WRAP UP too. Here is that subroutine as presently written:

```
600 REM--SUB WRAP UP
610:: PRINT "CONGRATULATIONS, YOU GOT IT"
620:: PRINT "THE SECRET WORD WAS "; S$
780 RETURN
```

What kind of block Right now, the body of the subroutine is an action block. What kind of block is needed to print either a winning message or a losing message? The branch block will do the job. Here is the WRAP UP subroutine with the needed changes:

```
600 REM--SUB WRAP UP
601:: IF G$ = S$ THEN 605
602::: REM--FALSE
603:::: PRINT "YOU LOSE"
604:::: GOTO 615
605::: REM--TRUE
610:::: PRINT "CONGRATULATIONS, YOU GOT IT"
615:: REM--END IF
620:: PRINT "THE SECRET WORD WAS "; S$
780 RETURN
```

The indents have changed because of the branch block. Notice that the branch block tells the computer to print CONGRATULATIONS, YOU GOT IT if G$ = S$, that is, if the guess is correct. If G$ <> S$, the computer prints the message YOU LOSE. Either way, the computer prints the secret word on the screen.

Final Thoughts

You have finished planning and refining the GUESSING GAME program. The final version is in Session 66, where you will enter it into the computer and experiment with it. Although you received step-by-step instructions for the GUESSING GAME program, you learned the basic rules for writing programs on your own. If you follow the steps outlined below faithfully, you will soon be writing complicated programs without help.

How to develop a program

1. Always start with a simple, top-level, main routine. Use English phrases to describe the tasks. Avoid thinking about details at this time.

2. Translate each English phrase in the main routine into one or two BASIC statements. If more are needed, use a GOSUB statement to a subroutine where you will spell out the details later.

3. Write skeleton versions of the subroutines. Include debugging messages. Run the program and check that the parts of the program are performed in the right order.

4. Fill in the details of the subroutines. If a task looks too complicated, use a GOSUB statement to a new subroutine that gives the details.

5. Within each routine, use only action, loop, and branch blocks. Do not use GOTO or IF statements in any other way.

6. Debug the program and add refinements where needed.

Good programs don't just happen. They require careful planning and faithful attention to block structures. These ideas are important in any language, not just BASIC. At first, it may take you longer to write short programs using block structures, but learning to use them is well worth it. You will save time and avoid trouble later on.

1. You changed a subroutine to clear the secret word from the screen. What helped you decide which subroutine to change?

2. Why can you be reasonably sure that the change you made to clear the secret word from the screen will not affect other parts of the program?

3. Before you added the counter variable C to the GUESS WORDS loop, how many guesses would the program permit?

4. Suppose you ran the program in its final form (see page 351) and pressed the (RETURN) key when asked to enter the secret word. What would the computer do?

5. In the final version of the program, what will happen if you guess the correct secret word on the tenth try?

6. What part of the program would you change to have the computer tell the winner how many guesses were used?

7. Suppose the rules of the game were changed so that you could win only if you guessed the secret word correctly *on the tenth guess*. What changes would you have to make in the program?

8. How would you change the program to have the computer give instructions if a user asked for them?

Final Changes **66**

IN THIS SESSION YOU WILL:	• Make further refinements to program GUESSING GAME and debug it. • Play the game. • Save the program.

Making Further Changes

First, change the program to include the refinements you made in the subroutines during the last session. The indents and renumbering software tools will help you make those changes. **Start the computer with your diskette as usual.**

BRUN WRITING TOOLS

This makes &INDENT, &UNDENT, and &RENUMBER available.

LOAD GUESSING GAME

Load the program you saved in Session 64.

LIST 100, 399

This is the main routine and first subroutine.

Make the changes in subroutine SECRET WORD. The new version is shown on the next page, with the changes printed in color. Be sure to use &INDENT and &UNDENT to fix the indents. Run the

It is very satisfying to see a well-written program run correctly.

program and make sure that subroutine SECRET WORD works correctly. Try entering a long word.

```
100 REM--PROGRAM GUESSING GAME
110:: GOSUB 200:   REM--SECRET WORD
120:: GOSUB 400:   REM--GUESS WORDS
130:: GOSUB 600:   REM--WRAP UP
140 END
190:
200 REM--SUB SECRET WORD
210:: HOME
215:: REM--LOOP
220:::: PRINT "WHAT'S THE SECRET WORD";
230:::: INPUT S$
231::: IF LEN (S$) <= 3 THEN 235
232:::: PRINT "TOO LONG"
234::: GOTO 215
235:: REM--END LOOP
240:: HOME
380 RETURN
390:
400 REM--SUB GUESS WORDS
405:: LET C = 0
410:: REM--LOOP
420:::: PRINT "WHAT IS YOUR GUESS";
430:::: INPUT G$
435:::: LET C = C + 1
440::: IF G$ = S$ OR C = 10 THEN 500
450:::: GOSUB 800: REM--HINT
490::: GOTO 410
500:: REM--END LOOP
580 RETURN
590:
600 REM--SUB WRAP UP
601:: IF G$ = S$ THEN 605
602::: REM--FALSE
603:::: PRINT "YOU LOSE"
604:::: GOTO 615
605::: REM--TRUE
610:::: PRINT "CONGRATULATIONS, YOU GOT IT"
615:: REM--END IF
620:: PRINT "THE SECRET WORD WAS "; S$
780 RETURN
790:
800 REM--SUB HINT
810:: IF S$ < G$ THEN 850
820::: REM--FALSE
830:::: PRINT "LATER THAN "; G$
840:::: GOTO 870
850::: REM--TRUE
860:::: PRINT "EARLIER THAN "; S$
870:: REM--END IF
980 RETURN
```

Now make the changes in subroutine GUESS WORDS. Be sure to indent it properly. Run the program and test whether it stops after ten guesses.

Now make the changes shown for subroutine WRAP UP. Run the program and see whether it gives the correct winning and losing messages.

Your program should work perfectly. As a final improvement, however, you might want to renumber the lines of each subroutine you changed. Renumbering will make room for any future changes you might want to make. Here are the steps:

```
LIST 200, 399
```
Check subroutine SECRET WORD.

```
&RENUMBER 200, 399
LIST 200, 399
```
That should renumber SECRET WORD.

```
LIST 400, 599
&RENUMBER 400, 599
LIST 400, 599
```
That should renumber GUESS WORDS.

```
LIST 600, 799
&RENUMBER 600, 799
LIST 600, 799
```
And that renumbers WRAP UP.

Final Program Testing

Play the game several times and check that the final version of the program works well.

When you have practiced using the program, save it on your diskette so you can show your handiwork off to others.

Computers and Work

IN THIS SESSION YOU WILL:
- Learn that most jobs today involve working with information.
- Learn how the computer is affecting jobs in the factory, office, and home.
- Learn that computers create important new social problems.
- Learn about careers and job prospects in computing.

A Century of Working

In the last hundred years, we have seen three rapid, dramatic changes in the type of work that most people do. The computer plays a big role in the change happening today.

100 years ago Your great-great-great-grandparents probably lived on a farm. A century ago, more than half of all American workers were still farmers, but big changes were under way. Farm machinery was making it possible for fewer and fewer people to grow more and more food. The factories that made farm machinery and other products needed workers. So there was a vast movement of people from the farms to the factory towns.

50 years ago Your grandparents probably grew up and worked at jobs in a city. Fifty years ago the majority of work was in manufacturing trades: welding, sewing garments, operating looms, building houses, and working on an assembly line. Only two people out of every ten were farmers then. People in cities had money to spend and needed new services: grocery stores, laundries, department stores, entertainment, and education. Jobs in service industries grew rapidly.

Today Even fewer people work on farms today; less than one job in 30 is a farm job now. The number of manufacturing jobs is also shrinking: There are more jobs in service industries today than in manufacturing. The biggest new growth today is in the number of information workers—people whose main work is handling and processing information: secretaries, bank clerks, office managers, accountants, lawyers, and teachers. Fifty years ago, only two people in ten were information workers. Today, half the workers in the United States are information workers, and the trend is continuing.

Computers and Jobs

Farm machines made farm work easier and more efficient. Factory machines made factory work easier and more efficient. It should not come as a surprise that information machines—computers—are making information work easier and more efficient. But computers are also changing farm work and factory work.

The modern farmer To be a successful farmer, you need more than land, good weather, and machinery. You also need information. You need to know what risks you run by planting too early or too late, how much to spend on fertilizer, when to apply it, whether to use pesticides, and so on. To get help with decisions such as these, many farmers are buying small computers. They run simulation programs and study the effect of a decision before they make it.

Factory robots Many jobs on a factory assembly line, such as inserting bolt number 37 into hole number 23 and tightening it, are repetitive and boring. These mechanical jobs can often be done better and more cheaply by **robots**. Factory robots are different from the robots you see walking around in movies. A factory robot is a device, such as a mechanical hand or arm, that performs various motions. A computer is programmed to send output signals that tell the robot what to do. Some robots also send back information about what the robot is touching to the computer. Robots are very attractive to factory owners because they never get bored or sloppy, they work 24 hours a day in unheated rooms with no lights, and they never stay home sick.

The modern office The people who work in an office do little or no physical labor. They do not grow food or build things. Instead, they work almost entirely with information: letters, memos, reports, budgets, and expenses. Computers are now essential tools for handling office information. Letters are typed on a **word-processing system**, a computer used mainly for writing, editing, and typing letters and pa-

Computer-controlled robots can do much of the work of building a car.

Computer-based word-processing systems are replacing typewriters in the office and at home.

pers. Memos are entered directly into a computer **message system**. The person getting the memo can read it immediately on the computer screen in her or his office. Computer software helps people plan budgets, estimate expenses, and study reports.

The computer on the desk More and more workers have computers at their fingertips. The bank teller checks your bank account on a computer screen. The travel agent uses a computer system to reserve tickets on an airline or rooms at a hotel. The checkout clerk at the supermarket uses a cash register connected to a computer. Real estate agents use an on-line data base to help clients find the house they want. Newspaper reporters search data bases for news information and then write their stories on a computer system. Mail-order and telephone-order clerks enter each order into a computer system.

Computer jobs at home Why do office workers have to go to the office? Until now, the main reason has been that the information they needed was at the office. Networks of computers now make it possible to do most office work wherever there is a computer and a telephone. For this reason, many people today can work at home; they use computers to get and send information. Handicapped people, parents of young children, and other homebound people now are able to enter the work force.

Problems for Society

Computers are changing our work habits in both good and bad ways. Computers create opportunities, but they also pose problems that must be solved.

Boring work Not all computer applications lead to exciting jobs. Data entry is an example. Thousands of people spend all day reading numbers from sheets of paper and entering them into a computer. This work is often necessary, but it does not make people happy.

Loss of jobs We should be happy that a robot can keep a human being from having to do dull, repetitive work on an assembly line. But what happens to the person who used to do that dull job? Does another job automatically appear? If not, what should such a person do? Most studies show that new technologies create about the same number of jobs that they replace. Farm machines replaced farmers but created new jobs in farm-machinery factories. Computers replace some workers but create new jobs for programmers. Unfortunately, the person who loses a job to a computer system is not usually the same person who gets a job as a programmer.

Need for education   Experts predict that the demand for people with computer skills will remain far ahead of the supply for many years to come. Schools and colleges, therefore, are under strong pressure to teach more computer courses to more students. We also need to retrain people who lose their jobs to computer systems. Yet our educational system is short of funds and teachers able to handle the new computer courses.

Unequal opportunity   Computers do not affect everyone in the same way. Not everyone has the same chance to benefit from the computer revolution. A child in a neighborhood where parents are unemployed or work in manual jobs has a much lower chance of learning about computers than a child in a neighborhood where parents work in information jobs. The first child is likely to grow up with only manual skills at a time when there are fewer and fewer manual jobs. The second child is likely to be ready for the new information jobs. This inequality is a problem for the whole society.

Computer Careers

As we said, demand for people with computer skills is far ahead of the supply. Now is a good time to think about a career in computing. In this section, we look at careers that involve close work with computers and at the education needed for each career.

Office information systems   As offices and small businesses make greater use of computers for word processing, messages, and data processing, they usually need someone to manage the entire information system. Such a person needs to understand the work of the office or the business as well as the role of the computer. A general knowledge of word processing and computer accounting is important.

Application programming   People who write special-purpose programs for other people are called **application programmers**. They usually know two or three computer languages, such as BASIC, COBOL, Pascal, or FORTRAN. A college degree in computer science or a business degree with four or five computer courses is good preparation for this work. You will need a good math background for either degree.

System programming   As you know, BASIC on your computer is itself a set of computer programs: the LIST program, the RUN program, and so forth. These are called system programs, and people who write them are called **system programmers**. They also design data bases and the programs that use data bases. System programmers need to know the same things that application programmers know. In addition, they need a stronger computer-science background, including knowledge of machine languages and computer design.

Computer engineering The people who design and build computer hardware are called **computer engineers**. They usually prepare for this work by studying electrical engineering and computer science in a five-year college program.

Your Future

You now have a solid understanding of what a computer can do. You also know how to tell a computer to do some of the things you want it to do. In other words, you are computer literate. If you enjoyed this experience, you are probably wondering what to do next. There are more things to do and learn. You are ready for additional books and courses. But you are also ready to explore on your own. If you have access to a computer, begin to explore it. Experiment. Try your own ideas. As we said on page 1, the purpose of literacy is to set you free to do things on your own. Do them!

QUESTIONS

1. What was the main type of job in the United States a century ago? Fifty years ago? Today?
2. What kinds of machines were important a century ago? Fifty years ago? Today?
3. How do farmers use computers?
4. How are computers used in factories?
5. What is a word-processing system?
6. What is a computer message system?
7. How does a computer make it possible for an office worker to work at home?
8. Are all computer jobs interesting and exciting? Explain your answer.
9. Do computers take away jobs from people? Explain your answer?
10. Why is it a problem if too many people in a society have only manual skills?
11. What is the difference between an application programmer and a system programmer?

Part 9

There were no new BASIC words introduced in this part.

BASIC Vocabulary (Shaded Areas Show Standard BASIC Words)

Commands		Statements			Functions
Program	Diskette	Action	Action	Control	
RUN	LOAD	INPUT	SPEED=	GOSUB	INT
LIST	SAVE	LET	FLASH	RETURN	SQR
NEW	DELETE	PRINT	INVERSE	END	RND
DEL	CATALOG	REM	NORMAL	GOTO	LEN
CONT	LOCK	PLOT	COLOR=	IF	MID$
BRUN	UNLOCK	HLIN	TEXT	FOR	
&INDENT		VLIN	GR	NEXT	
&UNDENT		HOME			
&RENUMBER					

New Ideas

application programmer A person who writes special-purpose programs for other people, usually in a language such as BASIC, COBOL, or FORTRAN.

computer engineer A person who designs and builds computer hardware.

message system A computer network system for exchanging messages between users in different places.

robot A device, such as a mechanical hand or arm, controlled by computer.

system programmer A person who writes programs, usually in machine languages, that allow the computer to process BASIC programs, handle large data bases, and edit text.

word-processing system A computer system used mainly for writing, editing, and typing letters and papers.

Part 9 • Review   363

Index

Photo Credits